The
INSTITUTE OF BRITISH GEOGRAPHERS:
the first fifty years

by
Robert W. Steel

LONDON
INSTITUTE OF BRITISH GEOGRAPHERS
1984

The Institute of British Geographers

The Institute of British Geographers is Britain's foremost professional body for geographical research, serving a membership drawn from those in higher and further education, research and administration, concerned with the teaching, development and application of the subject.

Enquiries about the Institute's activities, membership, or any other matters should be addressed to:

The Administrative Assistant,
Institute of British Geographers,
1, Kensington Gore,
London SW7 2AR.

Telephone (01) 584 6371

© 1984 INSTITUTE OF BRITISH GEOGRAPHERS
ISBN 0 901989 36 3

Printed by Henry Ling Ltd., at the Dorset Press, Dorchester, Dorset

Preface

During the autumn of 1976, when David Thomas was Secretary of the IBG, I was invited by him to initiate a session at the RGS at which a few founder members of the IBG recorded on tape some of their memories of the IBG, especially of its early years. Three members were able to attend—R. O. Buchanan, K. C. Edwards and A. E. Smailes—but H. C. K. Henderson was prevented by poor health from making the journey from his home in South Wales to London. Buchanan's contribution was especially valuable because of his very senior position in the profession and because of his long and very close association with the IBG, particularly during its formative years. What he recorded supplemented very considerably the information given in his Presidential Address on 'The IBG: retrospect and prospect' (*Transactions* 20, 1954, 1–14).

Some months later I was asked to prepare this history of the Institute. Indeed, in the words of a Council minute of 3 January 1978, which I saw only quite recently for the first time, I was named as 'the Institute's historian'. At that time it was thought that the fiftieth anniversary celebrations would be in the year 1984 and in that belief I undertook to do the work, knowing that I should be retiring from the Principalship of the University College of Swansea in September 1982. Subsequent research showed that 1983 not 1984 was the critical year but even when this somewhat vital piece of information was rather belatedly relayed to me, the Council was still thinking in terms of a celebration, first at the Annual Conference in Edinburgh and then at a special gathering in London in April 1983. The decision not to hold a London meeting was taken by Council only at its meeting on 5 January 1982.

In the event everything—apart from the publication of this history—was telescoped into the Annual Conference in Edinburgh during the first few days of January 1983. Circumstances had made it quite impossible for me to make any significant progress with the work of the history during the last two years of my Principalship which coincided with my term of office as Vice-Chancellor of the University of Wales as well as with the crisis in higher education that dominated the lives of all of us in British universities following on the receipt of the UGC letters in July 1981. At least this volume is appearing towards the end of the celebratory year, 1983, as a tribute to all that has been achieved by the Institute and by its members, on behalf of the subject, over the fifty years since the Institute was founded in 1933.

In his Presidential Address in 1954 Buchanan expressed the hope that ' a detached, impersonal, critical history ' of the Institute might ' well be produced for the jubilee of the Institute or for its centenary '. For him, however, such an attempt was impossible because of what he described as ' the peculiarity ' of his position in that he had been continuously in office for the whole of the first twenty-one years of the Institute's life apart from the year 1952. As a result he had developed, he wrote, ' if not a possessive parent complex, at any rate an intimacy of detachment that is quite inimical to an aloof, impartial examination of the record '. In fact my own account is perhaps no more ' detached, impersonal and critical ' than Buchanan's and for not dissimilar reasons. My own association with the Institute, and my personal knowledge of nearly every actor on the IBG stage over the past half-century, has not made it easy to stand back and take a completely dispassionate view of developments over the years. While not an original member of the Institute (I was at school in the sixth form at the time of the IBG's foundation), I joined the IBG in 1938 and was a member of Council or an Officer between 1947 and 1960 and then again an Officer between 1966 and 1968, when I was in successive years Junior Vice-President, Senior Vice-President and then President. I suspect that I have attended almost as many Annual Conferences as any other member, although not with the same regularity since I ceased to be Professor of Geography in Liverpool in 1974. With such a close association, and with my involvement with so many individual geographers, it is not easy to be ' detached ' or ' impersonal '. ' Critical ' one could be; but even this is hard to achieve when one knows how much the Institute has depended, at all stages in its development, on the voluntary effort and willingness of scores of geographers, the majority of whom one is glad to count among one's friends. It is their work, loyalty and inspiration that has made the Institute what it is today.

I have interpreted my brief as the preparation of a history of the IBG, not of a history of the subject as an academic discipline during the past fifty years. I have, therefore, made no attempt to discuss the remarkable and exciting development of the subject during that period, except insofar as this is reflected in the growth in the strength, influence and potential of the Institute. It might have been easier had I written the whole account chronologically but the end product would have been very dull for most readers had it become a straightforward historical account based chiefly on the Minutes of successive meetings of the Council of the IBG and Reports of the Annual General Meetings. It seemed more sensible to provide, following a relatively brief chronological account in Part I, an assessment in Part II of the trends and special activities of the first fifty years of the Institute's life along with some indication, in Part III, of the possible developments in the immediate future. This approach has involved some, though not, I trust, excessive repetition. It also means that there is the omission of the names of some who might otherwise have expected mention in relation to a particular event at a particular time in the development of the IBG.

The extant records of the Institute provide a very inadequate basis for a full historical account. They consist largely of the minute books together with reports printed in the volumes of the *Transactions* and *Area*. It is hardly surprising that some of the early records—of, for example, the first gatherings of geographers from which the Institute emerged—are scanty. After all, could the pioneers have anticipated the subsequent developments that arose from their meeting together? How many of us, especially in academic life, keep full records of meetings in which we are involved especially as, if we are honest, we must admit that many of them lead to nothing further? And of those who are secretaries, how many of us produce minutes quickly and in full, and how often do we rely on our memories and write them up on the day before the next meeting of the body concerned? Nevertheless it must be admitted that for a very successful learned society, the state of the IBG's archives is very poor. Papers have remained uncatalogued and unsorted for many years. Many of them that no doubt are important are inaccessible, and therefore unknown, among the jumble of receipts, vouchers, and other similar material stored in a room above the IBG's office in the RGS's house in Kensington Gore, London. This situation is perhaps inevitable in an organisation where the officers have always been scattered over a number of different universities throughout the country and with only a very limited staff (an administrative assistant and occasional part-time help) in the central office. Whether this unfortunate state of affairs in an otherwise highly successful learned society can be remedied in the future, perhaps by calling on the help of some retired members of the IBG resident in London, should be a matter of concern to the Council and to the membership at large, and a few observations on the problem based on first-hand (and often frustrating) experience are given in Appendix K.

The information available in the records and in the Institute's publications has been supplemented by discussions with former Officers, and by a very considerable volume of correspondence with individual members about specific points or the major features, as they saw them, of their period of involvement in the Institute as Officers, Members of Council or, on occasions, as ordinary members with particular interests. It would be impossible to refer by name to all those who have helped me in these ways. I thank them all for their assistance and at the same time apologise to those who, after taking much trouble to deal with my enquiries, find that I have made but limited, and perhaps quite inadequate, use of the information that they provided. Even with the willing help of so many individuals certain blanks remain. There is, for example, no photograph of one of the earliest of the Institute's Officers, H. A. Matthews, who died in 1943; and despite many letters of enquiry, and finally an appeal for information in *Area*, it has not been possible to provide the information for two of the founder members—G. B. G. Gray and Miss B. M. Tunstall—that (with a good deal of effort) has been given the other original or founder members of the IBG listed in Appendix C.

There are many people and institutions who deserve my thanks, and the Institute's, for help of different kinds, in the preparation of this history, over and above the members of the IBG to whom reference has been made above. Valuable information, much of it previously unrecorded, was provided by Jean Eames, closely associated with the development of the Institute over almost twenty years between the mid 1950s and the mid 1970s and the first administrative assistant

(1965–73). Her successors in that office, Wendy Greenwood and Alison Hind, have been very helpful in providing records and files from the central office and searching for papers and answering queries. Useful information on the publishing and printing sides of the IBG was given to me by two who have been linked with the Institute over many years and who were elected honorary members of the Institute during the 1960s—E. O. Giffard (formerly of George Philip and Son Ltd.) and W. J. Furneaux (Alden Press (Oxford) Ltd).

Financial help, which has considerably relieved the IBG's funds, has been given by The British Academy (one of whose ' small grants ' I was awarded in the session 1980–81) and The Leverhulme Trust (one of whose Emeritus Fellowships I hold for 1983–84 for ' work towards the completion of studies on the history and development of geography as a discipline in the twentieth century '). To both of these bodies, who do so much to sustain academic research in Britain, I record my thanks and indebtedness, and the Institute's.

The University College of Swansea has, both directly and indirectly, assisted in many ways, both while I was Principal and subsequently since my retirement. My former secretary, Joan Lewis, and her assistants in the Principal's Office, Margaret Fox and Christine Williams, helped in the preparation of this history in many different ways over several years. Most of the typing and re-typing of drafts in recent months has been done by Christine Williams and by Betty Thomson of Birkenhead who was, until her retirement, a member of the office staff of my former department in the University of Liverpool. The figures were drawn by Guy Lewis of the Swansea Department of Geography and the photographic skill of Ted Price in the same department was used with good advantage on the sixty photographs which came to me in, literally, all shapes, sizes and colours.

Since the history is appearing in the same style as *Area*, it has been seen through the press, with great patience and understanding, by Mark and Sarah Blacksell, and Mr George Hill of Henry Ling Ltd, has been generous in his help and advice and has produced the book in a remarkably short space of time so that it would appear before the end of the year in which the Institute celebrated its jubilee. I am grateful to Alan Wakelam for the cover design.

My special thanks are due to members of my family, particularly my daughter Elizabeth and, above all, my wife Eileen, both of them geography graduates. The phrase ' but for whose help and encouragement, this book would never have been completed ' has never been more true than in the case of this history since there would have been no progress whatsoever during many of the latter months of my Principalship had it not been for my wife's preliminary work on the minute books and the records; while in my retirement she has given every possible assistance to a husband who has been even more preoccupied with the affairs of the Institute than he was in earlier years when we had a young family and he was responsible for the editing of the IBG's publications. Our hope is that the outcome of our combined labours, with the willing assistance of many others, will be seen as worthy of the high standing of the IBG and of the loyalty and the scholarship of the many geographers who are its members.

Swansea, 1983   Robert W. Steel

Contents

List of Plates

List of Figures

List of Abbreviations

BGRG: British Geomorphological Research Group
ESRC: Economic and Social Research Council
GA: Geographical Association
IBG: Institute of British Geographers
INQUA: International Quaternary Association
NERC: Natural Environment Research Council
RGS: Royal Geographical Society
RSGS: Royal Scottish Geographical Society
SSRC: Social Science Research Council

Notes

Names. Normally initials are used when a name is first mentioned. Titles (Professor, Dr, Mr etc.) have been eliminated, partly to save space but also because in many instances titles change with the passage of time. A Mr may become a Dr and sometimes ends up by being a Professor. Subsequently, names only (without initials) are generally used in the same chapter; but initials may re-appear in a later chapter for a name already mentioned. Whenever possible, women are given a Christian name to distinguish them from men.

In the interests of brevity, the adjective Honorary or Hon has not been put before the titles of officers—Secretary, Treasurer, Editor, etc.—since all IBG officers are honorary.

References. The IBG style of referencing has been followed as far as possible. But since most of the references are to IBG publications, particularly *Transactions* and *Area*, full bibliographical details have not always been given, especially where references to the same paper or monograph appears in the same paragraph. The date of publication has not always been placed after an author's name where the date is obvious from the context.

A complete list of references has not been provided at the end of the volume since nearly all the necessary information is given either in the text or as notes at the end of individual chapters.

About the author

The author is one of the early graduates of the Honour School of Geography in the University of Oxford and was Senior Lecturer in African Geography and a Fellow of Jesus College, Oxford, until 1956. He was John Rankin Professor of Geography in the University of Liverpool from 1957 to 1974 when he was appointed Principal of the University College of Swansea. Between 1979 and 1981 he was also Vice-Chancellor of the University of Wales. He retired in 1982.

Robert Steel became a member of the IBG in 1938, and was a member of the Council from 1947 to 1960, serving as Assistant Secretary and then Editor from 1948 to 1960. He was elected President of the IBG in 1968 and an Honorary Member in 1974.

He is the holder of honorary doctorates of the Universities of Salford and of Wales and is an Emeritus Professor of the University of Wales. He was awarded the CBE in 1983. Since his retirement he has been Chairman of the Board of the Wales Advisory Body for Local Authority Higher Education and is a member of the SSRC.

PART ONE

THE HISTORY OF THE IBG

I

Before the IBG

A history marking the completion of the first fifty years of the IBG is not the place to describe at length the position of geography as an academic discipline at the time of the founding of the IBG in 1933. At various times histories of the development of the subject have been published[1] and these, together with the personal memories of some of the most senior members of the Institute[2], help to provide the background against which the beginnings of the IBG must be seen. As D. R. Stoddart (*Transactions,* NS 8, 1983, 1–13) states, ' the foundation of the Institute of British Geographers came as the culmination of the movement to establish geography in British universities which began with Keltie's report to the RGS in 1885 and Mackinder's subsequent appointment to Oxford in 1887 '. J. S. Keltie's report was commissioned by the society ' in reference to the improvement of geographical education ' (Keltie, 1886)—a wholly admirable objective—and from it stemmed not only H. J. Mackinder's appointment (at the relatively young age of 26) to a Readership in the University of Oxford but also the establishment of a lectureship in Cambridge in 1888 and, indirectly, the development of geography in several other universities through the stimulus thus given to the subject. A lecturer was appointed in Manchester in 1892, and lectureships were established early in the twentieth century at Aberystwyth, Edinburgh, Glasgow, Leeds, Liverpool, Reading and Sheffield, while L. W. Lyde was appointed to a professorship at University College, London in 1903. Chairs were also created for individuals at University College, Reading in 1907 (H. N. Dickson) and Oxford in 1910 (A. J. Herbertson) before the beginning of the First World War in 1914. During and immediately after the War, honours schools of geography were recognised in several universities, at Liverpool (1917), the University College of Wales, Aberystwyth, and the London School of Economics (both in 1918), Cambridge (1919), Manchester (1923) and Sheffield (1924), and chairs were created in Liverpool and Aberystwyth in 1917, and at Birkbeck College, University of London, in 1920. Thereafter there were numerous widely scattered developments, though it is noteworthy that Oxford, which with the RGS's encouragement had done so much early on, did not elect its first Professor of Geography until 1931 (44 years after Mackinder's appointment) or establish its Honour School of Geography until 1933.

Most of these newly-established departments were very small, at least by the standards of the 1980s, and their ancillary (clerical, secretarial and technical) staffs were minimal, if indeed they existed at all. The real pioneer geographers— those who had been trained in other disciplines, as geologists, biologists, histor- ians, and classicists, among others, and who had moved over into geography— were very few in number. They approached geography, and appreciated it, from many different viewpoints, and their significance and contribution has been assessed by H. C. Darby in the special Jubilee issue of the *Transactions* ('Academic geography in Britain: 1918–46', NS 8, 1983, 14–26) and by those who have collaborated (Darby is one of them) in *British Geography, 1918–1945: issues and ideas*, edited by R. W. Steel and to be published in 1984 by the Cambridge University Press. R. O. Buchanan (1954) observed, in his survey of the early years of the IBG ('The IBG: retrospect and prospect', *Transactions 1954*, 20, 1–14), that 'staffing . . . was on a very meagre scale judged by present- day standards, but the increase in the total number of academic geographers dur- ing the 1920s was, nevertheless, quite remarkable. Most of the appointments, even to responsible posts, were relatively young men, men with ideas and energy, men who were conscious of their opportunities and their responsibilities, even though they were heavily overburdened with teaching and administrative duties'. These were in fact the group from whom the IBG recruited its founder and other early members, and they were the ones whose enthusiasm for their subject and zeal for better publication outlets ensured the Institute's survival in the years immediately before the outbreak of the Second World War when both member- ship and financial and other resources were so slight.

Stoddart (*Transactions*, NS 8, 1983) has developed the theme that the holding of the 12th International Geographical Congress in Cambridge in 1928 helped to develop among geographers in Britain at the time 'coherence and a sense of identity' (p. 1). Twenty-six of them contributed in 1928 to the publication by the Cambridge University Press at the time of the Congress of the volume, *Great Britain: essays in regional geography*, edited by A. G. Ogilvie. Of these, 14 attended the Congress and 13 later became Founder Members of the Institute— P. W. Bryan, C. B. Fawcett, W. Fitzgerald, H. J. Fleure, W. W. Jervis, R. H. Kinvig, W. S. Lewis, A. G. Ogilvie, Hilda Ormsby, O. H. T. Rishbeth, P. M. Roxby, R. N. Rudmose Brown and A. Stevens. Stoddart (*op. cit.*, p. 12) gives a list of 35 academic geographers who are known to have attended the Congress and suggests that these were the 'geographers who were to dominate the subject in British universities for the next quarter of a century' (p. 1), even though the leading members of the British contingent were Fellows and Officers of the RGS including Sir Charles Close, Sir Percy Cox, Sir William Goodenough and Sir Halford Mackinder. Certainly the Congress enabled British geographers to meet prominent figures in other countries, such as J. W. Brigham, W. W. Atwood, S. W. Boggs, Isaiah Bowman and D. W. Johnson from the United States; and Emmanuel de Martonne, Emmanuel de Margerie, A. Demangeon, A. Cholley and M. Sorre from France (Germany, it should be noted, had not yet been restored to its membership of the International Geographical Union, even though ten years had passed since the end of hostilities in 1918).

Darby, who was present at the Congress as a person who had just graduated in the Geographical Tripos at Cambridge, has recently suggested that *Great Britain: essays in regional geography* was ' an achievement of the greatest interest in the history of British geography' (*Transactions*, NS 8, 1983, 16) since it was ' a self-conscious production that showed the subject " as it was " in Britain in the late twenties '. ' We might not be far wrong ', he suggests, ' in thinking that it had something of the character of a manifesto, a declaration of intent, a promise of the future . . . The mere fact that the Congress met in Britain at the time sustained and invigorated the growing subject. There were 21 departments of geography in existence when the book was being prepared, and another three were added before the year 1928 was over. It had been a fine summer, and when the geographers returned to their universities they did so with their heads held higher than before ' (p. 16).

There is, therefore, ample evidence about the special significance of the Congress, yet this growing body of university geographers had no formal association of its own, and many individuals found it difficult to secure publication of the results of their research. Alice Garnett's published reflections on this period are of special interest (*Transactions*, NS 8, 1983, 27–35), as she was so closely involved in the many discussions, formal and otherwise, that led ultimately to the founding of the IBG. Many of these discussions appear to have focused upon the nature of the relationships that exist between university geographers and the institutions and societies already in existence, including the RGS and the GA. She, with characteristic forthrightness, was adamant in her view ' that if formed, from the start a new society must be independent and beholden only to its members for all financial needs ' (p. 30). She was sure (as were others, too) that any new organisation could not be the concern of a body such as the RGS, notwithstanding the spirit expressed by Sir Halford Mackinder—a life-long Fellow of the Society though never its President—at an RGS meeting in 1931 when he said, ' We have now reached a time when possibly there might be formed some circle of students, say, within this Society, who would build up a philosophical geography originated by observation and speculation no doubt, but tested by criticism (Garnett, p. 30).

Yet, as Garnett points out (p. 30), ' though some two hundred names were listed as British representatives attending the congress at Cambridge not even forty were university teachers, and of the latter only twenty-six elected five years later to become founder members of the IBG! ' Moreover three of those who were to play a very important part in the founding of the Institute—R. O. Buchanan, H. A. Matthews and S. W. Wooldridge—were not even present at the Congress.

Undoubtedly a desire for more opportunities for publication lay behind the move towards the formation of a new society to cater specifically for these needs. Publication facilities were lagging behind the growing demand for outlets, and this was the great spur to the establishment of an organisation that would provide room for work that was deemed worthy of publication but was not offered space in existing journals such as the *Geographical Journal, Geography*, and the *Scottish Geographical Magazine*. To many of the young academic geographers of the time, the RGS appeared to stress exploration and mountaineering, and writing about the less well-known parts of the world, and few academic papers were published. The then Secretary of the Society, A. R. Hinks, FRS—described by Stoddart (1983, 2) as 'formidable and frequently irascible'—was thought by some to be opposed to certain types of geographical writing, though recent writers (e.g. Freeman, 1981; Steers, 1982; and Garnett, 1983) have suggested that his attitude derived from his emphasis on the importance of maintaining academic standards. Perhaps after the passage of more than fifty years, it is pointless to pursue these matters, for which there is all too little documentation and possibly rather too much speculation. Perusal of the pages of the *Geographical Journal* in the early 1930s does not reveal a wealth of writing by academic geographers, though in the *Journal* for 1933, the year in which the Institute was founded, there are, as Stoddart points out (1983, 2) 'characteristic papers on the Rub 'al Khali, headhunting in Formosa, and Gino Watkins's kayak' along with 'academic offerings by, among others, H. C. Darby, A. C. O'Dell and E. C. Willatts'.

The GA, very properly, had particularly the needs of those teaching the subject in schools as its major concern. Attendance at its conferences by university geographers of all ages was warmly advocated by H. J. Fleure, the Association's Honorary Secretary, and others, and for many geographers, as Garnett states (*op. cit.*, p. 28), 'annual participation in the programme of lectures, discussions and social gatherings became an essential activity in the yearly round'. Indeed, after the establishment of the Institute, IBG and GA meetings were for many years associated with one another in the same building, the London School of Economics, so that this valuable and traditional link of geographers was maintained until the IBG at a much later date concentrated its conference efforts on an annual residential meeting held normally outside London. But the Association's publication—*The Geographical Teacher* until 1926 and thereafter *Geography*—offered only limited scope for papers reporting the results of geographical research by university teachers, and despite efforts made by Fleure, with the collaboration of P. M. Roxby, during the 1920s (and reported by Garnett, *op. cit.*, pp. 28–9), the GA did not provide the publications medium for which the university geographers of the period were searching. Buchanan, looking back on these times after a lapse of some twenty or more years notes that *Geography*, 'under the inspiring editorship of Professor H. J. Fleure, and reflecting the massive growth of the Geographical Association, had blossomed from a terminal into a quarterly periodical of enlarged size, and generous treatment was given to academic contributors; but the editor had already gone as far as he could without sacrificing the legitimate professional interests of the great body of teacher members, and no further concession seemed possible. ' But he thought that the situation in Scotland was probably easier than it was in England and Wales, with the *Scottish Geographical Magazine* in his view (though some would dispute this) 'hardening its policy in favour of work on Scotland or work by geographers in Scotland'. Thus he believed that 'the publication pinch was less acutely felt in the Scottish departments of geography, and for that reason there may perhaps have been less enthusiasm in Scotland for the new venture' represented by the establishment of the IBG than there was elsewhere.

The significance at this time—and for many years afterwards—of the meetings of Section E (Geography) of the British Association for the Advancement of Science must not be overlooked. Indeed Alice Garnett suggests (1983, 29) that during the 1920s 'attendance at the September meetings of Section E came to carry greater importance for academic geographers than the January GA conferences. ' In her view, 'the encouragement afforded by these meetings for research, the reading of research papers, and discussions, with the added incentive of field days at the weekend, played an immeasurably important part in laying the foundations for our future independent development; indeed, as our numbers increased, Section E meetings could be likened to embryo IBG gatherings—at least in spirit if not at that time in professional content. '

The beginning of the 1930s was the start of an economic recession, it should be remembered, that is comparable with (and some would argue worse than) that facing Britain and the world during the 1980s; and it was in such circumstances that the IBG was born and started the life that has now reached the respectable age of fifty. There was an increasing number of university geographers, many of them both young and active, even ambitious for promotion and advancement. They were anxious to meet regularly and formally for the discussion of shared problems and of their research, and to have a forum of their own, associated with, but not dominated by, cognate groups and societies such as the RGS, the GA and Section E (Geography) of the British Association for the Advancement of Science. Above all, they were concerned about the need for additional outlets for the publication of their papers based upon their research, in a variety of fields, the results of which they were anxious to share with the public. Rightly or wrongly, most of them believed that they were not receiving a fair deal from the editors and editorial boards of existing periodicals. There is clear evidence that some papers failed to pass the scrutiny of either the RGS or the GA, and rejection letters, however worded, inevitably cause frustration to those who, like the geographers of the late 1920s, were seeking outlets and who realised that their only hope of promotion within the university, or of advertising the virtues of their subject as an academic discipline outside the university world, lay in publication.

There is, however, very little archival material on which to base one's assessment of the situation more than half a century ago, though the personal reminiscences and reflections of some of those who have published their memories, such as Alice Garnett (*Transactions*, NS 8, 1983, 27–35), along with briefer notes by S. H. Beaver (36–7) and E. G. Bowen (38–40), are of great interest. Many of the discussions that took place at that time are unrecorded, and at this distance in time it is perhaps wiser not to refer to individuals by name. It is known that one or two geographers in established positions took the view that there was no need for a new organisation. They argued that they, personally, had had no difficulties in finding outlets for their papers in the *Geographical Journal* or elsewhere. There were others who were hesitant because they feared that a new professional organisation might have bad effects on established institutions such as the RGS and the GA. This concern for established bodies was commendable, as was the anxiety of many individual geographers to avoid doing anything that might weaken the significance of the annual summer meetings of Section E

(Geography) of the British Association for the Advancement of Science. But a considerable body of opinion felt that new outlets for publication were important and must be found, so that they were prepared to achieve this objective irrespective of the consequences. Whether the impact of a new institution on old-established societies (the RGS had just celebrated its hundredth anniversary, and the GA had been founded in 1892) entered very seriously into the consideration of many of the geographers of the time is somewhat doubtful for few of the pioneers who became Founder Members can have anticipated the growth of the Institute which, in any event, for the first fifteen years or so of its existence hardly resembled at all the IBG that we know today—apart from the dedication of its members and their determination to ensure the maintenance and the growth of the Institute once it had been established.

The IBG's first historian who was so closely associated with the Institute's first two decades, R. O. Buchanan, surveyed its history down to 1954 in ' The IBG: retrospect and prospect' (*Transactions*, 20, 1983, 1–14). A twenty-first birthday he saw as ' no unimportant occasion in the life of an individual or of an institution ', and he thought it fitting to survey those twenty-one years ' to bring to the younger members some idea of the story of the early hopes and struggles of their organisation, and to attempt some assessment of what has been accomplished and what are the tasks that lie ahead ' (p. 1). ' It is almost always difficult to put a finger precisely on the beginning of a movement or an organisation ', he wrote ' but for the IBG I am going to risk the selection of a day in January 1931 when Dr S. W. Wooldridge, Dr H. A. Matthews (then of Birkbeck College, later of Bedford College, London) and I were lunching together '. This seems to have been a working lunch in the best sense of the term, although Buchanan himself suggests that it differed from others of its kind ' only in the fact that a decision was taken to try to change the situation ' (p. 2). The talk turned on the research work that geographers were doing and the lack of opportunities for publishing the results. A month later a more formal meeting with other geographers from the London colleges, mostly in their thirties, was held in King's College on 18 February 1931.[3] As there are no minutes, we must rely on Buchanan's memory which produced eleven names: S. W. Wooldridge, H. J. Wood, S. H. Beaver and W. G. East (from the Joint School of King's College and the London School of Economics); R. O. Buchanan, R. E. Dickinson and G. Tatham (University College of London); H. A. Matthews and H. C. K. Henderson (Birkbeck); D. K. Smee (Bedford); and B. M. Tunstall (East London College, now Queen Mary College). The meeting was called ' to discuss some form of organisation to serve the common interests of geographers '. Arising from it, Wooldridge was asked to prepare a memorandum for C. B. Fawcett, Head of the Department of Geography at University College London, in which the need for a new organisation to publish the research that academic geographers were doing was stressed. Fawcett was asked to discuss the memorandum with the senior members of the staffs of the Departments of Geography in the London Colleges and also took it (in an amended form, it seems) to the annual meeting of the Heads of Departments of Geography held on 24 September 1931 under the chairmanship of A. V.

Williamson of Leeds. He also reported on the matter to the Council of the RGS. Meanwhile the proposals were also considered at (in the words of the document 'Proposals for consideration of university geographers') 'a special meeting of as many as could be reached of the junior members of Geography staffs of British Universities at the centenary meetings of the British Association for the Advancement of Science', held in London in September 1931. Out of these meetings there emerged a joint committee of ten representatives of all grades of university geographers 'to explore the position and to make a report and recommendations' for the formation of what was described as an 'Association of University Geographers'. Although no minutes of this meeting seem to have survived, it is apparent that the Joint Committee was constituted as follows: J. N. L. Baker, R. O. Buchanan, H. J. Fleure, A. A. Miller, P. M. Roxby, R. N. Rudmose Brown, C. B. Fawcett, Ll. Rodwell Jones, O. H. T. Rishbeth and S. W. Wooldridge.

The circulation of the note about these proposals did not have an overwhelmingly warm reception or a convincingly encouraging reception. Only 43 firm promises of membership were received along with a number (unspecified) of 'doubtfuls' and ten firm refusals (there does not appear to be any record of who those ten were!). But it was decided to press forward even though, with the proposed subscription of £3 per annum—which some regarded as being, according to Garnett (1983, 31), 'prohibitively high'—the new association, dedicated to the publication of research, would have an assured income of only about £150 (not, even in those days, a princely sum). A general meeting of geographers held in London in January 1932—presumably during the Annual Conference of the GA—agreed to form a 'University Group of Geographers' (a change from the earlier title discussed, an Association of University Geographers). A small working committee was set up to deal with those matters not resolved by the earlier committee and to report, if possible, during the next meeting of the British Association for the Advancement of Science to be held in York in September. There is no record in the IBG archives of the exact membership of the committee or who was chairman, but J. N. L. Baker, C. B. Fawcett, H. J. Fleure, Alice Garnett, A. G. Ogilvie, P. M. Roxby, J. A. Steers and S. W. Wooldridge met at various times during the course of the next few months.[4] They produced a report for a meeting that took place in York on 2 September 1932. Following the incorporation of various amendments approved by the meeting in York, it was circulated as Enclosure I attached to the Agenda for the meeting of the IBG called for 3 January 1933, and a letter (dated 30 November 1932) inviting attendance at the first meeting was signed by A. G. Ogilvie and S. W. Wooldridge as chairman and secretary respectively of the Inaugural Committee. The amended report was prepared and a group set up at York, consisting of Fleure, Ogilvie, Steers and Wooldridge, together with P. W. Bryan, C. D. Forde, Ll. Rodwell Jones and H. A. Matthews. They also prepared a statement (Appendix B) on the steps that had been taken over the years to 'obtain an additional outlet for advanced work in Geography', beginning with plans by A. J. Herbertson and G. G. Chisholm which proved abortive because of the outbreak of the First World War (I have found no record of these earlier efforts by geographers to form some kind of professional association).

In view of the significance of this report and the accompanying statement they are reproduced in full, as Appendix B on page 142 exactly as they were distributed to potential members in November 1932. It is especially noteworthy that it is recorded that ' a considerable body of unpublished research work exists ' and that, right at the outset, the Committee felt it desirable to make clear that ' the proposed activities of the Institute, both in the matter of meetings and publications, are not in any sense to be regarded as competing with those of other geographical bodies and journals, but rather as supplementary '.

As Enclosure 1 of Appendix B makes clear, the Institute's ' objects in view ' included, besides the all-important independent publication of research, the holding of meetings. These would include the reading and full discussion of papers at a meeting to be held in January; short visits to various Schools of Geography and to localities offering opportunities for work in the field; and an annual business meeting to be held either in the autumn (at the British Association centre for the year) or in January in London.

Shortly before the inauguration of the Institute in January 1933, the Council of the RGS met on 19 December 1932 and discussed the formation of the new society. The President (Admiral Sir William Goodenough) made a statement on the proposal which had been circulated to some members of Council ' for a proposed Institute of British Geographers whose aim would be, without interfering with the work of the Society, to encourage the publication of academic theses and to further the aims of university schools of geography '. Four members of the Council with special links with academic geography are recorded in the Minutes as participating in the discussion, though they made, in Alice Garnett's words (1983, 33), ' little or no contribution that might be regarded as helpful. ' Sir Halford Mackinder believed that ' the movement should not be discouraged ' though he thought that the promoters could scarcely have considered seriously the cost of publication. E. G. R. Taylor thought that the promoters felt ' the need of more narrowly professional publication for more technical papers not of interest to the Society '. Kenneth Mason was not convinced that ' the movement could be financially practicable or of real benefit '. C. B. Fawcett informed the Council that the junior members of the academic staffs felt that their professional prospects depended on the publication of research, though he was convinced that the amount of serious work awaiting publication had been greatly exaggerated. The President is recorded as summing up the discussion ' as showing agreement that the Society should give the proposed new organisation what encouragement and advice was possible, ' and the Secretary of the Society, A. R. Hinks, whatever his personal or official views may have been, became a Founder Member of the new Institute—unlike some university teachers who, as Garnett says, ' were at pains to express disinterest ' and who did not join then or, in some instances, at any later date (Kenneth Mason, my own professor in Oxford, was one of those who never joined even though he was in post until 1952 and in that period two of the Institute's residential conferences, the first and the third, were held in Oxford, holding their lectures in his own School of Geography).

Notes

1. A selection only of these accounts, some published many years ago and others quite recently, include the following:

    Bowen, E. G. and others (1968) ' A retrospect, 1917–18 to 1967–8 ', xix–xxxvi, in Bowen, E. G., Carter, H. and Taylor, J. (eds) (1968) *Geography in Aberystwyth: essays written on the occasion of the Departmental Jubilee 1917/18–1967/68* (Cardiff)

    Brown, E. H. (ed.) (1980) *Geography yesterday and tomorrow* (Oxford)

    Cameron, I. (1980) *To the farthest ends of the earth: 150 years of world exploration* (London) (The history of the Royal Geographical Society, 1830–1980)

    Dickinson, R. E. and Howarth, O. J. R. (1933) *The making of Geography* (Oxford)

    Freeman, T. W. (1961) *A hundred years of Geography* (London)

    Freeman, T. W. (1967) *The geographer's craft* (Manchester)

    Freeman, T. W. (1980) *A history of modern British Geography* (London)

    Gilbert, E. W. (1972) *British pioneers in Geography* (London)

    Mill, H. R. (1951) *Hugh Robert Mill: an autobiography* (London)

    Steel, R. W. (1967) ' Geography at the University of Liverpool, ' in Steel, R. W. and Lawton, R. (eds) (1967) *Liverpool essays in Geography: a Jubilee collection* (London).

    Steel, R. W. (1970) ' Geography in British universities ' in Balchin, W. G. V. (ed) (1970), *Geography: an outline for the intending student* (London), 147–62

    Taylor, Griffith (1951) *Geography in the twentieth century; a study of growth, fields, techniques, aims and trends* (London)

2. Some of these are included in the special number of the *Transactions* of the Institute of British Geographers, published at the time of the Edinburgh conference of the IBG (*Transactions*, 8, 1983). The authors are H. C. Darby, Alice Garnett, S. H. Beaver and E. G. Bowen, and there are accounts by M. J. Wise of three of the Founder Members of the IBG: R. Ogilvie Buchanan, Sir Dudley Stamp and S. W. Wooldridge.

3. R. O. Buchanan (*Transactions*, 20, 1954, 3), D. R. Stoddart (*Transactions*, NS 8, 1983, 2) and Alice Garnett (1983, 30) give the date as 8 February 1931; but since this was a Sunday, I think it improbable that a group of 11 geographers (Garnett's figure), enthusiastic or concerned though they undoubtedly were, met on such a day (would King's College, London, have been open on a Sunday in 1931 in any event?). I have taken, therefore, the date of Wednesday 18 February 1931, to which there is a reference in a typewritten document in my possession (headed ' Proposal for consideration of university geographers ' and dated 29 October 1931 in which there is the following reference: '. . . following informal discussions among the junior staffs of the London Colleges, a meeting was held on Wednesday 18 February, 1931 '

4. According to Garnett (*Transactions*, NS 8, 1983, 31) the first committee consisted of ten members, six of them heads of departments. Five of the committee were London-based, which appears to have caused concern in some quarters. The membership of the second committee was deliberately broader and only four of the eight were heads of departments and only two were London-based (Fawcett and Wooldridge). Ogilvie was nominated as chairman but since he could not always attend, meetings were often chaired by Fawcett, in whose room at University College London the Committee usually met.

II

The birth and early years

The previous chapter has attempted to provide a picture of the position of geography as an academic discipline in the years immediately prior to the birth of the IBG in January 1933 and to describe some of the preliminary steps taken by the geographers who were to be among the founder members of the new Institute.

The first meeting of the Institute took place at 11 am on Tuesday 3 January 1933 at the London School of Economics. Ll. Rodwell Jones was unanimously elected chairman of the meeting and H. A. Matthews was appointed minute secretary. The minutes report that the meeting ' was well attended ', and the report from the York meeting of the inaugural committee was discussed clause by clause, so that very detailed consideration was given to the proposed constitution, including the composition of the Council, the method of election of members to Council, the functions of the Council and its relationship to the Editorial Board. There followed a discussion of the title of the new organisation and the size of the subscription. The minutes record that ' without a definite proposal the meeting affirmed the choice of the Institute of British Geographers ' and—' again with no definite proposal to the contrary, it was nevertheless affirmed—with acclamation—that the recommendation of the inaugural committee for an annual subscription of 10/6d should stand '. The following officers were unanimously elected: President, C. B. Fawcett; Honorary Secretary and Treasurer, A. A. Miller; and Honorary Assistant Secretary, H. A. Matthews. Six members of Council were elected: J. N. L. Baker, R. O. Buchanan, H. J. Fleure, Ll. Rodwell Jones, P. M. Roxby and S. W. Wooldridge. They were charged with a consideration of the report of the inaugural committee and of the proposed constitution, aided by a drafting committee. When the meeting resumed in the afternoon under the chairmanship of C. B. Fawcett the newly elected President reported that he had received a letter from Sir Halford Mackinder expressing his interest in, and support for, the new Institute. He also reported the receipt of a letter from the President of the RGS (Admiral Sir William Goodenough) expressing his goodwill towards the Institute but regretting that he had not been notified of its initiation. The afternoon then concluded with papers read by A. Stevens, W. G. East and S. H. Beaver. Tuesday 3 January 1933 had, therefore, been both the first Annual General Meeting of the IBG and the first of the 44 annual conferences so far held in early January of each year, apart from the six years' gap of the Second World War.

The first meeting of the Council was held at the Imperial Institute on the following Saturday (7 January), four days after the holding of the inaugural meeting, and presumably after the conclusion of the GA's Annual Conference of January 1933. It is unnecessary, fifty years later, to record in detail all the matters discussed at a meeting that lasted $2\frac{1}{4}$ hours beyond noting that a drafting committee for the formulation of the constitution of the IBG was established and that relationships with other geographical bodies were discussed at some length. No action was to be taken to conflict with the interests of Section E (Geography) of the British Association for the Advancement of Science (business and Council meetings might be held then but there would be no sessions for the reading or discussion of papers). It was noted that there was a possibility that the RGS, now with increased publication facilities, might consider publication by members of the IBG (although the RGS would exercise control of what was published); and the GA might also be able to publish research monographs or articles in *Geography* on behalf of members of the IBG. But the general feeling of the Council inclined towards regular publication, for the time being annually, of ' a journal or memoir containing three or four articles of 15,000 to 20,000 words together with reports of meetings and abstracts of papers read for discussion '. This, it was estimated, would cost about £60 per annum if 500 copies were printed. There was to be no ' editor ' but a ' convener ' who would act as chairman of the editorial board. The subscription was fixed at 10/6d, at least until the time of the next General Meeting, this being a sum that it was considered would be ' sufficient to cover the probable expenses of the Institute until then '. It was agreed to invite voluntary donations towards an initial publication fund.

The President and Secretary agreed to draw up a circular letter ' to be sent to all past and present members of the Staffs of Geography Departments in the Universities and University Colleges and to certain others, containing:

   i.   A summary statement of events leading up to the formation of the IBG, and of the present position.

   ii.   A brief statement of policy, especially of policy with regard to publication.

   iii. The personnel of the Council and Editorial Board.

   iv. An invitation to membership.

   v.   A request for initial payment of 10/6d (where not already paid).

   vi. Inviting donations towards the initial publishing fund.

   vii. Inviting members to submit to the Editorial Board

       a) material for publication in the Memoirs;

       b) material for discussion at meetings of the Institute. '

When the Council next met in Liverpool on 19 April 1933, the Secretary reported that ' the total membership of the Institute to date was placed at 39, a figure which fell far short of the number who intended to join, and which might reasonably be expected to increase substantially in the near future '. But as it had been previously decided that ' all present members of the staff of departments of geography in Universities and University Colleges are entitled to become original members of the Institute ', others were able to send ' intimation of intended membership ' to the Secretary-Treasurer. As a result there is a list of 73 ' original ' members listed in the first IBG publication, *Transactions*, with which was combined publication no. 2, *The pastoral industries of New Zealand* by R. O. Buchanan (1935). After the 1934 Annual Meeting new members had to be proposed and seconded by a member and elected at a business meeting. The 73 original, later called founder, members came from 21 universities, and 25 of them were members of the staffs of various colleges in London. Eighteen of these founder members are alive today, and some of them are still active in their retirement and attend meetings of the IBG from time to time. All of them were invited to the fiftieth anniversary dinner held in the University of Edinburgh in January 1983, and three (J. A. Steers, S. J. K. Baker and D. D. E. Rodgers) were able to attend, and in the speeches that followed, Steers responded to the toast of those who had been the original members of the Institute.

The list of Founder or original members is printed as Appendix C (p. 145). The years of birth and, where applicable (as it is unfortunately in a very large number of cases), of death have been added whenever the information could be found; but in two cases (G. B. G. Gray and B. M. Tunstall) it has not been possible to provide any of this information despite extensive enquiries from a variety of possible sources. At the second meeting of the Council, Fleure suggested that the printing estimate of £60 noted at the first meeting ' might reasonably be reduced to £45 '. At the third meeting held at Leicester during the annual meeting of the British Association, arrangements were discussed for the programme of the Annual General Meeting which would include the reading and discussion of papers and a field excursion in the Chilterns on the Sunday under the leadership of S. W. Wooldridge. It was also decided to recommend that, if a publication were available by the time of the meeting, the annual subscription should be fixed at £2.

The pattern of meetings established in the first year of the Institute's existence was closely followed in subsequent years. Thus the second general meeting was held in London on 6 January 1934 (the minutes do not mention the number of members present), with a meeting of the Council held on the previous evening and lasting, the minutes record with unusual precision, from 5.15 to 6.58 pm; and later in the year Council met in March at University College London (jointly with the Editorial Board), in Marishal College, University of Aberdeen, in September (during the British Association meeting), and in November, again at University College London. Approval was given to the publication of Buchanan's monograph (on the pastoral industries of New Zealand) and of Henri Baulig's ' paper ' on the changing sea-level (in fact a series of four lectures delivered during November 1933 in the University of London) ' subject to a favourable report from a second referee '. An agreement for the publication of these two memoirs was reached with Messrs. George Philip and Son. It was reported that ' owing to the large numbers of papers submitted it would be necessary to arrange for a further half-day meeting ', and a total of eight papers was accepted for the enlarged programme.

There were 29 members present at the General Meeting held on 1 January 1935. Nearly half a century later it is of interest to note E. G. R. Taylor's reference to ' the large grant that had been obtained from the University of London ' as a subvention for the publication of Baulig's lectures (the grant from the University's Publication Fund was in fact £60); A. C. O'Dell's suggestion that, in the interests of cheapness of production, consideration should be given to ' the phototillnograph process which was largely used in the USA and by certain British societies ' (this in Buchanan's handwriting but with a large pencilled question mark alongside it—could it be photolithography to which reference was being made?); and the report on future publication from the President that stated that ' no works were in hand (possibly because members were holding back in order to see the first monographs) but that a number of pieces of work were known to be possibilities '. There is also an interesting item relating to a paper from an IBG member in Aberystwyth which suggests that dissatisfaction with postal services between England and Wales is nothing new. The minute records that ' The paper that was to have been given by Mr. W. Fogg on " Figuig: an oasis of the Moroccan Sahara " had been delayed in the Post Office during the holiday rush, and had to be omitted.' The meeting also agreed on ' the desirability of avoiding January 1st as a date for the meeting '.

A year and a day later, on 2 January 1936, the attendance was marginally greater—33 (the names are listed in the minutes) compared with 29 in 1935. The total membership of the Institute had risen to 83. The convener of the Editorial Board reported that most of the Board's work had been done of necessity by correspondence and that ten ' pieces of work ' had been submitted (two of them by non-members). Of these one had been withdrawn and three had been recommended for rejection by referees, leaving six still under consideration, in some cases subject to ' substantial reorganisation of the form of the work ' as recommended by the referees.

The IBG's concern for research in associated fields and other institutions at this early stage of its existence was indicated by the unanimous adoption of the following resolution: ' That the Institute of British Geographers has heard with pleasure of the constitution of the East Malling Agricultural Station research committee which has under consideration proposals for undertaking work in microclimatology '. Earlier on, the Council had received a letter from E. G. R. Taylor indicating (i) the desirability of asking the British Museum authorities to consider placing the map collection in one department in order to facilitate its use by students of geography and history, and (ii) the desirability of giving official support to the foundation of a Cartographical Society '. In this instance, however, it was decided that ' the letter be left on the table for further information '.

As in the previous year, Council met during the GA conference in January at the London School of Economics, during the British Association meetings in September (when at a meeting in the Lads' Club in Norwich it was reported that only 32 of the total membership of 75 had paid their subscriptions) and at University College London in early December. Once again it is recorded that there was a ' lack of any accepted work '—a surprising situation in the light of the background to the establishment three years earlier of a body with the specific and indeed urgent task of providing publication outlets for geographers.

Shortly afterwards, however, the publications side of the Institute's work was changed very considerably with the prospect of several new works: Alice Garnett's monograph, published later as *Insolation and relief; their bearing on the human geography of Alpine regions*, and L. E. Tavener's *Land classification in Dorset*, and a possibility that Dorothy Doveton's work on the human geography of Swaziland might also be available to the Institute for publication. Sales of publications, up to 30 September 1935, were 182 copies (including 80 to members) of publications no. 1 and 2 (*Transactions* and Buchanan's *The pastoral industries of New Zealand*) and 216 copies (147 to members) of publication no. 3 (Baulig's *The changing sea-level*). During 1936 Council met on four occasions—in London in January and again in July, when arrangements were approved for the IBG's first field meeting to the Lake District based on Windermere (eleven members and two guests attended); in Blackpool in September; and in London in October. At the Blackpool meeting, held at the Raike's Parade School, the possibility of undertaking the publication of shorter articles was discussed at length, and in the light of later developments in the life of the Institute it is noteworthy that it was agreed:

i.   that it was desirable to have a permanent record of the activities of the Institute;

ii.   that regularity of publication should be a main aim;

iii. that, if shorter papers were accepted, they must be limited to papers that had been read before the Institute.

The balance of opinion was, however, ' in favour of continuing the present policy of using available funds for the publication of memoirs '. There is a familiar ring about the minute that records that ' Mr. J. N. L. Baker stressed the necessity of speeding up publication, and drew attention to the serious delays that had sometimes occurred after pieces of work had reached the referee's hands '. It is interesting, too, to note that at the October Council meeting it was reported that ' no nominations for President or for Council members had been received '.

Thirty-one members were present at the Annual General Meeting on 6 January 1937 when R. N. Rudmose Brown of Sheffield was elected to succeed Fawcett as President. One member drew attention to what was described as ' a serious decline in the number of financial members ' and suggested that the current membership fee of £2 per annum might be rather high, but the officers disagreed with this point of view, believing that the 9 subscriptions in arrears for 1935 and the 27 for 1936 would eventually be paid. At the subsequent Council meeting a significant point about the standards expected for publication was established when it was noted that ' the Institute policy was not to reserve publication for works of outstanding excellence and originality such as might be necessary as grounds for admission to the fellowship of an exclusive learned society '. Arrangements were set in train for a field meeting in Derbyshire to follow the annual meeting of the British Association in Sheffield; and the

President reported on talks that he and his fellow officers had had with E. O. Giffard, Educational Liaison Officer of George Philip and Son and a member of the Institute, to consider ways and means of stimulating sales of the Institute's publications. There was also discussion of the most effective way for the Institute to protest, on behalf of geographers generally, at the threatened discontinuance of publication of the Ordnance Survey 5th (Relief) edition of the one-inch map. At the November meeting of the Council, I was elected a member of the Institute even though it was only five months since I had graduated in the Oxford Honour School of Geography (there was no category of research student membership at the time). It was also reported that the editor of *The Annals of the Association of American Geographers.* D. Whittlesey, had suggested a possible exchange of publications between the AAG and the IBG.

A poorly attended Annual General Meeting on 6 January 1938 (a total of only 22 members) learned with satisfaction that during the previous year three monographs had been published (Garnett, Tavener and Doveton). It was thought more than likely that several other works would be offered to the Institute quite shortly although nothing was at present under consideration by the Editorial Board. But during the year the Council met on only two occasions—in London after the Annual General meeting and at Cambridge during the British Association meeting in August; and there was a lack of response by members to the proposed field meeting which J. A. Steers had been prepared to lead at the end of the British Association week, so that plans for it had to be abandoned. There was, however, a good prospect that the monograph on the London Basin by S. W. Wooldridge and D. L. Linton would be published, even though the Officers were concerned that ' George Philip's estimate for an edition of 500 was 9/9d per copy, and not far short of £250 in aggregate '; and this anxiety about the cost persisted notwithstanding the likelihood of grants in aid of publication being forthcoming from both the University of Edinburgh and the University of London. It was noted, however, that ' if such grants did in fact materialise, the net cost to the Institute would be probably not more than £180, and this, though heavy, could be supported. ' This concern on the part of the Officers no doubt reflected both the precarious nature of the Institute's finances and also the international tension that characterised the nation in the months between the Munich ' settlement ' of September 1938 and the outbreak of the Second World War in September 1939.

Arrangements were made for the Annual General Meeting for the afternoon of Thursday 5 January 1939 ' to be continued on Friday 6 January if sufficient papers were available '. Thirty members attended at the London School of Economics to listen to papers and to participate in the business meeting during which J. N. L. Baker was elected President in succession to R. N. Rudmose Brown. I was present for the first of the many IBG conferences that I have attended. Baker had been my undergraduate tutor in Oxford and was supervising my research on the human geography of Sierra Leone, and he had persuaded me that membership of the IBG was ' a good thing '. Indeed he had generously paid my subscription out of the supervision fee levied by the University of Oxford and given to him (he had done the same for A. F. Martin and possibly other

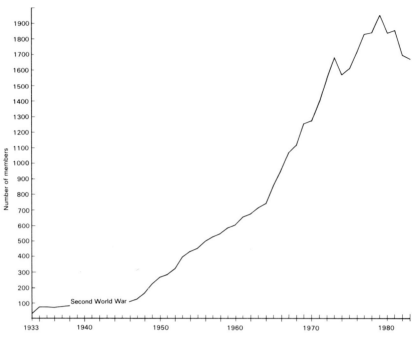

Figure 1. Membership of the IBG, 1933–83. The numbers include student membership (now averaging between 200 and 300 per annum). The decline in membership from the peak of 1945 in 1979 is a reflection of the consequences of the economic recession and its impact upon higher education. At various times the subscription for ordinary and student members has been increased but only occasionally has this been accompanied by a marked drop in membership. Even in the 1980s the decline in total membership has been caused, at least in large measure, by a number of student members not seeking ordinary membership when they completed their time as postgraduate students. Some at least of these have, unfortunately, failed to secure employment, so that their resignation from membership of the IBG is understandable.

research students as well). I recall that, on my arrival at the lecture room in the London School of Economics, he was anxious to introduce me to someone in my own age-group. He picked on D. L. Linton—nine years my senior but looking youthful, as he always did, with his striking and handsome appearance (lest readers should think that his choice might have been S. H. Beaver, my senior by eight years, I ought to say that almost certainly he was serving the GA—whose Conference Organising Secretary he was—as likely as not operating the lantern, as slide projectors were known in those days, and not, therefore, attending the reading of the papers at the IBG).

The Council met later in the day and was informed that 'the following works, finished or in progress were offered to the Institute': A. F. Martin, ' Newfoundland '; R. W. Steel, ' Sierra Leone '; A. E. Smailes, ' Population and settlement in north-east England '; and H. A. Matthews, ' Chilean climates '.

In the event, and in part at least because of the outbreak of war later in the year, none of these manuscripts was received by the Institute. Indeed the first that I knew of the discussion of my work on Sierra Leone was when I read the minutes of this meeting of the Council when I started my work on the preparation of this history of the IBG!

Also at the meeting there was discussion about the desirability of circularising training college lecturers in geography with a view to their becoming members, as well as of those university teachers of geography who were not already members; and the Treasurer was instructed to look into the possibility of subscriptions being paid by Banker's Order. At the subsequent meeting of the Council held at University College London on 6 March 1939 it was reported that the circular had resulted in replies from one training college teacher and one university non-member; and, not for the first nor the last time, there was an instruction to the Secretary ' to express to the publishers the Council's anxiety over the delay in the publication of the Wooldridge and Linton memoir '.

The minutes of the Council meeting of 5 January 1939 were not confirmed and signed by the President until 27 September 1945 and the minutes of the Annual General Meeting held on the same day were not signed as a correct record until 5 January 1946. These facts need to be underlined in an account of the history of the first fifty years of the Institute for it must always be recalled that in effect for six years the IBG was dormant, if not moribund, with all its officers, and most of its members, having other tasks and other concerns to fill their time during the period of the Second World War. The IBG began almost a second existence in late 1945, though it was able to build on the foundations laid so firmly, and so devotedly, by the pioneer geographers in the Institute during the 1930s.

It is for that reason that I have concentrated on more of the detail of Council discussions and Annual General Meeting deliberations in the early years than is possible, or desirable, for the later years of consolidation and expansion. The Institute of pre-war years was small in membership and not very strong in its influence, overshadowed in many respects by the long and great tradition of the RGS and the considerable activity among those teaching the subject, particularly in schools, in the GA. Membership was small (Figure 1) since, at least in the early years, it was assumed that only university teachers qualified. The total membership in December 1938 was 81, all but thirteen of whom were university teachers, and for a variety of reasons not all of these wanted to join—some, it appears, because they saw the new body in competition with, and even antagonistic towards, the RGS and the GA. Nearly half a century later it seems pointless to dwell on these attitudes or to attempt to refute the argument, although it should be recorded that it is a matter on which a number of correspondents among senior geographers still alive today have addressed me, some with considerable vehemence. The feeling, however unjustified it may have been, did exist and influenced the decision of some to have nothing to do with the Institute at this time. It would be invidious to refer to some who stood out and refused to belong in these early days, especially as several of them decided to join during the post-war period by which time it was clear that the IBG had a very specific role to play in the geographical world and so needed all the support, in universities and elsewhere, that it could command. What is significant is that nearly all of the active and influential geographers of pre-war years joined the Institute, many as founder members, as listed in Appendix C, including A. E. Trueman, Professor of Geology (and Geography) at the University College of Swansea who later (after some years as Professor of Geology at Glasgow) became chairman of the University Grants Committee. The Institute's minute books are almost the only archival records of this period. It is doubtful whether many letters on IBG matters were written at the time, and these would mostly have been hand-written, which explains why there are no copies (and almost no files). Two letters, both from Baker to Buchanan, have survived, and they appear to have travelled rather more quickly than they would today. On 5 July 1938 Baker wrote from Oxford to Buchanan in London about his fears as to whether the Institute could survive financially (the letter begins ' Have you any time to think about the IBG? I am a little concerned about its future '). Two days later he could send a supplementary letter, having already had a reply from Buchanan. One wishes that more of such letters had survived for the final paragraph of the first letter reads:

' I have for some time been turning over in my mind the project of an atlas. The Historical Association derives a large revenue from the sale of a small historical atlas and I wondered if we could produce an Atlas of Political and Economic Geography. It would be quite a simple black and white affair with perhaps a few pages of suitable text. If we could make it a joint effort, so much the better. We must between us have plenty of material. What do you think about the idea? If we could do it I think Philip would publish it and we might make quite a bit out of it. I don't know of anything that would compete directly with it. Let me have your views. ' A PS adds: ' I don't mean our two selves, but " An Atlas of Economic and Political Geography, issued by the Institute of British Geographers, edited by . . . " ' But for the outbreak of war in the following year such an atlas might very well have materialised, and it could have been a significant indication of what the IBG was capable of doing.

Some personal reminiscences of certain founder members of the IBG appear in the special issue of *Transactions* published in January 1983. What the analysis of all these records underlines is how fragile and povery-stricken the Institute of those early days was. In the words of the Editor of *Area*, reporting on the fiftieth anniversary annual conference at Edinburgh on January 1983, the realisation of ' how precarious its early years have been and how modest were the aspirations of the founders put talk of present crises very much in perspective '. The important message of those years is that, despite all the difficulties, the Institute survived and so was able to form the basis for the upsurge and expansion that characterised the immediate post-war years and the slightly later period of expansion in higher education. As Buchanan (1954) put it in his presidential address in the twenty-first year of the Institute's existence, ' the pre-war period of quiet consolidation had given a firm foundation for the spectacular development of the post-war years ' (*Transactions* 20, 7).

The other special interest in these early records lies in the nature (and even the intensity) of the discussions in both Council and the Annual General Meetings. There is perhaps less difference between the 1930s and the 1980s than we sometimes think—or perhaps it is that geographers, like leopards, do not change their spots. The matter of the constitution looms large in the debates of the 1930s and the same names appear and reappear as the proposers of motions and amendments. There were numerous discussions about the composition and functions of the Editorial Board and an insistence that there should be fair and proper, yet at the same time very rigorous, consideration of work submitted to the IBG with a view to publication. It is interesting, too, to observe the establishment of some of the very procedures—the nomination of Council members by the Council for example—that nearly half a century later have been subjected to the careful and critical scrutiny of members of the Institute, many of whom see this as an undemocratic process that called for substantial modification, if not complete abolition.

The emphasis laid on field work and the importance given to the organisation of field meetings are noteworthy. It was one of the ways in which the link between the new Institute and the then strong and long-established meeting of geographers under the auspices of Section E of the British Association for the Advancement of Science was maintained and indeed strengthened, with field excursions arranged (as recorded above) in the Lake District and the Peak District. The lack of support for a post-Cambridge field meeting was noted but the officers were undeterred and arrangements were in hand in 1939 for an excursion to follow the British Association's meeting in Dundee. In fact it was abandoned after two days because of the deteriorating international situation and the imminence of general war following on the German invasion of Poland at the beginning of September 1939.

Though there were no formal meetings of the IBG between March 1939 and September 1945 the Officers remained in post although all three of them (Baker, Buchanan and Matthews) were in the Services during most of that time and so were not in a position to play an active part in any matters relating to the interests of the IBG. As Buchanan (1954) pointed out '. . . the outbreak of the Second World War ended the activities of the Institute for six years ' (*Transactions* 20, 7). There were, however, some developments relating to the suggestion, referred to above (p. 17), that exchanges of publications should take place between the IBG and the Association of American Geographers. Whittlesey, the editor of the *Annals of the Association of American Geographers*, had promised to raise the matter at the meeting of the Council of the Association of American Geographers towards the end of December 1937. The minute book is silent about the subsequent negotiations but some of us became beneficiaries of the exchange arrangements made and Buchanan, in his presidential address of 1954, refers to ' an agreement that was its own tribute to the patience and goodwill in negotiation of Professor Derwent Whittlesey on the American side and of Mr J. N. L. Baker on our side ' (*Transactions* 20, 13). By it each member of the two organisations received without further payment the publications of both. Unfortunately, as Buchanan points out, when the war broke out it became difficult to sustain Institute activities in any way, and even a Council meeting could

not be arranged. Nevertheless the President obtained Council approval by correspondence to a reduction of the subscription from £2 to one guinea (£1 1s)
so that members might continue to receive the *Annals* from the USA in default
of Institute publications to exchange for them. Unfortunately this expedient
served its purpose for only a very limited time since it was ended by the inability
of the American Post Office in war conditions to continue to accept the *Annals*
for transmission to Britain. Attempts to revive the scheme shortly after the end
of the war failed because of the radical change in the situation in North America
consequent upon the merger in 1949 of the Association of American Geographers
and the Society of Professional Geographers. Eventually, however, alternative
arrangements were made, at a much later date and in a very modified form.

No publications appeared between the Wooldridge and Linton monograph,
Structure, surface and drainage in south-east England (1939) and *Transactions and
Papers, 1946* (1946), and members paying subscriptions annually became in
effect lapsed members. Those paying £2 by Banker's Order—the Treasurer had
evidently found that such a method was feasible and about 15 members appear
to have taken advantage of it—accumulated a credit balance with the Institute,
though even the total sums involved were very small in relation to the subscription today—in fact the largest individual balance recorded was only about half
of a member's subscription for a single year in 1983.

Note

1. Alice Garnett (1983) ' IBG: the formative years—some reflections ', *Transactions* NS 8, 27–35
    S. H. Beaver (1983) ' Recollections of a founder member ', *Transactions* NS 8, 36–7
    E. G. Bowen (1983) ' Some early impressions ', *Transactions* NS 8, 38–40
    See also M. J. Wise (1983) ' Three founder members of the IBG: R. Ogilvie Buchanan, Sir
        Dudley Stamp, S. W. Wooldridge, A personal tribute ', *Transactions* NS 8, 41–54, and
        H. C. Darby (1983) ' Academic geography in Britain, 1918–1946 ', *Transactions* NS 8,
        14–26

III

The post-war revival and consolidation

The last meeting of the Council before the Second World War had been held at University College London on 6 March 1939 under the presidency of J. N. L. Baker and with four other members of the Council present. The Minutes end with the significant words 'the meeting then adjourned', and it was not until 27 September 1945 that the Council met again. Baker was still President and Buchanan Secretary and Treasurer, and H. J. Wood was also present; but the Honorary Assistant Secretary, H. A. Matthews, had died during the war, and the first item of business was a reference to his death. Matthews had been the first Assistant Secretary of the IBG in 1933 and 1934 and had been re-appointed to that office in 1939. He was the only one of the founder members of the IBG to be a casualty during the war while serving in the Meteorological Branch of the Royal Air Force, and Council's resolution reads as follows: 'The President referred to the loss sustained by the Institute and by the subject in the death of Dr H. A. Matthews, and it was agreed that the Secretary should convey the Institute's profound sense of loss to Mrs Matthews.'

The Second World War saw the end of many institutions and the newly established, and still very infant, IBG might well have been one of its casualties but for the devotion of a team of its members with a real faith in their subject and a confidence in the way in which they saw the Institute helping in the post-war revival and growth of geography. To appreciate the miracle of the Institute's survival after 1945, when in Alice Garnett's words (1983) 'a new "IBG Phoenix" arose, vastly increased in size and strength from the ashes of World War II' (*Transactions* NS 8, 34), it is necessary to appreciate the scene in the academic world at the time. The War had destroyed (or at least very seriously disrupted) much of the university system as it existed in Britain in 1939, so that many universities were in considerable disarray, and it would have been easy for them, and their much depleted staffs, to have concentrated wholly on the teaching of the greatly increased number of students, including many returned ex-servicemen, to the total exclusion of research activities and the building-up of their disciplines. Departments of geography, never large in the inter-war period, had lost many of their staff. Many university geographers had, in one way or another, been involved in work in the national interest, but it is even harder now than it was for Buchanan in 1954 to make what he termed 'an

assessment of the contribution of Institute members to the war effort'
(*Transactions* 20, 14). He wished then that a suggestion made in 1946 by
the then President (J. N. L. Baker) that a record be compiled of the war
service of IBG members had been followed up, and in default of such a list he
summarised what had happened as follows (*Transactions* 20, 14):

'... while many served in fields quite alien to their professional expertise (notably as
fighting sailors, soldiers or airmen) others quickly proved their value in closely related
services (meteorology, survey and cartography, for example) while increasingly the intelligence services of the fighting forces availed themselves directly of the trained ability of
geographers, whose contributions ranged from such durable productions as the Geographical Handbooks of the Naval Intelligence Division, to such ephemeral but vital items
as split-second operational interpretations of air-photographs'.

Other geographers became temporary civil servants and in particular served
in the Ministry of Town and Country Planning, created in 1943; while others
continued to be involved in the administrative and teaching functions of
universities which succeeded, throughout the war years, in remaining open and
receiving students, many of whom were, however, in residence for only a
relatively short period.

There was at the time a great deal of talking about the creation of a new society
at the end of hostilities—typified perhaps particularly by the victory of the
Labour Party in the General Election of July 1945—and several geographers
were involved in the production of some of the blueprints for this new
society. E. G. R. Taylor, for example, had been involved with a group of younger
geographers even before the outbreak of war in the preparation of background
material for the Barlow Report on *The distribution of the industrial population*
(Cmd. 6153, 1940) (see p. 106) and she was always a strong advocate for a
National Atlas of Britain as a basis for planning, and as a member of the
Consultative Panel of the Ministry of Town and Country Planning contributed
to the discussion of regional organisation and the location of industry.[1]

L. D. Stamp, assisted by many other geographers, had been involved throughout the 1930s in the Land Utilisation Survey of Britain and in 1942 he was
appointed chief adviser on rural land use to the Ministry of Agriculture. He was
Vice-Chairman of the Scott Committee that reported in 1942 on *Land utilisation
in rural areas* (Cmd. 6378) and the nature and tenor of the whole report indicates
his role in that committee as its moving spirit.

With hindsight, nine years after the end of the war, Buchanan (*Transactions,*
20, 1954, 14) was able to state that 'There seems little reason to doubt that
the enhanced reputation of the subject at the end of the war owed much to the
recognition of the value of geographers' contributions to the war effort'. But in
the immediate aftermath of the war, it was by no means clear what was likely
to happen to disciplines such as geography, and the chaos in universities as
ex-servicemen flooded back to complete their university courses, or, with the
help of ex-service grants, to begin their higher education, created many problems
and uncertainties in universities throughout the country.

Looking back on these post-war years, one can discern a remarkable growth
in universities generally—and perhaps particularly in departments of geography—

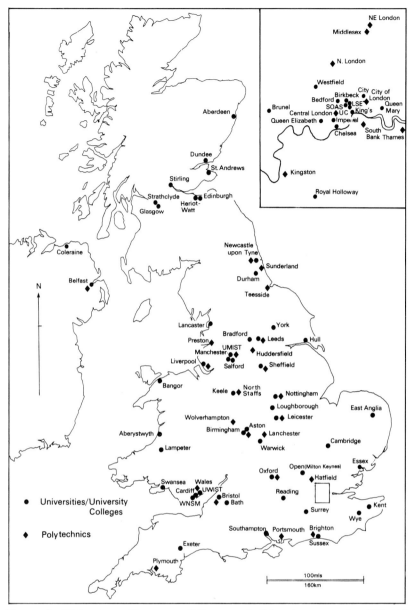

Figure 2. Universities, University Colleges and Polytechnics in the UK. All universities in Great Britain are included, together with the constituent institutions of the two federal universities of London and of Wales, and all those polytechnics which have identifiable groups of geographers. The inset shows the location of the colleges and polytechnics in the Greater London area (including Brunel University and the City University) apart from Wye College (Kent), which is part of the University of London. The Central Institutions of Scotland are not shown. The following abbreviations are used: UMIST—The University of Manchester Institute of Science and Technology; UWIST—The University of Wales Institute of Science and Technology; WNSM—The Welsh National School of Medicine. The New University of Ulster at Coleraine and the Ulster Polytechnic in Belfast are included though they are in process of merging in a new 'Polyversity' with campuses in Belfast, Coleraine and Londonderry, to be known as The University of Ulster.

and undoubtedly it was a time of very considerable expansion in the geographical profession. It was, of course, nothing on the scale of that following on the publication of the Robbins Report of 1963 (*Higher Education,* Cmnd. 2154, 1963) and the founding of a number of new universities during the 1960s. But there were modest developments following 1945, which included the establishment at Keele, near Newcastle under Lyme, of a new university institution, the University College of North Staffordshire (now the University of Keele), with Geography as one of its Foundation Chairs; and these provided a firm platform from which there could, at a later stage, be a large forward leap for the subject (Figure 2).

The number of staff appointments increased considerably as a result of the increase in student numbers with the return of the ex-servicemen, and several departments which had been minute in pre-war days suddenly grew to a reasonable size; but in general the student increases were not matched by an increase in resources. In those days no-one referred to staff/student ratios or to what it is now fashionable to call ' student-contact hours '. Indeed many university teachers thought that the main purpose of their having jobs in universities was to teach students and to develop academic and social relationships with them. There was in fact little time to devote to research in those days, and there were almost no facilities to undertake it. No-one talked of academic staff/technician ratios because, as often as not, there were no technicians in the modern sense of the term, although many departments had that invaluable aid, the general handyman, who willingly and very effectively undertook any jobs that needed to be done. Secretarial help was minimal. When I was Acting Secretary of the Institute in 1948–49, and later during my years as Editor of the *Transactions*, it was necessary for me, a member of the staff of the Oxford School of Geography, to seek outside help with the typing of letters, and both I and the Institute owe a great debt of gratitude to the wife of the minister of my church in north Oxford who very willingly gave up time, for almost nothing, to assist the Institute and one of its officers with essential secretarial work.

Many departments had to find additional space for increased student and staff numbers or to create it by the sub-division of larger rooms. Geography departments were often located in old houses for there were few purpose-built departments at that time (Cambridge was, I think, the main exception, though there may have been others). Laboratories and space for map-drawing classes had to be found, these being newly created needs for many geographers at the time. It is as well to recall that the best-selling book by F. J. Monkhouse and H. R. Wilkinson, *Maps and diagrams*, which was first published in 1952, was a new type of student text for it was in fact the published version of the Cartography courses that the two authors gave in the Department of Geography in the University of Liverpool. With expansion in the early 1950s, the Liverpool Department, based in a beautiful Victorian house in Abercromby Square, had to spread into an adjacent house. The department in Newcastle upon Tyne, at that time still a part of the University of Durham, occupied a series of houses in Sydenham Terrace; and R. F. Peel, on going from Cambridge to the newly-established Chair of Geography in Leeds, embarked upon a massive conversion of some adjoining private houses which became the home of the rapidly growing Department of Geography in that University. One of the post-war Departments of Geography that was specially designed for the purpose by its first Professor of Geography, W. G. V. Balchin, and his colleagues, was that in the University College of Swansea where the Natural Sciences Building, opened in 1955, housed the departments of Geology, Botany and Zoology, as well as Geography.

New and converted buildings belonged, however, to the expansion period of the 1950s, and in the immediate post-war years there was little indication that such an enlargement of departments of geography would be taking place. The Institute had, as has already been indicated, become dormant during the Second World War and many may have doubted whether it could be revived. Membership was small (still less than 100) and there was no central organisation or institutional infrastructure. There were minute books for Annual General Meetings and for the Council's deliberations, and a large book recording the payments of subscriptions and the state of the Institute's account. There was no depository for the possessions of the Institute, and the stock of publications was kept by the Institute's publishers, George Philip and Son Ltd, at their Willesden depot. Facilities were indeed minimal and no-one then could have foreseen even in the wildest of dreams what is, by comparison, the size , wealth, complexity and even sophistication of the IBG in its fiftieth year.

That the Institute was first resuscitated and then grew steadily in the post-war years—in parallel as it were with the development of geography as a discipline that was increasingly accepted as a proper subject for university study—was largely due to the efforts of a handful of devoted geographers with a real faith in their subject, and to the support that they received from colleagues, both those who had been in university posts throughout the war and those who were returning from the services and from other forms of war-time employment (and some from prisoner-of-war camps in Europe and Asia) and from new recruits to the profession. Baker and Buchanan had been Officers of the Institute before the outbreak of war and they took immediate steps, from their posts in Oxford and University College London respectively, to secure the revival of the Institute by calling a meeting of the Council in London on 27 September 1945, within less than seven weeks of the end of the Japanese war. They received considerable support from those serving on the Council (to which they had been elected as long ago as 1939 or earlier). Among those who especially deserve mention were A. G. Ogilvie, who from the very early days of the IBG appears to have acted as a spokesman for the Institute among his colleagues in Scotland[2], A. A. Miller and S. W. Wooldridge. Whether election to the presidency of a learned society is regarded as an honour given for ' services rendered ' or not (and whatever the Institute's view of presidential office may have been over the first fifty years of its existence), it is worthy of record that between 1939 and 1953 the Presidents of the IBG were—in this sequence—Baker, Miller, Wooldridge, Ogilvie and Buchanan; and it is right that, in the course of the celebrations of the Institute as it exists today after half-a-century of activity, special praise should be paid to those geographers of the immediate post-war period who toiled to bring about the revival of the Institute, greatly helped by the faith of other founder members, the majority of whom were still active at the end of the Second World War. But it was, above all, the enthusiasm, devotion and confidence of a few who were particularly far-sighted and, in the best sense of the term, ambitious, that ensured a future for the Institute. Not even they, however, could have hoped to see an IBG as numerically, even financially, strong and as academically diverse as it is today.

With the resumption of activities after 1945, as normally as anything was in those difficult yet exciting days in both national and university life, it would be tedious to record, even to summarise, all the matters discussed by the Council of the IBG at its meetings or the items of business dealt with at Annual General Meetings. The latter have always drawn a higher proportion of the total membership than is customary in learned (and indeed most other) societies and they have often been somewhat more informal affairs than is usually the case with such business meetings. In Council the same matters recur with remarkable frequency and many of them have been discussed with a different emphasis as a consequence of the changing composition of the Council over the years.

Thus in the Council meetings immediately after the restarting of the IBG in 1945 these are among the items of business that came up for review:

i.   members' subscriptions (the minute reads ' in view of the strong financial situation of the Institute and the present difficulties of members, especially junior members, it was agreed to recommend to the Annual General Meeting that the subscription be reduced from £2 to £1 '). The Institute's cash-in-hand at the end of the war appears to have been £511. 0. 9, this sum reflecting in part the accumulation of subscriptions paid by Bankers' Orders by a few members during the war years;

ii.   the resumption of the January meetings of the Institute, making arrangements so that IBG activities would not clash with those of the GA; publication policy which the President agreed to review at the Annual General Meeting;

iii. a discussion of arrangements for Departments of Geography to receive gifts of a selection of current Geographical Section of the General Staff (GSGS) map series from the War Office, as a result of the efforts of E. C. Willatts, Maps Officer in the Ministry of Town and Country Planning;

iv.   the appointment of referees for papers submitted to the Institute with a view to publication, and consideration of referees' reports (business that took up a very high proportion of Council's time for a number of years until it agreed to give greater authority to the Editor both in the choice of referees and in the decision as to what should be published); and

v.   the possibility of renewing the arrangement for the exchange of publication between the IBG and the Association of American Geographers, the wish being expressed that, with the cessation of hostilities and the partial relaxation of pressure upon shipping across the North Atlantic, this much-appreciated exchange programme would be resumed as soon as possible.

In the immediate post-war period R. O. Buchanan was the outstanding figure. He himself recorded many of his views when the Institute was twenty-one years old for his presidential address, delivered in 1954 (*Transactions* 20, 1–14) was in his own words ' some attempt . . . to survey . . . twenty-one years, to bring to the younger members some idea of the story of the early hopes and struggles of their organisation, and to attempt some assessment of what has been accomplished and what are the tasks that lie ahead '. He did not see this as ' a detached impersonal, critical history ' because, as he put it, ' for the whole of those twenty-one years, with the solitary exception of the year 1952 ', he had been continuously in office. He felt, therefore, that he had developed, ' if not a possessive parent complex, at any rate an intimacy of attachment that is quite inimicable to an aloof impartial examination of the record '.

Buchanan was surveying a shorter period and a much smaller and less complex organisation than the IBG is after fifty years of existence. But he was very intimately associated with it at a time when he knew everyone and was well aware of all that was going on, and this history will not attempt to repeat all the significant aspects of the IBG's development that he dealt with in his presidential address. Tribute must be paid to the commanding figure that he was throughout those early years, and in the post-war years when his advice was constantly sought by Officers of the IBG even after he had left office. The traditions that he established continued for a number of years, certainly throughout the 1950s, and those of us in office during that period (and there were far fewer changes then than has been the case in more recent years) were conscious of his continuing influence and perhaps somewhat averse to changing the pattern of organisation that had served the Institute so well in its earlier years. Thus the business of Council remained remarkably similar, not only while Buchanan was an Officer but in subsequent years as well. Perusal of the Council minutes, all of which are handwritten until A. E. Smailes had them typed after the first meeting at which he was present as Buchanan's successor in the Secretaryship (27 April 1951), shows how much time was devoted to certain matters which in more recent years have been dealt with by smaller groups of members or by executive action on the part of the Officers. Arrangements for conferences were discussed at length, sometimes in the presence of a representative of the department responsible for the local arrangements. The election of new members is listed, and even on occasions the names are given of those who were deemed to have ceased to be members of the IBG through failure to pay their subscriptions, (some surprising names appear in these lists!). There are frequent references to the importance of maintaining good relationships with other geographical societies; and there are discussions, sometimes extending over more than one Council meeting, about the criteria for eligibility for membership.

A very high proportion of Council's time was taken up in dealing with publication policy and the content of the *Transactions*. The Minutes record not only the names of authors and the titles of their papers but also the persons invited to act as referees; and in many cases there is a record on the discussion arising from these reports. This emphasis on the importance of publications is indicative of the basis for the Institute coming into existence and it underlines the continued concern of the Council as a whole, and of its individual members, to ensure that this side of its activities was properly and fully maintained. The Editorial Board of earlier days had not been very successful in its operation, and Council undertook a responsibility which in many societies would have been delegated early on to a smaller group. In the 1950s it was still possible for Council to operate in this way though it did mean that some meetings were very lengthy, and in many instances the editor's recommendation was eventually accepted but only after prolonged, and even occasionally heated, discussion. As is made clear elsewhere (see p. 60), the system had to change at a later date because of the pressure of other business and because it was essential that more authority should be placed in editorial hands. But for the 1950s it was a system that worked very well, and no-one, including the editor, seemed anxious to change it.

I was particularly associated with this side of the Institute's activities throughout most of my service as a member of the Council, or as an Officer of the Institute, between 1947 and the beginning of 1961. My election to Council took place in unusual circumstances. A number of the younger members of the Institute were concerned about the nature of the Council's nominations for new members of Council. They thought there were too many professors and too many readers, and not enough ordinary members. They saw Council nominating as its successors people who might, in their view, be too establishment-dominated. On the evening before the Annual General Meeting of 1947, as I was about to leave for my home in Oxford (and with no intention of returning to London for the AGM the following morning) I was tackled by Eila Campbell and Gladys Hickman, and asked if I would let my name go forward for election as an ordinary member of the Council. In my absence on the following morning, I was nominated and seconded by the two of them and, somewhat to my embarrassment, elected. E. G. R. Taylor, a formidable person by any standards, said at the meeting, so I was informed afterwards, that she knew nothing about Mr Steel but she understood that he was young and was at Oxford, and that was good enough for her! The fact that I had been elected in a ballot and that the person defeated was a professor who had given me considerable encouragement in my African research, did not help, though subsequently the professor became a member of Council in his own right and we served happily together for some months.

In normal circumstances I suspect that I would have served my three years as an ordinary member of Council and then disappeared from view. Buchanan was, however, taking study leave in the session 1948–49, and returning to his native home in New Zealand for the first time for many years. The Minutes indicate that the Assistant Secretary, W. V. Lewis of Cambridge, was to be asked to take over from Buchanan and be Acting Secretary for the period. Lewis decided that he could not undertake these additional responsibilities and the choice fell on me, whether as the second name on the list of possibilities (the Minutes are silent on this point) or as the youngest member of the Council who could not reply negatively after everyone else had been asked and refused, I shall never know. Thus I found myself Acting Secretary of the IBG within months of election to the Council, and I enjoyed the experience though it did cause me a considerable amount of additional work at a time when the teaching load in the University of Oxford was particularly heavy. I had contact with many geographers, most of them senior to myself, during that year, and I suspect that that experience had a good deal to do with the shaping of my future career.

This history of the IBG should not be autobiographical but it is necessary to explain my early involvement with the IBG. While I was Acting Secretary I had responsibility for much of the editorial work since Buchanan had had to leave a number of publishing matters unfinished when he left for New Zealand. I also found myself responsible, as the local organising Secretary, for the first-ever residential conference of the IBG, held in my own College in Oxford, Jesus, in January 1949. Again it was a very valuable experience for a comparatively young man, and I hope that all those who have followed me as Local Secretaries for IBG conferences share with me in thinking that the work is very worthwhile, provided that all goes smoothly with the conference arrangements and that people are as appreciative, and understanding, as they certainly were at this first conference held outside London.

When Buchanan returned, Lewis indicated that he did not wish to be re-elected as Assistant Secretary, with responsibility for the finances of the Institute, and I was nominated in his stead. This meant that for a year I looked after the finances while continuing to do much of the editorial work, and Council decided that it would be appropriate that I should take on further editorial responsibilities although, without a constitutional change, a new office could not immediately be created. Council agreed on 5 September 1950 that ' it was most desirable that Mr Steel should remain responsible for the editorial work, and the Secretary was therefore instructed to approach Mr A. E. Smailes for his consent to be nominated by Council' [as Secretary]. At a meeting on 3 November 1950 the composition of Council and the duties of Officers were discussed. The Secretary referred to ' the greatly augmented work and responsibility involved in the editorial duties. The point had come when it ought to be considered whether the editorial work should not devolve upon a specifically appointed editor, with a seat on the Council in his own right, instead of being merely one of the items to which the Secretary and the Assistant Secretary had to attend. If that were agreed, a constitutional amendment would be necessary to provide for editorial status, to abolish the non-functioning editorial board of the existing constitution, and to increase the membership of the Council from nine to the consequent ten '. Because of the need for the approval of any amendment by the Annual General Meeting, followed by a postal ballot, ' it would still not be possible to make a formal appointment to the position of Editor until January 1952. Meantime Mr Steel would continue to be responsible for the editorial work '.

One of my first acts as the Officer responsible for editorial work was to negotiate an agreement with a new printer. There were some prolonged discussions in Council, and with various firms, including George Philip and Son Ltd, but eventually the decision was taken in the light of estimates submitted, whereby that of the Alden Press in Oxford was less than half that submitted by our publishers, and considerably below the figure tendered by another firm of printers who had considerable experience of work with learned societies. The move to the Alden Press was a particularly happy one from my point of view because of the proximity of the firm to the Oxford School of Geography, of which I was at that time a member of the staff, and because of the great personal interest taken in this new work by Raymond Alden and by W. J. Furneaux, who became their Managing Director quite soon after the Institute moved its business to his firm. The immediate post-war years were marked by considerable difficulties in the publishing world, as much concerned with the supply of material as with labour problems, and the Institute was affected by these just at the time when Council had taken the important decision to publish in future papers in preference to monographs—a reversal of pre-war policy but in keeping with the special needs at the time when many shorter papers were being offered for publication by a rapidly growing membership. The Honorary Secretary had always had responsibility for editorial work and for negotiations with the Institute's publishers/printers, George Philip and Son Ltd. George Philip, with a superb international reputation in all matters cartographic, were not particularly geared for the Institute's needs or for the special post-war problems of publishing. Volumes were taking too long to appear, a situation common to many other learned societies at the time, but the Council became increasingly concerned with the delays, especially in view of the dominant importance of publishing as an Institute activity. The Alden Press had little experience of work with learned or scientific journals, and (as I discovered later) Bill Furneaux's special interest in the IBG stemmed from his desire to build up a new image for the firm and to work in new fields of activity. In fact in the course of ten years the firm's involvement in the publication of journals from learned societies increased enormously, and Bill Furneaux has always attributed this to the experience that he and his colleagues had with *Transactions*. If the Alden Press benefited in the long term, then the IBG certainly profited greatly from the concern that was shown for their publications during this period when it was very important to maintain both the high standards of production characteristic of the pre-war years and the rigidity of printing schedules at a time when many journals were appearing much later than should have been the case.

Other matters relating to the editorial interests of these years are discussed elsewhere (pp. 56–9) but there were other features of the IBG at this period that call for attention. The beginning of residential conferences is significant in that the Institute has never reverted to the non-residential conferences that were typical of the early years of its existence. Even on the two occasions when the Institute has returned to London, it has been on the basis of residence being provided for a high proportion of the participants in a College (Bedford College in 1952), or in several halls of residence in Bloomsbury (1969 when the conference was based particularly on the Department of Geography at University College London). The first conference in Oxford was an outstanding success, and although the total number of members present (92) was small compared with the much greater numbers that have attended more recent conferences, the proportion of the total membership involved in the conference was high, a feature that has remained true of conferences ever since.

There were difficulties in the early days, some anticipated and others unforeseen. Since the first conference had been held in Oxford, it was not unnatural to think of Cambridge as the venue for the second conference, and a decision to accept an invitation from Cambridge was taken by Council at its meeting in Oxford on 9 January 1949. It was felt that the disadvantage of holding the meetings outside London was less than might have appeared when residential conferences were first discussed, and the Minute reads ' the advantages of meeting in Cambridge were so obvious that, despite some regrets at the severance of the link with the GA, Mr Farmer's suggestion that the conference be held at St John's College was welcomed. He was left ' to prospect the position in Cambridge ' and at a later meeting (6 May 1949) he reported that 'St John's would provide accommodation for the men, and accommodation for the women would be arranged, probably at Girton '.

At the next Council meeting held in Newcastle upon Tyne at the conclusion of the Annual Conference of the British Association for the Advancement of Science, a woman member of the Council, C. P. Snodgrass of Edinburgh, ' reported the view of some of the members that accommodation arrangements that separated the women and the men were unacceptable and urged that an approach be made to Newnham College which, it was suggested, was prepared to accept mixed parties '. The Council, however, felt that ' it would be churlish to refuse a generous offer because of individual disapproval of Cambridge organisation and customs. The Secretary undertook, however, to see whether improvements in this aspect of the arrangements could tactfully be secured '.

In the event the conference met in Cambridge, with, so far as I can recall, a majority of the men in St John's College while all the women members, together with the male members of the Council and some other men, were housed in St Catharine's College. It was a highly successful conference, and this, together with the success of the Oxford conference in the previous year, ensured that residential conferences continued in future.

It is of interest to note that an overseas guest of the Institute was present at Cambridge in the person of Professor Humlum of Denmark. Though described as ' the guest of the Institute ' the Minute of the Council records that ' the Secretary was instructed to make it clear to Professor Humlum that the Institute was not able to contribute anything to his expenses '. Happily the financial situation of the Institute improved in subsequent years, and overseas guests were properly entertained and financed by the Institute in ever-increasing numbers.

The 1950 conference was to have been held in London though it was to be of a residential character. There were difficulties, and as Assistant Secretary I am recorded as saying (15 March 1950) ' that if suitable London arrangements could not be made, he felt sure that a meeting could be arranged at Oxford again '. The Secretary's Minutes record that ' the general feeling was that an offer from Oxford should be regarded as a last resort, when all other possibilities, including Liverpool for instance, had failed '. Nevertheless the conference was held in Oxford, this time with J. M. Houston as Local Secretary, and the proposed London meeting did not take place until 1953, based upon Bedford College, since in 1952 the IBG met for the first time ever outside England in the University College of Wales at Aberystwyth.

Arthur E. Smailes, then Reader in Geography at University College London but later Reader and then Professor of Geography at Queen Mary College, London, succeeded R. O. Buchanan as Secretary in January 1951 and he remained in that office until January 1962. He thus served the Institute for longer than any of his predecessors or successors. The 1950s were a period of consolidation for the IBG following on the immediate revival of the post-war years and before the growth that took place during the 1960s as a direct result of the huge expansion in higher education provision that was marked by the foundation of new universities, the granting of university status to a number of Colleges of Advanced Technology, and the designation of thirty polytechnics in England and Wales as well as of the ' Central Institutions ' in Scotland. To some members more familiar with the activity of these later boom years in higher education, the earlier period may have appeared almost one of stagnation; but for those who had seen the foundation of the Institute and appreciated the precarious nature of its existence during those early years, the 1950s were marked by several significant developments. The Institute was able to build on the basis provided for it by the expansion in size of departments of geography in universities and by the consequential increase in the size of membership (and ultimately of the financial resources available to it). There was increasing participation by the Institute in national affairs (see pp. 106–7) and the building-up of significant international relationships, particularly through the seminars that began during the 1950s with the Anglo-Polish meeting of 1959 (see pp. 97–8).

Simultaneously there was a strengthening of the financial base of the Institute begun by Farmer and continued by H. C. K. Henderson, who succeeded Farmer as Assistant Secretary in 1956 and whose title was later (1960) changed to that of Treasurer, to indicate his special field of responsibility. It must be emphasised, however, that the Institute continued to operate—of necessity—on a financial shoe-string. Discussions in Council about the meeting of the expenses of Council members had never been very satisfactorily resolved. Reference has already been made to the Council's somewhat brusque reaction in 1950 to the expenses incurred by a distinguished visiting geographer to an IBG conference. On 5 January 1952 it was recorded that ' the expenditure of up to £20 per annum towards defrayment of expenses incurred by Council members in attending meetings of Council was approved. It was decided that members should submit a periodical statement of their expenses and an equitable apportionment of the grant should be made '. This meeting took place in Aberystwyth, not one of the most accessible of venues for an Annual General Meeting or for a meeting of the Council, and clearly it was not anticipated that any member of Council would claim expenses for attendance at it.

Three years later A. F. Martin's proposal ' that the travelling expenses (third class rail) of members of Council in respect of their attendance at Council meetings should be met by the Institute in full ' was agreed, and ' a subsistence allowance of up to 25/- for a night necessarily spent away from home might also be claimed '. It is perhaps worth noting that third class still existed in those days, the second class having been eliminated from travel some years before.

At the Annual General Meeting held at the end of 1955 in the University of Reading, and arising from the Officers' presentation of their reports, it was recorded that ' members again expressed concern about the heavy burden of work that fell upon the Honorary Officers as a natural outcome of the growth of the Institute and its increased publishing activity'. There was a proposal from E. M. J. Campbell and D. K. Smee ' that a sum of up to £150 per annum should be available to provide clerical and other assistance for the Officers as needed ' and this was unanimously agreed by the meeting. This sum was, of course, increased on future occasions so that the position today is very different from what it was then. Nevertheless it was not until much later, and some years after the appointment of an administrative assistant to serve in the central head-quarters of the Institute in London, that Council decisions were taken to make reasonable secretarial help available for its Officers in their different places of work. Even now it may be questioned whether the amount of assistance provided, and the remuneration carried by it, are in any way adequate for the needs of the Institute as it goes into its second half century. But the advances since the 1950s have undoubtedly been considerable and it is as well to be reminded in the 1980s how conditions generally have improved.

Publication remained during these years the Institute's principal *raison d'être* and, as preceding paragraphs (pp. 31–2) and the chapter on IBG publications (especially pp. 57–9) make clear, there was, in the early 1950s, an up-dating of the publications programme, which had suffered severely during the period of great difficulties in the printing trade in the immediate post-war years. Nevertheless feelings of dissatisfaction about the volume of publication were expressed by some members at the annual conference in Aberystwyth in 1952. A group of ' Young Turks '—most of whom later became professors in various universities, together with the Fellow of an Oxbridge College and the Registrar of the second largest university in Britain—mounted a campaign to press the Council to publish more papers more quickly. Council gave careful consideration to the proposals before deciding that such an enlarged programme was not feasible at the time in view of the financial limitations imposed upon it by its publishing and other commitments and the time constraint placed upon an editor for whom it was not possible to provide any paid editorial assistance. But it did not resist in any way the suggestion that a new and independent publication might be launched by this group of geographers: indeed it went on record as expressing the Institute's goodwill towards the new venture, welcoming the journal as ' essentially a supplementary Bulletin in no way intended to draw off support from the Institute and its publications '. Thus *Geographical Studies* came into existence, the first number appearing in 1954. It was printed by the Alden Press, the IBG's printers since 1952, and among the authors in the first issue were A. A. Miller, President of the Institute in 1947, and P. R. Crowe, who had had papers published in three out of four successive issues of the IBG's *Transactions*.

The first editorial, by C. A. Fisher, referred to the 'Third Generation' of geographers, and it deserves to be read even after the passage of nearly thirty years because of the light that it throws on the situation in the geographical world in Britain in this post-war period. Fisher (*Geographical Studies*, 1, 1954, 1) saw the first generation of geographers as being those who had been ' schooled in one or other of nearly all the major disciplines then taught in the universities— mathematics, chemistry, geology, botany, zoology, history, economics and classics ', who ' were united in their revolt against narrow specialism and in their insistence on the supreme importance of the " world view " '.

The second generation, consisting of those who were taught, at least in part, by these pioneers, Fisher saw as ' undeniably privileged '. They benefited, he suggested, ' from close contact with minds of exceptional calibre, and were often not merely spectators but active participants in the continuing task of building up the geographical synthesis in which their teachers were engaged. Moreover, having been taught by men who had themselves been disciplined in one or more of the specialist branches of learning, their feet remained firmly on the ground even though their heads might occupy a more exalted position ' (*op. cit.*, 1–2). This generation was the first to study geography at undergraduate level; they included (though Fisher did not make this point) a high proportion of the founder members of the Institute.

The geographers of the third generation—in which Fisher appears to have included himself although he had graduated in Cambridge before the outbreak of war—were faced, he thought, ' with far greater opportunities than those which confronted their predecessors. The battle for recognition has been won; the barriers to the promised land have been broken down; all that remains is to enter into the heritage which is ours and to build soundly for the future.' He saw difficulties, however, since the third generation, trained only by geographers, was taking over the synthesis ready-made. It was spared ' the intense intellectual effort by which its predecessors unwittingly added to their mental stature and, furthermore, it lacked any first-hand experience of the rigorous discipline of specialist studies ' (Fisher *op. cit.* 2).

What, then, was the response of the third generation to these challenges? Fisher offered a series of suggestions in the conviction that ' if a geography department does nothing more than bring together under one roof a body of people whose combined interests reach out across the barriers into several of the major specialist fields yet who nevertheless share the " world view " in common, it will abundantly justify its place in any university '.

And it was, his editorial continued (*op. cit.*, 3) ' in this belief that *Geographical Studies* is being launched by a group of third generation British geographers. We need hardly say that it makes no claim to speak for the members of that generation as a whole, nor does it seek to limit itself to the publication of their work or to the expression of any particular viewpoint. On the contrary, we hope that it will stimulate constructive controversy and we shall welcome material from whatever source, certainly not least from geographers overseas, many of whom have already shown a lively interest in our proposals. For if *Geographical Studies* can contribute something to a discussion and clarification of the major issues with which all geographers the world over are faced today it will, we submit, be fulfilling a useful purpose '.

Six issues of *Geographical Studies* appeared between 1954 and 1959 and some very significant papers were published, many of them being frequently cited in other learned journals. But despite the valiant and devoted efforts of the Editorial Board, the supply of papers gradually dwindled while the costs of publication increased steadily, so that in 1959 the decision was taken to suspend production. By then the Institute was producing more—including, in 1957, the first of its post-war monographs, G. J. Butland's work on southern Chile—and there was a considerably reduced gap between the date of submission and the date of publication.

The initial success and then the demise of *Geographical Studies* is relevant to the history of the IBG because it is a reflection of some of the special problems in the years immediately after the War that faced those working in universities, and of the willingness of a few geographers to respond to the challenge of a difficult situation. Its disappearance in 1959 is also a sign of the increasing success of geographers in securing publication space in journals associated with cognate disciplines—the *Agricultural History Review,* for example, or the *Quarterly Journal of the Geological Society.* This in itself was an encouraging sign of the recognition by colleagues in other subjects that geographers had important contributions to make to the progress of their own disciplines. Perhaps it is also worthy of note that at no time was any rancour shown by the Institute's officers, or the rank and file membership, towards the new journal; indeed rather the reverse. As Editor of the *Transactions* at the time, I am happy to place on record that all the geographers active in the launching of *Geographical Studies* were close friends of mine in the early 1950s and have remained so to this day, since all of them are still alive apart from Fisher who died in 1982; and Charles Fisher and I, throughout most of this period, were collaborating closely as joint editors of a volume of essays.[3]

There was, therefore, a great deal happening during the 1950s, some of these activities being more appropriately recorded in other sections of this volume. Compared with later periods there were fewer changes of officers although a regular infusion of new blood came to the Council through the election of new Ordinary Members of Council. The Institute's finances at the time did not permit any major new initiatives—and the fate of *Geographical Studies* underlines the problem and uncertainties of these years. Continuity was certainly provided by the two combinations of Smailes, Farmer and Steel and, later, Smailes, Henderson and Steel—much as Buchanan's presence as an officer had done in earlier years (see Appendix D). With hindsight, one can see that more regular changes of officer might have been beneficial to the Institute, had the right people been willing and able to take on the responsibilities of office at the time. But the most appropriate tribute possible to a long-serving Secretary was paid at the Annual General Meeting in Liverpool in January 1962 when the following resolution was carried unanimously: ' That the Institute thanks Professor Smailes warmly for his most valuable services as honorary Secretary during the past eleven years. It deeply appreciates his tireless energy in promoting the advancement of geography. '

Notes

1. Taylor, E. G. R. (1938) 'Geographical distribution of industry', *Geographical Journal*, 102, 22–39; Taylor, E. G. R. (1940) ' Plans for a national atlas, ' *Geographical Journal,* 105, 96–108.
2. There is a significant comment on Ogilvie by Baker (President 1939–47) in Baker, J. N. L. (1959) ' A. G. Ogilvie and his place in British geography' in Miller, R. and Watson, J. W. (1959) *Geographical essays in memory of Alan G. Ogilvie,* 6; ' . . . but for his (i.e. Ogilvie's) tactful and sympathetic help the early days of the Institute of British Geographers would have been much more difficult than they were. '
3. *Geographical essays on British tropical lands.* This was—after inordinate delays, not all of them the fault of either the editors or the contributors—eventually published in 1956 by George Philip and Son Ltd, who were still the Institute's publishers (though no longer its printers).

IV

The years of expansion

A. E. Smailes was, as already noted, Secretary of the Institute for longer than any of his predecessors or successors. His eleven years of service saw the Institute through the all-important period of post-war consolidation. He was followed by Geoffrey North of the University of Manchester. North's period of office was short for he found it difficult to combine the increasingly heavy demands of the Institute's job with his commitments in the University of Manchester as a lecturer in the Department of Geography; and the situation was made worse for him when he was invited to become warden of a hall of residence, St Anselm's. The position had been reached in the Institute where it was no longer possible for it to be effectively administered from three dispersed offices in different departments of geography even with the grace and favour, and maximum possible support, of the various heads of departments concerned. During the early months of 1963 there was a breakdown of communication between the President (S. H. Beaver) and the Honorary Secretary, and North resigned during the summer of 1963. W. Kirk, as a member of the Council at the time, was asked to take over the arranging of the forthcoming Annual Conference in the University of Keele in January 1964, and during the remaining months of 1963 he was Secretary-designate. He was confirmed in this office by the Annual General Meeting in January 1964 and thereafter remained Secretary until 1972.

During Kirk's secretaryship the Central Office, with a full-time administrative assistant, was established in London, with much practical help from L. D. Stamp who had been President of the IBG in 1956 and who was President of the RGS at the time. There is no doubt that the IBG could not have survived during the following years, with a virtual doubling of the membership, and a tremendous proliferation of its activities without this administrative reorganisation, some of the details of which are discussed elsewhere (pp. 117–20).

Other professional aspects of the Institute's activities were very considerably developed while Kirk was Secretary. The concept of a Director of the IBG, mooted in 1964, and discussed by the Council then and subsequently, was eventually—though not necessarily ' finally '—turned down by a narrow majority, at the Annual General Meeting of 1979 (see pp. 49–50). The hopes that Kirk and his colleagues entertained in the years following 1964—that the Institute would play an increasingly important role in national policy—were only partially fulfilled. The Institute was able to participate in a number of national discussions. It was given representation on the Map Users' Committee of the Ordnance Survey. The Secretary, helped by M. J. Wise and others, brought about a far-ranging reform of the British National Committee for Geography with the creation of a sub-committee dealing with home, as distinct from international, affairs (though this would appear to have become moribund in recent years as a result of the deliberate policy of the National Committee). A joint committee for ONC (Ordinary National Certificate) and HNC (Higher National Certificate) awards in Cartography, Planning and Surveying was established, and Kirk and I served on it for a number of years. There were also IBG submissions to various Government bodies on library provision, local government reorganisation and other matters, some details of which are given on pp. 109–10 as examples of the Institute's increasing participation in public affairs. In Kirk's own words ' we improved the professionalism of the services the Institute offered to its members ' during these years while there was a tremendous increase in the publication sales service to an international market, largely through the energies and activities of K. M. Clayton.

Other developments during Kirk's time as Secretary, some of which are elaborated elsewhere, include the launching of a Newsletter for the information of the members of the IBG. This later was transformed into *Area*, one of the great success stories of the Institute. There was a large increase in the activities of the study groups which Kirk saw as having a special role to play in the organisation of theme sessions at Annual Conferences. He also saw the groups as an opportunity of maintaining contact and continuity in the months between Annual Conferences. The growth in activities of these study groups transformed the Institute and, in general, there were great gains. It was a controlled development under the aegis of the Institute with specific rules that had to be followed by each group, and even the special problems posed by the strength and activity of the British Geomorphological Research Group (the BGRG) were sorted out, with much help from D. L. Linton, one of the founder members of the group. In recent years the fissiparious tendencies have, in the view of some, become a little alarming at Annual Conferences when there are so many concurrent sessions. But there is no doubt that the groups promoted a great surge of intellectual activity and publication, and drew many young enthusiasts into the affairs of the Institute, and provided very important academic links with members of associated disciplines. As Kirk himself observes, ' it is difficult now to conceive of an Institute without its study groups and working parties '. Other developments included the increase in the numbers of foreign seminars, for which the Anglo-Polish Seminar provided a model, and the Indo-British Seminars were developed following on the links established between British and Indian geographers at the New Delhi Congress of the International Geographical Union in 1968, helped by generous financial support from the Paul Cadbury Trust and the Commonwealth Foundation. Annual Conferences increased remarkably both in size and range of activities. There were interesting contrasts between the smaller and more intimate conferences in what, at least in English eyes, were 'remoter areas', including St Andrews and Aberdeen in Scotland and Belfast in Northern Ireland, and the larger conferences held in more central locations, such as London in 1969. Host departments were increasingly involved in the planning stages as the numbers attending conferences continued to increase, and several new features were added, including the appointment of distinguished guest lecturers, the invitations to younger European geographers to attend, and the forum for young research workers. There is no doubt that all these developments were of great benefit to the Institute and its membership as a whole. The organisation of conferences became so complex that eventually, in the 1970s, a special conference organiser had to be appointed within the Council to work in close liaison with the local conference organiser in the host university or polytechnic. The Heads of Departments' meetings, which had usually been held during IBG conferences, were no longer scheduled in the IBG programme since there was inadequate time or space for such activities; and in recent years the business of this conference of heads of departments has been transacted at a specially convened annual meeting held in London.

While Kirk was Secretary there was also a significant change in the conduct of the editorial business of the Institute, which has always been one of its major preoccupations. It became increasingly difficult for Council to scrutinise every item for publication as it had done in the past. After B. H. Farmer's retirement from the editorship in 1966, editors reported to Council rather than submitting every item to Council for its decision. Such a change was inevitable with the increase in the number of issues of *Transactions* produced and, later, with the establishment of Special Publications (from the outset with a different editor from that of the *Transactions*) and with the development of *Area* as a regular publication that came out more frequently than the Council met.

Kirk's own assessment of the period when he was in office between mid-1963 and 1972 is that ' it was an exciting and very rewarding time in which, during the time of expansion, most Officers of the Institute felt the creative urge to build up an Institute second to none in the world. Size brought its own problems but these were for overcoming and the length of service of Officers did give an element of continuity and experience in problem-solving and policy formation '.

By the end of the 1960s there had been great advances in the much enlarged Institute from the period in the 1950s when the IBG was still small enough for Council to deal appropriately—though not necessarily particularly effectively— with all the business. By the creation of an editorial board with delegated powers in 1968, the Council streamlined its business very considerably taking away from it what during the years following the war had constituted the bulk of its agendas. The Editorial Board had power to determine editorial policy within the terms of the constitution and in the light of financial constraints, to appoint referees, to approve publication and to advise the Editor on the planning of the *Transactions* and of Special Publications and, in association with Study Groups, of occasional other publications.

This very important step forward was not, however, by itself sufficient to deal with all the problems faced by Council with the continued growth in the size of the Institute and with its increased involvement in the sphere of public policy.

In 1973 a Conference Committee was established to plan and organise the programme for the Annual Conference (co-ordinated by the local secretary and the Secretary) and the accommodation of members and the financing of the conference (in association with the Treasurer). A small Nominations Committee was created to receive, consider and recommend to Council nominees for election to office and to the ordinary membership of Council. Both of these committees reported to the Council although essentially as a means of transmitting information and seeking approbation for matters in the detail of which the whole Council could not be directly involved. A joint GA/IBG Working Party on Geography and Higher Education had terms of reference that included discussion of matters referred to it by the IBG and the GA, especially those relating to geography in universities and polytechnics and the professional status and careers of graduate geographers. An *ad hoc* committee on geography in planning education was established for discussions with the education committee of the Royal Town Planning Institute. Representatives of the Institute sat on a number of national bodies, including the British National Committee for Geography, the Registrar-General's Geographical Advisory Committee, the committees in England and Scotland dealing with technical education, and the Ordnance Survey map-users' conference. Liaison was also maintained with the RGS, the GA, the SSRC, the NERC, the British Universities Heads of Departments Conference, and certain overseas geographical societies (notably the Association of American Geographers and the Canadian Association of Geographers).

International seminars were under the direction of the Council who appointed an organiser, to work in close association with the Secretary, to develop the seminar programme and, in the case of seminars held in Britain, to organise the physical details, usually in association with one or more departments of geography, and without access to any IBG funds for the development and running of such conferences ' (see also p. 100). Study groups functioned largely as academic sub-divisions of the Institute, operating within constitutions and financial arrangements controlled by Council. They were to organise meetings (at the Annual Conference and on other occasions) and to initiate publication for consideration by the Editorial Board while, from time to time, in association with or at the request of Council, they represented the IBG on matters within their particular field of competence (see also Chapter VII).

All these activities were reported directly to Council so that matters concerning study groups and international seminars appear very frequently in Council agenda. There was also always a relatively large volume of business introduced by the Secretary who, together with the Treasurer, had only Council to whom he could refer business or consult over matters of policy.

The previous paragraphs summarise the administrative situation in the Institute as it had evolved during the 1960s and as it existed at the time when Richard Lawton was elected Secretary in succession to Kirk in 1972 and the Secretariat moved from Leicester to Liverpool. He was inheriting a large organisation with a substantial and active membership, as shown by attendance at Annual Conferences and the growing activities of the Study Groups. But it was clearly at a stage in its development when continuing growth would necessitate certain organisational changes. Both Council and members needed to be more actively and fully involved in the Institute's affairs. He believed that Presidents and Vice-Presidents should have a more direct role to play, and that some of the detailed work and the decision-making power should be shared by Honorary Officers. He also saw a need to move towards procedures which kept a balance between the ultimate authority of Council and the officers, particularly in major policy matters, and the responsibility of groups with delegated authority (whether committees, study groups, the committee charged with the arranging of the Annual Conference, seminar committees, etc.) to do their work within the framework of the general policies of the Institute.

During his period of office (1972–5), various alternatives presented themselves and each contributed towards the necessary reshaping of the Institute in the mid-1970s. He concentrated on the creation of a newer and sounder administrative organisation and a more widely based policy and decision-making structure. He saw the necessity for better and more information to be made available to members if they were to be involved in as widespread a manner as possible. There was also a need for a reappraisal and a clearer definition of the role of Honorary Officers, and for a reassessment of the objectives and activities of the Institute, more than forty years after its initial establishment.

Lawton's basic aim was, in his own words, ' to reshape the IBG to be responsive to members' wishes, to become a more effective and professional organisation, and to expand its influence by working in close association with other geographical societies, to promote the cause of Geography and Education, in the scientific world, and in public affairs. '

Before his election as Secretary he had been well aware that the IBG was run by its Officers and, to a less degree, Council though he had not appreciated how little was actually on paper other than in Council minutes. Officers had to work from their home bases so that organisation was decentralised. This over the years has been recognised as inevitable and, properly supported and co-ordinated, it could be a strength in an Institute with limited reserves and only a small budget.

Fortunately the Treasurer, D. R. Diamond, and the incoming President, J. T. Coppock, were of the same mind as Lawton in his zeal to continue the restructuring of the IBG along the lines set by his predecessor, Kirk, and so a great deal was achieved in a relatively short period. Within less than two months of Coppock becoming President a paper, dated 21 February 1973, was issued for the consideration of the Council since this seemed to be ' an appropriate time to look at the whole structure of Council's business and to consider whether further reorganisation and delegation of business should now be taken '.

The paper is discussed here at some length since it is concerned with a committee structure that, in essence, still exists and which is, therefore, the basis of the IBG's organisation as it moves into the second half-century of its existence. The 1973 paper suggested several reasons for such a review being undertaken at that time. It could be argued, the Officers said, ' that too much time is taken at Council meetings by detail, which is not easily handled in such a large body and which may be frustrating to members, since it leaves too little time for discussion of policy '. ' Inadequate use is being made of the expertise of Council members, who are thus insufficiently involved in the Institute's affairs; while, as the Institute becomes more involved in the sphere of public policy it will often be necessary to take rapid decisions, for which present procedures are too leisurely. It is also recognised that considerable administrative burdens are being placed on honorary officers. Any reorganisation must, therefore, try to spread these burdens a little, while at the same time avoiding harmful fragmentation of policy and decision-making '.

The Officers believed that the conduct of business could be considerably streamlined by delegation of specified powers to new committees (along the lines of the already existing Editorial Board), subject only to reporting to Council and to periodic review. These committees would represent the main areas of interest in the Institute. They would have their own chairman (usually an Officer) and would involve *all* members of Council in some active committee work; and they would deal with much of the Institute's detailed business. Thus Council would be left free to concentrate upon broader policy issues which could then be delegated to committees and/or officers for action. The committees would report to Council and operate within clearly defined areas of responsibility.

The greatest need, however, in the view of the Officers was for a Finance and General Purposes Committee, which would be able to make necessary decisions between Council meetings. This committee might consist of the President, Secretary and Treasurer, together with two or three ordinary members and be responsible for carrying out much routine business and for co-ordinating policy matters (including some that involved honorary officers and *ad hoc* committees). They also suggested the possibilities of a ' liaison committee ' which would maintain links with other learned societies and government, and a standing committee for study groups. Alternatively they suggested that—alongside the Finance and General Purposes Committee—there might be a sub-committee or small working party or ' task force ' whenever a particular need arose, with the duty of investigating and making recommendations.

These proposals were discussed at length by the Council who set up a small committee to make recommendations ' on the organisation of Council business '. It is unnecessary to detail these or to discuss the different points of view raised by these considerations, but it is important to note that much careful thought was given to these important matters at this stage in the growth of the Institute, and that final conclusions were reached by the Council meeting late in 1973 and endorsed by the Annual General Meeting in January 1974. It was decided that there should not be a Finance and General Purposes Committee so that ' financial and general policy would remain in the hands of Council '; but there were important recommendations ' that the trend towards wider involvement of Council and the membership in the conduct of the Institute's business be continued (for example, by co-option); ' ' that Committees of Council should have delegated powers over their specific areas of responsibility, subject to report to Council and the lodging of copies of all reports with the Hon Secretary and with the Central Office of the IBG; and that the President and Officers of the Institute should be empowered to act over matters of concern to the Institute and to professional geographers when there was insufficient time to consult Council or its Committees, subject to full report to Council. The President, Secretary and Treasurer were to be *ex officio* members of all Committees, and Committees were to be given powers to co-opt as specified in their composition. The Committees of Council constituted were as follows: Editorial Committee; External Relations Committee; Study Group and Research Committee; Education Committee; Nominations and Membership Committee; and Conference Committee. The members of the sub-committee saw their proposals as comprehensive and possibly too ambitious for immediate implementation; they did not consider that they went ' beyond activities in which the Institute was already engaged, to a greater or lesser extent '; and they believed ' that they would help towards a more vigorous pursuit of these activities, as well as the development of new areas of interest '.

It may be helpful to record a little of what each of these Committees of Council was to do. The Editorial Committee, which later became the Publications Committee, was a recognition of the development of a high degree of autonomy for the Editors of both *Transactions* and *Area*, within the current financial and publications policies of the Institute. This went hand in hand with the devolution of much of the time-consuming work of the editors to paid editorial assistants. It also played an important part in co-ordinating the publishing activities of study groups, balancing the arguments about different types of publication, and even periodically debating the wisdom, or otherwise, of the splitting of *Transactions* into, for example, physical geography and human geography components.

The External Relations Committee was not only to look after the European seminar programme (see pp. 99–100) but also to advise Council about its links with other geographical and scientific societies, including The Royal Society, and with Government and other bodies, over matters of scientific, professional and public concern to geographers. This committee was largely responsible for the initiatives with which the Institute spoke on behalf of professional geographers, and the new thrust is evident not only from J. T. Coppock's Presidential Address in 1973 on geography and public policy, but also in the addresses given by M. J. Wise (1975), J. W. Birch (1978) and M. D. I. Chisholm (1980) among others[1].

The Study Group and Research Committee was designed to be a new and active focus for the academic drive of the Institute, which could be effectively linked with the IBG's activity as a whole. The committee was designed to prevent breakaway movements on the part of individual study groups. There were lengthy negotiations with various groups, especially with the BGRG, and eventually Council spelt out the procedures for the formation of study groups, providing a model constitution and laying down what the financial arrangements must be (see pp. 92–6).

The establishment for the first time of an Education Committee was of considerable significance since it was a recognition of the fact that the Institute's membership was constantly widening and diversifying, for whereas at one time nearly all members of the IBG had been associated with universities, there was increasing strength from the polytechnics and from the institutes and colleges of higher education. Relationships with the GA (which also has a Higher Education Section Committee) suggested the desirability of a Joint Higher Education Committee. This has worked well and was later important in developing the relationships between the two societies and all those interested in higher education. It also played a significant role in the lengthy negotiations over the National Conference for Geography and Higher Education and, more recently, in the development of the Higher Education Learning Study Group.

A Nominations and Membership Committee was necessary to take out of Council debates the question of nominations, especially of officers. The IBG, as most learned societies, springs to life only intermittently to nominate for membership of Council, and in a growing membership it was important to give careful and consistent thought to Council membership and to be very sure that the nomination of Presidents would be of persons who were actively interested in the Institute and would bring both academic distinction and commitment of leadership to its affairs. In more recent years there have been further developments of a nomination and election procedure, and this method, first used in 1980, has moved it closer to that used, for example, by the Association of American Geographers which gives full opportunities for members to participate in elections.

The Conference Committee, later headed by the newly created office of Conference Secretary, arose from Lawton's first experience of co-ordination for the large conference in the University of Birmingham, in 1973. From this he discovered the importance of the closest possible liaison between the Council and the local organising committee, and also the extent to which the programme depended upon the activities and plans of the Institute's Study Groups. Very soon afterwards Council decided to create a new post, that of Conference Officer, who would be *ex officio* chairman of the Committee.

These discussions in Council—and the ideas behind the restructuring of the Council's committees—are reported at length in this history of the Institute because, in marked contrast to much other Council business, they are well documented. They also indicate very closely the concern of the Officers and the Council for an organisation and administration of the Institute appropriate to the growth in membership that marked the early 1970s and to the challenges that had to be faced at that time. The membership at large was not as happy as the Council hoped that it would be with these changes, though it must be admitted that members generally were silent about their anxieties except in discussion among themselves and on those occasions when criticism and complaint always show themselves most markedly—at the Annual General Meetings which, over many years, have always attracted quite remarkably large attendances. This well-established fact is surely an indication of the strength and vigour of the Institute as a meeting place for many geographers, and it is a very useful safety valve for the kind of organisation that the IBG has become, even if it does create difficulties, from time to time, for the Officers and the Council.

Alongside the restructuring of the committees serving the Council, it was also necessary to develop an effective administrative system to put into action both organisation and policy in the new situation where a much larger and more complex organisation had to be cared for by the Secretary and the other Honorary Officers. There clearly had to be changes, not for their own sake, but to allow the Institute to work smoothly in accordance with its objectives and the wishes of its members. The natural link with the RGS, through the proximity of the headquarters of the two institutions, was a very valuable asset and pointed towards the development of the closest possible ties with both it and the GA. But the small office established in London could not run all aspects of the IBG's work, especially with its Honorary Officers in different parts of the country. In practice, therefore, the London Office concerned itself with financial, membership and publication matters. The Editors, now supplied with some professional help, proceeded with their business of publication from their respective bases. The Honorary Secretary continued to run things from his department, with modest part-time secretarial help. The IBG still had to work on a shoe-string budget even if the sums available for the support of its officers were on a much more generous scale than they had been twenty years or more earlier. Lawton felt strongly that there should be an Executive Secretary based on headquarters, who would be able to give continuous thought, and most of his energy, to the affairs of the Institute, freed of the many other demands upon a full-time academic geographer. The decision, after much discussion, not to proceed with such an appointment, based largely on financial arguments, came after Lawton had retired from his office as Honorary Secretary, but it was he who, with the Treasurer, prepared the way for such a post and ensured that at least the necessary financial resources were in large measure available when the matter was thrashed out by the Annual General Meeting in 1978 (see pp. 121–2).

An important change that occurred during Lawton's period of office was the move away from the informality of the Annual General Meetings that traditionally had been characteristic of these gatherings. Officers' reports had always been presented verbally, often with considerable humour; this indeed was the recognised way of communicating with the membership at large on this special occasion in the year, but it did mean that there was no more than a summary record in the archives—a drawback not only to the historian of the first fifty years of the Institute but also an inadequate way of keeping members, whether present or absent from the Annual General Meeting, informed of what the Institute was doing. With the full encouragement of his fellow officers Lawton ensured that the Agenda, with supporting papers in the form of full Minutes of the last Annual General Meeting and detailed reports from each of the Officers, was circulated in advance with the notice of meeting. This gave members an opportunity to debate issues, to challenge or to suggest policy, and indeed to tell Council what they wanted and what they expected. Simultaneously there was much fuller reporting in *Area* of the activities of seminars and conferences, and of the actions taken by representatives on various national bodies. Thus the membership at large was better informed than at any previous time of the affairs of the Institute, and this may well explain why—in marked contrast to the experience of some other learned societies—the membership has held up in recent years notwithstanding the many difficulties experienced in higher education, including the trimming down of the staffs of universities and polytechnics and the problems of employment faced by many of the younger members of the IBG, especially those who have joined as student members.

In the mid-1970s, therefore, the Institute was more active, academically and professionally, than ever before, not because of an administrative reorganisation but because of the wishes and the zeal of its members. It fully maintained its traditional role among professional geographers as a special forum for the discussion of research and for publication. Its membership, no longer synonymous with ' university geographers ', included recruits from the other sectors of higher education and from among geographers who were working in government service and in planning. There is no doubt that this broadening of the membership worked very much to the advantage of the Institute and was reflected in the type of activity and the contributions made to both academic research and to applied policy-type issues. It meant that the IBG of the 1970s was very different from the body of earlier years. Some of the senior members may have regretted these changes, especially as, inevitably, the Annual Conferences were much larger and more impersonal than they had been in the decade immediately following the Second World War. Others, while welcoming the way in which academic activities were obviously flourishing, particularly through the development of study groups, feared that through the study groups some specialists were possibly ' turning inwards upon themselves ' at the expense of the activities of the Institute as a whole. But in terms of its strength and influence, there is no doubt that the Institute profited from these developments and that the policy was correct. The gains were far greater than the losses, and publication—still the hallmark of the Institute's success and its major contribution to academic excellence in the subject—remained very active and varied with the standing of both the *Transactions* and *Area* being very high, not only within Britain but internationally. Of similar significance was the Institute's increasing involvement in issues of public policy (Chapter X), growing co-operation between members of the Institute and representatives of other disciplines, and the widening of the IBG's links with American and Commonwealth geographers as well as with those in Europe, an increasing number of whom accepted invitations to be the Institute's guests at the Annual Conferences.

David Thomas, the first Professor of Geography at St. David's University College, Lampeter, University of Wales, was elected to succeed Lawton as Secretary at the Annual General Meeting in January 1976. Lawton agreed to clear up a number of matters before Thomas finally took over from him and the records were transferred from Merseyside to mid-Wales. Thomas inherited from his predecessor a lively organisation which, while he was in office between 1976 and 1979, grew steadily in terms of membership although activity expanded at a much faster pace, largely (in his view) because of the continued success of the Institute's study groups, annual conferences and overseas seminars, and through the encouragement that came from increasing co-operation with the RGS and the GA, as well as with other related bodies.

The activities of study groups expanded so much that in effect they took over the Annual Conference. Some of them began to produce their own publications and to levy fees accordingly, and others started to engage in seminars and conferences overseas with comparable groups, particularly in Europe and North America. Annual Conferences continued to grow in size, and that at Newcastle in 1978 attracted about 800 participants (residents and day visitors). That almost half of the total membership should appear at some time or other during the conference must be quite exceptional among learned societies. It is no doubt indicative of the value put upon this annual opportunity for the exchange of views and information by the membership at large. The considerable number of day visitors has caused the Council some concern and creates certain problems in both catering and communication; but perhaps it is inevitable in view of the high cost of conferences and the increased accessibility of meeting places in centres such as Newcastle, Coventry and Birmingham.

Seminars with overseas groups had developed to such an extent that as many as three of these were taking place in a particular year. They continued to concentrate on contacts with European, particularly East European, countries, but there were also seminars with North American and Indian geographers. The number of overseas visitors attending the Annual Conference continued to increase, and this gave younger colleagues from abroad an opportunity of establishing a relationship with the IBG which would not have taken place otherwise.

Thomas, like Lawton, worked hard to encourage the closest possible links with other geographical societies, at home and overseas, though he recognised that there was a limit to the extent of collaboration possible, especially as it was discovered that the overlapping membership (between IBG and RGS) was almost negligible so that no advantage was to be gained by the joint collection of subscriptions. The Joint (GA and IBG) Higher Education Committee met regularly and produced several publications including the guide to degree courses in geography which is now issued annually as *A matter of degree* and published by Geo Abstracts.

The restructuring of committees earlier in the 1970s, described above (pp. 43–6), had assumed the appointment of some type of an executive committee but the failure of the Council to carry the membership as a whole on this issue resulted in some rethinking; and Thomas was responsible for bringing forward the paper that made the case for the appointment of a full-time, or at least a part-time, Executive Officer. The sum required was thought to be about £5,000 per annum over five years; and it was believed that a charitable trust might be prepared to put up money for an experimental period to add to the balance in the IBG accounts already created by the Officers for this purpose. The matter was discussed during the Conference in Hull in January 1978. The arguments in favour of the Council's recommendation, put forward by the Officers, were that the scale of operation of the IBG demanded such an appointment; that the Institute needed to become more effective and professional to provide its members with the services that they required; and that the Institute ought to be in a stronger position to influence national policy. The opposition to the proposal, largely led by K. M. Clayton, a former Treasurer and in 1983 the Senior Vice-President of the Institute and thus President-designate for 1984, was considerable. On the initial show of hands, it appeared that the appointment had been approved but a whole series of procedural points were raised, during which a number of members left the meeting, and when the count eventually took place the Council had lost by a small majority (103 for, 115 against, with 13 abstentions). In retrospect it was perhaps as well that this was the outcome because at the time it was not possible to foresee the way in which inflation would eat into the Institute's resources, especially at a time of ever-rising costs of publication and administration. Moreover it was not anticipated that new circumstances in higher education would have the effect of slowing down the increase in the size of the membership of the IBG which had, until then, been almost continuous over a long period. Nevertheless, the possibility of an appointment of an executive officer must be kept in the forefront of IBG thinking in the coming years. Acceptance of the idea that the work done by the Secretary should remain a part-time function of a senior academic in a university or polytechnic department of geography appears to imply that the Institute is not going to change its present form to any appreciable degree. Put differently, it suggests that, as one former Secretary of the Institute has put it, the IBG would tend to cruise along but would not be capable of giving the appropriate lead in public opinion or in policy making.

J. C. Doornkamp of Nottingham followed Thomas and was Secretary from 1979 to 1982. Increased financial support was given for research initiatives by different study groups, the sum of £2,000 per annum being made available to them, and discussions continued between the Officers of the leading geographical societies in Britain (see pp. 111–13). A new venture for the Institute, the publication of *The atlas of drought in Britain, 1975–6*, was widely acclaimed, one review being headed ' Drought atlas of brilliant originality '. Financially, however, the publication was not a success and in the end, after considerable discussion and some anguish in the Council, the atlas was sold at a price considerably below that originally fixed.[2]

The voting procedures to which reference was made (p. 46) were established with a transferable vote system and the establishment of the principle of a postal ballot for vacancies on Council. Any member was free to nominate candidates to hold office as well as to fill Council vacancies. In fact the new method of election had the opposite effect from that which had been intended by the enthusiasts for the change since for three years no ballot was needed because there was no excess of candidates over vacancies, and only single names came forward for the different offices that fell vacant. It was not until 1983 that there was a ballot for the office of Junior Vice-President (to succeed to the Presidency in 1986) with two candidates, while seven members were nominated for three vacant places on the Council.

Despite critical comments from some members on the form and size of the Annual Conference, a high proportion of the membership continues to attend the Annual Conference, suggesting that the formula for these gatherings worked out over the years cannot be wholly inappropriate. There was considerable debate in Council and at Annual General Meetings about the form of the *Transactions*; in particular there was pressure from some quarters for *Transactions* to be split into physical geography and human geography parts. Such a move was encouraged by some members, notably R. J. Johnston, now the Secretary of the Institute

(*Area*, 12, 1980, 19–20). But it was debated in the pages of *Area* (see, for example, Steel, 1980, and Watson, 1980³) and resisted by the Council generally, and especially by the Editor of *Transactions*, D. R. Stoddart.

Doornkamp notes that during his time in office the economic difficulties of higher education showed themselves in a variety of ways. In earlier years the Institute had received, in effect, a hidden subsidy from the departments in which the Honorary Officers worked, but increasingly it became necessary for the finances of the Institute to be cared for in a different way and quite separately from those of the departments most closely associated with the work of the Officers. It was also noted that a number of the younger academics were reluctant to become members on a variety of grounds: that the subscription was too high, that they could not see what the IBG could do for the individual member, and that they questioned whether the value of the *Transactions* was commensurate with the size of the subscription. Despite these difficulties, most members continued to see the IBG as performing a very useful role on behalf of the discipline and those professing it. As Doornkamp observes, ' if the IBG did not exist, it would have had to be invented, ' surely a particularly pertinent comment from a recent Secretary.

R. J. Johnston of the University of Sheffield was elected Secretary at the AGM in January 1982. He was a member of the Council between 1977 and 1979 and, as noted above (p. 50), had been the leading protagonist in the debate on whether the *Transactions* should, or should not, continue in what had become its traditional IBG form. He was the moving spirit behind the formation of the Book Club launched by the Council in 1978. His enthusiasm and drive, and capacity for hard work, exemplified in his long list of publications, have spilled over into the affairs of the IBG to its great advantage. He has followed up many of the initiatives shown by the Council in recent years, such as the discussions with societies such as the RGS and the GA on the possibilities of closer liaison in a variety of ways, with each society working for the progress of the subject, often in very clear and well-defined spheres of activity. He has also been responsible for new leads, notably full collaboration in the Association of Learned Societies in the Social Sciences, whose aims are ' the monitoring, promoting and defending the position of the social sciences '. His concern for the future of higher education and for the employment prospects of younger members in the present economic situation in Britain are shared by the Council; and his contribution with E. V. Brack to the Jubilee issue of *Transactions* (8, 1983, 100–11) on ' appointment and promotion in the academic labour market ' was a very relevant survey of the academic geographers in British universities during the first fifty years of the IBG's existence. With J. C. Doornkamp, he has edited one of the IBG's publications produced to mark its jubilee year, *The changing geography of the United Kingdom* (1982, London).

Johnston and his fellow Officers were responsible for the organisation of the very successful and well-attended Jubilee celebrations in Edinburgh in January 1983 in close collaboration with the local conference committee. A full report of the conference is given in *Area*, 15, 1983, 68–70. The President was, very appropriately, J. Wreford Watson, who had been Professor of Geography in

Edinburgh (of whose Department of Geography he is a graduate) since 1954. At the AGM he was succeeded by the current President, J. W. House of Oxford. Apart from the presidential address on the 'soul of geography' and lectures related specifically to the celebratory theme of the conference, there was a guest lecture by Donald Meinig of Syracuse University, USA, on 'Geography as an art' and a lecture, sponsored by the publishers Methuen, on 'Planning the future—a national perspective' by Sir Wilfred Burns, former Chief Planner at the Department of the Environment.

P. Randell Baker, elected Treasurer in 1981, resigned his appointment because of continued absence, on secondment from the University of East Anglia to a special assignment with the Government of Fiji, and D. A. Pinder, who had been Acting Treasurer throughout 1982, was elected in his place. D. R. Stoddart completed six years as Editor of *Transactions* and was succeeded by M. Williams. M. Blacksell had already agreed to do a further year at Editor of *Area* but during 1983 R. Flowerdew was appointed as his successor from the beginning of 1984. The photographs of the officers in the Institute's jubilee year have been placed together (plate 7): J. W. House (President); R. J. Johnston (Secretary); D. A. Pinder (Treasurer); M. Williams (Editor, *Transactions*); and A. M. Y. Blacksell (Editor, *Area*).

Notes

1. Coppock, J. T. (1974) ' Geography and public policy: challenges, opportunities and implications ', *Transactions* 63, 1–16

   Wise, M. J. (1975) ' A university teacher of geography ', *Transactions* 66, 1–16

   Birch, J. W. (1977) 'On excellence and problem solving in geography ', *Transactions* NS 2, 417–29

   Chisholm, M. D. I. (1980) ' The Wealth of Nations ', *Transactions* NS 5, 255–76

2. *The atlas of drought in Britain: 1975–76* was edited by J. C. Doornkamp, K. J. Gregory and A. S. Burns and published by the IBG in 1979. It was described (*Area* 11, 1979, 1977) as ' probably the world's first systematic atlas study of the nature, incidence and effects of a natural hazard '. Despite a very favourable ' limited period offer ' of £15 to members before it was put on sale at £27.50, sales were relatively small for many months. M. Blacksell, in reporting on the Annual General Meeting of 1982, wrote ' The only item to raise spirits above the tepid was a surprise offer of the IBG's Drought Atlas at the unrepeatable price of £3 to participants at the Conference. Members could hardly believe their luck and departed with almost indecent haste. More than a hundred were eventually solid! '

3. Steel, R. W. (1980) ' A note of caution ', *Area* 12, 20–2

   Watson, J. W. (1980) ' An excursion on beach combing ', *Area* 12, 22–3

PART TWO

THE ACTIVITIES OF THE IBG

V

Publications

Publication has always been central to the objectives and activities of the Institute of British Geographers. 'Transactions', meant initially to be the public record of what the Institute had done and was doing, came to be the accepted title for all its publications over many years, even when the bulk of the volumes produced consisted of monographs or relatively short papers by members of the IBG. Indeed the title has remained for nearly half a century, and when a new style publication began in 1976 it was decided, after due discussion, to retain the title *Transactions* so that the series is now known as *Transactions New Series*.

It seemed, therefore, right that much stress should be laid upon the importance of both the old and the new series of *Transactions* and that their background should be described at some length. Later, however, other means of communication with the geographical world and with others, too, needed to be devised, and this took the form first of a house journal or 'Newsletter', and then from 1969 of *Area*, a quarterly that has been outstandingly successful, thanks to the support of members and the inspired leadership of the succession of editors. There has also been a demand for volumes relating to particular themes, and these have appeared sometimes within *Transactions*; and latterly, with the support of a commercial publisher but still within the general surveillance of the Council of the Institute, 'Special Publications' have been introduced.

For these reasons the section on Publications has precedence over all other aspects of the IBG's complex existence, and the position of this chapter does not simply reflect the perhaps understandable prejudice or bias of an author who was for more than ten years responsible for the editing of what at the time consisted of the complete publications programme of the IBG. As indicated elsewhere, a large part of the Council's Agenda has been devoted to discussion about publications, and it is a matter that has often exercised the minds of those attending the Institute's Annual General Meetings. Whether the right balance has been obtained, whether members receive in the form of publications 'value for money' in terms of the subscriptions that they pay, whether too much is spent on '*Transactions*', which some allege is essentially a volume for libraries and is not particularly wanted or appreciated by members, are still matters of controversy and debate. The following chapter does not attempt to answer these questions, or even to express opinions too forcibly on some of these issues. But it does endeavour to underline the continuity of a policy for the publication of academic research undertaken by the members of the Institute, and throughout it emphasises the care taken by those responsible—referees as well as editors and other members of the Council—for the maintenance of the highest academic standards in all the work issued over the name of the IBG.

The Transactions

In Buchanan's review of the development of the Institute during its first twenty-one years, he noted that 'the initial impulse towards its formation had come entirely from the search for a further publishing medium, though even before it was formed other functions were visualised' (*Transactions* 20, 5). These functions included the Annual Conference which has become so vital in the life of professional geography in Britain but, as I pointed out (1961) in my assessment of the Institute's publication policy made at the time of my retirement from office after ten years of responsibility for the editing of IBG publications, 'a major activity of the Institute continues to be the publication of papers and monographs. Indeed a very high proportion of the Institute's revenue is spent upon publications; and it is, therefore, most desirable that from time to time, not only the Council and its officers, but the membership at large, should take stock of the position and ask what is being received in the way of publications in return for the annual subscription' (*Transactions* 29, 129). Among these publications, the *Transactions* has always had a special place throughout the first fifty years of the Institute's existence; and, whatever its shortcomings, what is now a quarterly journal may indeed be considered by many to be 'the most distinguished, scholarly and authoritative in the field', to quote the words of D. R. Stoddart (1983), albeit a biased observer in that he was from 1977 to the end of 1982 the editor of the *Transactions* (*Geographical Magazine* 55, 41).

In the early years, Institute policy was directed towards the publication of monographs, apart from Baulig's *The changing sea-level* which, consisted of lectures delivered to the University of London in 1933. The selection based on the careful refereeing which has always been characteristic of the IBG, was clearly sound. At the time of my review (1961) I could state that 'none of the original volumes of pre-war years can be purchased today' apart from Dorothy M. Doveton's *The human geography, of Swaziland* (*Transactions* 29, 130). Nevertheless, the original publishers had, with IBG agreement, published a revised edition of S. W. Wooldridge and D. L. Linton's *Structure, surface and drainage in south-east England* in 1955, and the IBG itself had reprinted Baulig's lectures in 1956, using a photo-lithographic process.

In the post-war situation, however, the needs of the Institute's members were different. At the first Annual General Meeting after the end of the War (2 January 1946) the Secretary outlined the Institute's publication policy. Whereas pre-war publication was confined to monographs—'a policy adopted for various reasons that were good at the time'—'changed circumstances, particularly the announced intention of the Royal Geographical Society to revive its Supplementary Papers, made it advisable to consider whether the policy should not be broadened to include publication of shorter papers, at least to the extent of all papers read by members at the meetings of the Institute. ' This change was approved although—as so often happened in IBG deliberations—it is recorded that ' no vote was taken or asked for ' but ' there was general agreement with the President's summing up that the meeting had given to the Council the indication it needed of the general line to be followed. '

The ' decision ' having been taken, the Officers had to implement it. Shortage of supplies of paper and other problems in the printing trade were causing the IBG—in common with other learned societies—grave difficulties resulting in intolerable delays. The decision to print the date of submission of a paper came much later—not until 1965 in fact; and perhaps this was just as well for some papers published by the IBG took months from the date when they were received to the time when they appeared in print in the *Transactions*; and, as those who are involved in bibliographical references know only too well, *Transactions and Papers 1949* was not published until 1951.

These delays bothered the Council and Officers every bit as much as the members, including the authors of the papers in course of publication. The Council wanted to be involved in the initial appointment of referees; referees, many of them heavily overburdened with teaching and other university duties in the immediate post-war years, were not always as quick as they might have been, and some were notoriously indecisive in the framing of their recommendations; overworked Officers, notably the Honorary Secretary (who had at the time editorial responsibility within the Institute) were not necessarily able to give top priority to publishing matters; and manuscripts and maps, once arrived at the printers, seemed to remain untouched for months on end. Again and again Council expressed concern but the Officers' representations to the printers seemed singularly ineffective. The details of how the problem was solved need not be listed now though some are referred to on pages 31–2. In essence the solution lay in the designation of a single officer whose main, indeed sole, responsibility was for publishing, and an almost simultaneous change of printer. I was the officer concerned from 1949 onwards, and the first to be designated ' Editor ' (in 1952), and I was responsible, on behalf of the Council, for the move to the Alden Press (Oxford) Ltd, who remained the Institute's printers for the *Transactions* from 1952 until 1980. Thereafter I was Editor until the Annual General Meeting of January 1961 when I was succeeded by B. H. Farmer with whom I had already been closely associated in Institute affairs during the years 1952–56 when, as Assistant Secretary, he had been responsible for the financial side of the IBG (much of it, of course, directly concerned with the amount of money available for publication). It is unlikely that any member of the IBG will ever again serve for as long in any one office, and indeed what was in effect a ten-year sentence is not one that I would willingly wish on any colleague, much as I enjoyed the editorial work involved. There was indeed a very satisfying side to this particular task, which, as I have said elsewhere, gave me a host of friends and, so far as I am aware, created no enemies even when I had to write letters of rejection of papers to colleagues in other universities, many of them considerably more senior and experienced than myself.

As noted elsewhere, the Institute developed—and maintained for many years, long after my retirement from the editorship—a particularly close and happy relationship with the Alden Press, and especially with its Managing Director, W. J. Furneaux, who often attended part of the Annual Conferences of the IBG when they were held reasonably near to Oxford and who was very rightly admitted in the mid 1960s to Honorary Membership of the Institute in which he continues, now in retirement, to maintain a very real and live interest. Happily too, relations with the Institute's publishers, George Philip and Son Ltd, who (as is stressed on pp. 75–9) had stood so firmly alongside the Institute in its early days, and without whose help and encouragement the publication aspirations of the IBG could not have been fulfilled, continued on a most cordial basis even after the printing side of the Institute's activities had been separated from the publishing. This change had come about after estimates had been obtained from George Philip, the Alden Press and an Essex firm (see pp. 31–2), and Council had decided that the Alden Press offered the best alternative at a meeting held on 15 March 1950 when it was recorded that the Alden Press had the ' advantages of relatively low costs, of being under the Editor's eye at Oxford, and of being able to produce illustration work of a high standard '. This decision was confirmed on 5 September 1950 when the Council noted that there continued to be ' intolerable delays ' and ' unsatisfactory progress ' with the printing of no. 15 (the volume for 1949), for which the publishers stated that another three months before publication were still required. But not until 5 January 1952 was the Secretary instructed to give ' firm formal notice ' to terminate the agreement existing between the Institute and George Philip and Son Ltd as publishers. This disturbed the firm in view of the long association that it had enjoyed with the IBG from the beginning, and in a letter received in May 1952 E. G. Godfrey, Director and Managing Editor, expressed ' his concern at this action, in view of their earnest desire to give satisfactory service and their hope that a new agreement might be negotiated '. The Council minute records: ' In view of the firm's evident goodwill towards the Institute and keenness to retain the publishing, the Secretary was instructed to enter upon discussions with Mr Godfrey to find out whether a mutually acceptable agreement could be negotiated '; and at the subsequent Council meeting held on 1 November 1952 there is a minute reporting on ' a friendly interview with Mr Godfrey in May at which there seemed to be no obstacles in the way of framing a new agreement acceptable to the publishers and at the same time giving the Council of the Institute the freedom of action it required '. Two months later it is recorded that outstanding matters between the publishers and the Institute had been settled, whereby ' the Institute's freedom to sell or otherwise dispose of copies of the *Transactions* or parts thereof except to the Trade had been accepted fully '.

Thirty years later it is unnecessary to indicate the steps by which the backlog of publication was gradually dealt with nor the progress made as a result of the new printer's great interest in the work on which the firm was now engaged and the considerable expertise that it brought to the task which embraced cartographic as well as normal printing processes. Early on (in fact in the second number printed for the Institute by the Alden Press) Bill Furneaux and I embarked on a real adventure in cartography when we produced, with considerable success, A. A. Miller's 'three new climatic maps' (*Transactions 1952*, 17, 15–20) in several colours (and with perfect registration.[2] Eight years later we boldly embarked, in the last issue of *Transactions* for which I had editorial responsibility, on a pull-out map of the drainage pattern and erosion surface remnants of the south-western Lake District that had a total width of 30·5 cm.[3] In this same volume the shingle complexes of Bridgwater Bay straddled right across two pages of the *Transactions*, giving them a span of nearly 30 cm from one margin to the other.[4] Gradually there was a catching-up on the delays of the period 1949–51 with two volumes 1950 and 1951) appearing in 1952, the Alden Press's first year as the Institute's printers; and the firm went to great lengths in subsequent years to produce each volume by the end of the year bearing its date.[5] Throughout, they fully maintained this high standard of printing and production that had characterised the work of George Philip and Son Ltd in earlier years, and the firm remained the IBG's printers until 1980.

It is unnecessary to repeat points made by me in ' A review of IBG publications, 1946–1960 ' (*Transactions* 29, 129–47) except to refer to the willingness of my Oxford colleague A. F. Martin (and at the time a member of the IBG Council) to be Acting Editor for several months in 1955 while I visited various countries in southern and eastern Africa, and to the significance of the decision in 1956 to consider the ' possibility of reviving the pre-war custom of publishing occasional monographs as an addition to the regular publication of volumes of research papers '. Two important provisos were added—that such monographs ' were not merely theses or extracts therefrom ' and that ' there was a prospect of a university or some other body making a substantial contribution towards the cost of publication '. This modification of the outcome of the discussion of the Institute's publications policy in 1946 (p. 56) resulted in enquiries from a number of possible authors and to the acceptance for publication of, first, G. J. Butlands's *The human geography of southern Chile* (132 pp., 1957) and, secondly, M. R. G. Conzen's *Alnwick, Northumberland; a study in town-plan analysis* (122 pp., 1960). Both these monographs were widely, and favourably, reviewed and sold well by the standards of the times. In a sense they were the precursors of the Special Publications series of more recent years. They attracted grants on a larger scale than the more usual papers, many of which received some financial aid from the universities with which their authors were associated (normally of the order of £10 to £30—a useful contribution in those days towards the cost of the blocks for illustrations). Southern Chile received a grant of £100 from the University of Birmingham and some assistance from the Anglo-Chilean Society, and Alnwick was given financial assistance by the Sir James Knott Trust, His Grace the Duke of Northumberland, C. I. C. Bosanquet and William Robertson. It was at this time too that Council took decisions, referred to above (p. 56), about reissuing earlier volumes that had gone out of print.

The first index of all the published work of the IBG was compiled and published in 1956 as a result of the meticulous labours of a librarian member of the Institute, Miss A. M. Ferrar of the Department of Geography, University of Leeds. It has been widely used and much appreciated by many members, as have the second and third indexes, also prepared by Miss Ferrar (now of the

University of Hull) and published in *Transactions* 31, 1962, 169—85 and *Transactions* 42, 1967, 193–219. Since then there has been no further index since, as Stoddart remarks, ' Alas, in this computer age, eight years of effort have proved insufficient to bring up to date the last cumulative index of the Institute's publications, prepared in the traditional manner' (*Transactions* NS, 1983, 12).

I felt it appropriate to give an account of my stewardship as the Institute's first Honorary Editor before I handed over to B. H. Farmer in 1961 and not only reviewed the achievements of the IBG in the publishing field over nearly thirty years but also looked at some of the trends in different branches of the subject in the light of the papers offered to, and accepted by, the IBG (Steel, 1961). Aided and abetted by my daughter, Elizabeth, then aged 15, I went further and together we studied the ages of authors when their papers were published by the IBG. This led to the statement in the underline of one of the diagrams that ' some geographers, especially women geographers, show a reluctance to reveal their ages, and estimates have had to be made in a number of cases'.[6] The diagram revealed some interesting facts as did the analysis as a whole, and similar studies of the nature of published work and their authorship have been undertaken in other parts of the Commonwealth.

B. H. Farmer followed me as Honorary Editor and dealt with the first years of the period when the Institute was moving beyond the time when the volume of material and the financial resources available provided for only one volume of *Transactions* each year with the occasional monograph. He already knew about the financial aspects of the publishing side of the Institute's work through his years as Assistant Secretary responsible for the Institute's finances. He was familiar, too, with the traditional manner with which the Council had dealt with editorial matters: the appointment of referees by the whole Council after due consideration of at least the title, if not the content, of the paper; the reception by Council of the reports—and often there were more than two of these by the time Council was prepared to take a decision; and the decision, again by the whole Council, about acceptance or rejection. There was editorial discretion for many of the details and for the determination of priorities in publication; and in practice the Editor generally was able to guide the Council to what he regarded as the right and proper decision by, for example, summarising lengthy and detailed referees' reports. Time simply did not permit the reading aloud of all such reports at Council meetings such as happened when I first became a member of Council; but whereas in 1947 Council was concerned with only four or five papers at most (and was often appealed to, to suggest an additional author so that a volume would be of a reasonable size), Council was finding itself with a responsibility for the consideration of reports on a score or more of papers by the end of the 1950s, over and above the selection of referees for another dozen or more papers newly submitted to the editor or recently read during the Institute's conference.

There was, therefore, a move away from what might be termed ' the Buchanan system ', and the change was more easily effected by a new editor who had observed the working of that system without actually inheriting it directly. A changing situation called for a new approach and for different methods though the Institute remained unaware—or chose to remain in ignorance—of the administrative and financial changes that had eventually to be faced (some of them, however, not until the 1970s), if an adequate and ever-enlarging publishing programme were to be sustained in line with the steadily increasing membership of the IBG. Farmer, the new Editor, had forecast, when he was Assistant Secretary, ' a measure of stability of membership by 1955 ' (Buchanan, 1954, 38) and Buchanan as President in 1953 went on record as stating (p. 8), ' I still find it difficult to visualise a stable membership of much over 400, and Mr Farmer's estimate may yet prove right, with a figure of approximately 400 '. Yet by 1960 membership was already nearly 600 and there were signs of still further increases—though no officer, however, far-seeing, could have anticipated that the membership would have topped the 1,000 mark by 1966 to close on 2,000 by 1979.

Farmer was joined in 1965 by C. Embleton who was appointed to a newly-created post of Assistant Editor. He worked closely with Farmer for two years before himself being appointed Editor and he is better placed than anyone to assess the importance of the work done by Farmer as editor for the five years 1961 to 1966. ' I learnt, ' Embleton has written, ' a tremendous amount from him. I was always impressed by his able handling of the editorial office (though one should not be misled by that term—we had no other assistance apart from very part-time secretarial help!), by his courteousness in dealing with authors, by his meticulous attention to detail, and by the excellent relationships that he maintained with the Alden Press. At the Alden Press, the Managing Director, Mr Bill Furneaux and his colleagues, took a very personal interest in the IBG's publications, and gave us sound advice about the preparation of manuscripts, illustrations, and ways of economising in publication costs without losing the high-quality format that the IBG membership had come to expect since the inception of the journal. '

Embleton's editorship extended from 1967 (following two years as assistant to Farmer) to 1972, and he was first assisted by J. T. Coppock and then by C. E. Everard. An important forward step was the setting up in 1968 of an Editorial Board consisting of the Editor, the Assistant Editor and two other members of Council, to handle the increasing editorial business which hitherto had been conducted in full Council meetings. As the Board could meet more frequently than the full Council, and in more convenient places, this was a great help in speeding-up the pre-publication process. The time between first submission of a paper and its appearance in print averaged about twelve months. Since the Alden Press was still using letter-press, this meant that, with the sequence of press-reading, galley proofs, page proofs, revises and binding, six months was the minimum time for the printing operation; improvement in timing was, therefore, contingent on accelerating the earlier stages of refereeing and editing. Two referees were appointed by the Editorial Board for each paper, with a third in case of disagreement in their recommendations; and, occasionally, papers even went out for a fourth opinion.

From 1963 there were two issues of *Transactions* each year, and by 1968, sufficient articles of high quality appeared to be coming forward to justify increasing the number of issues to three per year. Indeed a change to three issues a year was imperative, in view of the fact, as the figures below indicate, that the number of papers accepted for publication had been rising steadily from about twenty a year in the early 1960s to about thirty a year by the late 1960s, if there was not to develop a backlog of papers awaiting publication, and if publication time was to be reduced. Later the number of papers submitted to *Transactions* began to level off at about 55–60 a year in the period 1968–73; as the ratio of acceptances at the same time showed a slight worsening (from 56% to 46%), the amount of material to fill *Transactions* never exceeded capacity. Three issues a year remained the standard until 1976 when *Transactions* became, as it remains, a quarterly journal.

Papers considered by the Editorial Board (Council before 1968)

	1972	1971	1970	1969	1968	1967	1966	1965	1964	1963	1962
Total considered	57	57	57	59	57	53	41	34	32	20	31
Withdrawn	0	1	0	0	1	1	1	2	2	0	1
Accepted	26	28	32	33	32	28	28	22	16	17	23
Rejected	31	28	25	26	24	24	12	10	14	3	7
% of papers accepted	46	49	56	56	56	53	68	65	50	85	74

Notes: these figures are for *Transactions* only and do not include ' Special Publications'. The 1966 figures exclude *Transactions* No. 39 (special volume).

The levelling-off in the number of papers being submitted to *Transactions* in this period was undoubtedly affected by the beginning of a new series of ' Special Publications '. ' Theme volumes ' had often been considered by the Institute but such volumes had always appeared in the *Transactions* series; an example is no. 39 (1966), ' Vertical displacement of shorelines in Highland Britain '. The first of the new series of Special Publications was issued in 1968 as a Memorial Volume to Sir Dudley Stamp, with the title *Land use and resources: studies in applied geography.* It contained both research articles and reviews, invited from seventeen geographers who had close connections with Sir Dudley, and it appeared in time to mark the 21st International Geographical Congress held at New Delhi in December 1968 in a country with which Sir Dudley had particularly strong ties. Other Special Publications at this time included *Post-glacial uplift in Arctic Canada* (1970), *Slopes: form and process* (1971), *Polar geomorphology* (1972), and *Social patterns in cities* (1973).

During his term of office Embleton introduced two significant changes in the Institute's publications—metrication and foreign-language abstracts. Metrication brought the Institute into line with standard scientific practice over units of measurement and enabled the Editor to establish a consistent style in the use of both units and abbreviations for them. The publication of abstracts in French and German, introduced in *Transactions 46* (1969), proved a bigger and more difficult headache. The Editorial Board in fact had originally intended to include abstracts in Russian (and one member also wanted them in Welsh!), but in the end it was agreed to make a start using just two languages. However, authors frequently claimed that they were quite unable to provide the translations, and it was said that there was no money to pay for any outside help. Printing costs were increasing, and in many instances authors either completely omitted to check the French or German in proof or gave these abstracts only cursory attention. Eventually foreign-language abstracts were discontinued after *Transactions 62* (1974)—a step much regretted by Embleton who, with others, believe that they are invaluable in bringing the work of British geographers before a wider European audience.

With the 50th issue of *Transactions* in 1970 there was a change in format, with the re-design of the cover using two-colour adaptations of photographs or diagrams, and with the adoption of new type-face and new-style headings in the contents. The re-design in fact helped to achieve further economies because it enabled more words to be fitted into a page without loss of legibility. The covers of this period in themselves deserve both study and appreciation, and the cover of no. 52 (1971) is one of the editor's own photographs of an Indian village near Bareilly, Uttar Pradesh.

In 1972, the possibility and desirability of splitting *Transactions* into two series, physical and human, were considered at length. This was an idea often discussed by members of the Institute, and the Editorial Board was urged to consider the matter, on both academic and financial grounds. There were precedents for such a step in other geographical serials, such as *Geografiska Annaler* in Sweden. After long discussions, the Editorial Board decided against the idea on the grounds that: (i) a division into physical and human geography is arbitrary, and cuts across certain fields of geography; (ii) there are areas of geographical study that cannot be placed into either category; (iii) there would be severe editorial problems in balancing the sizes of the two series—publication of one might have to be delayed, for instance, until sufficient articles had accumulated for the other; and (iv) it would have been necessary to increase the number of issues per year from three to four (two physical, two human), and this would have resulted in increases in costs of production. The issue remains alive and continues to exercise the minds of some members, including officers of the Institute (see pp. 50–1).

From the time of the Institute's first publication in 1935, editorial business had always been conducted without any permanent secretarial assistance. The University Departments of Geography, to which successive secretaries, editors and assistant editors were attached, generously (and to a large extent unknowingly!) provided secretarial facilities without cost to the Institute, apart from very limited financial assistance made available from time to time for outside and part-time secretarial assistance. By about 1970 payment for items of work done by secretaries outside departmental office hours was being re-imbursed by the Institute. It was clear, however, that such a system could not be long maintained with the steadily increasing burden of work arising from the growth in publication. Embleton calculated that he and his assistant editor were involved each year in the early 1970s in about 1,000 items of correspondence and a million words of proof-reading, in addition to the preparation of numerous agendas, minutes and reports. At long last, therefore, Council began to consider in 1973 the appointment of a paid editorial secretary and the establishment of an editorial office, since without such assistance no one would have been prepared to shoulder the burden of the editorship.

These problems were indicative of both the new scale of IBG publishing-activity, represented now by *Area* and ' Special Publications ' as well as by *Transactions,* as well as the pressure of work on many members of the Institute. Changes had been particularly marked during the period of Embleton's editorship and immediately afterwards while R. J. Price was editor. Indeed between 1965 and 1973 twenty-six issues of *Transactions* and ' Special Publications ' appeared, and 214 research articles were published in *Transactions.* The volume of publication was in fact roughly comparable with that of the previous thirty years of the Institute's history. Yet by adhering to the most rigorous procedure, there is no doubt that the highest standards of scientific publication had been maintained.

When Embleton's long period in office, first as assistant editor and then as Editor from 1965–72 was drawing to an end, it was hoped that the then Assistant Editor, C. E. Everard, would succeed him. Initially Everard agreed to accept office but ill-health prevented him from taking up the appointment. Thereafter, as many as fifteen members were approached and asked to consider nomination for the post. What concerned them was both the volume of work involved, and the lack of sub-editorial and secretarial assistance offered by the Institute. Eventually R. J. Price, a member of Council, agreed with some reluctance, to take over the editorial responsibilities for a limited period, with J. A. Patmore as assistant editor. Price produced the three volumes for 1973, while negotiations for the provision of appropriate editorial assistance were concluded within the Council. As a result B. T. Robson agreed to move from the editorship of *Area* to that of *Transactions* from the beginning of 1974. As the only member of Institute so far to have been responsible for the editorial work of both *Area* and *Transactions,* his assessment of the relationship between the IBG's two journals has special significance. He saw the comparison ' as a case of chalk and cheese ', with the journals aiming to do different things and the demands of each being very different. He also found a great contrast in the editorial role, with the Editor of *Area* controlling matters ' from the first twinkle in the eye to the final bedding-down at the press ', whereas *Transactions* ' had a momentum and gravitas whioch gave the Editor a necessarily more subservient role '.

There was at the time a good deal of uncertainty about the future of *Transactions.* Some long-established members of the Institute had suggested that it was a journal ' that nobody wanted and that certainly no-one read '. Others proposed a splitting of it into physical, human and, perhaps, ' generalist ' sections, and there was criticism that the IBG was producing a very expensive product that absorbed a large portion of its income without apparently meeting any kind of recognised need. Robson certainly did not agree with the whole of this analysis; indeed he was convinced that the despondency was at least ' a little misplaced ', impressed as he was by the extent to which *Transactions* were used for teaching purposes. He was sure that there was a future for *Transactions,* especially if three main problems could be tackled. These were the excessively long period between the submission of articles and their ultimate publication; the mixture of articles that meant that *Transactions* has no reading constituency; and the difficulty of attracting to *Transactions* what he saw as ' some of the more seminal articles which wanted to impress an audience of specialists within the peer group of some particular field within geography, or often within one of the overlapping fields lying between geography and other disciplines '.

Robson tackled these problems in a forthright manner. He did away with a formal Editorial Board, taking over many of its responsibilities himself. This enabled him on occasions to ensure that certain papers jumped the queue and so achieved rather speedier publication that would otherwise have been the case. He changed the format to an annual continuously paginated quarterly journal, and at the same time persuaded the Council to agree to an alteration in the title to the slightly cumbersome *Transactions of the Institute of British Geographers New Series (TIBG NS).* He also embarked on an attempt to alternate the traditional ' mixed ' issues with ' theme ' issues, starting with two experimental volumes, each with thematic sections. The first of these (*Transactions* 63, 1973) was concerned with geography and public policy and the second, *Transactions* 66 (1975), with landscape evaluation. Later there were fully thematic volumes on houses and people in the city (*Transactions*, NS, 1, no. 1, 1976), edited by Robson himself; man's impact on past environments (*Transactions*, NS, 1, no. 3, 1976), edited by L. F. Curtis and I. G. Simmons; contemporary cartography (*Transactions*, NS, 2, no. 1, 1977), edited by D. Rhind; and change in the town (*Transactions*, NS, 2, no. 3, 1977), edited by J. W. R. Whitehand and J. Patten. Two others followed but these came after D. R. Stoddart had succeeded Robson as editor: housing and employment in the inner city (*Transactions*, NS, 3, no. 1, 1978), edited by A. G. Champion and A. M. Warnes, and settlement and conflict in the Mediterranean world (*Transactions*, NS, 3, no. 3, 1978), edited by G. H. Blake. Stoddart produced one other theme volume on the Victorian city (*Transactions*, NS, 4, no. 2, 1979), edited by R. J. Dennis, but no other volume in later years had a specific theme until the special issue, edited by Stoddart himself, to mark the Jubilee of the IBG under the title ' The Institute of British Geographers, 1933–1983 ' (*Transactions,* NS, 8, no. 1, 1983).

The virtual disappearance of theme volumes during Stoddart's editorship is no doubt a reflection of the success of ' Special Publications ' (see pp. 74–5), which to a large extent fulfil the role intended by Robson in the theme volumes. He had wanted to attract articles on topical issues from workers who might not otherwise have looked to *Transactions*, with its traditional ' mixed ' collection of articles, as an appropriate outlet for their work. He also hoped to bring some of the geographical work being done to a wider audience who would not normally have read *Transactions*. He saw, too, an opportunity of encouraging some of the study groups to use *Transactions* as their vehicle for informing others of what they were doing. The theme volume experiment was partly successful although it did have the unfortunate consequence that submitted articles took even longer to appear in print as they waited for thematic issues to appear. It also raised questions of refereeing since it was not always as easy to apply the same stringent standards to the papers produced by potential authors for thematic issues as those applied to submitted articles.

With the development of ' Special Publications ', *Transactions* has in effect reverted to the older pattern of ' mixed ' articles and some members believe that it is still looking for a convincing role for itself, nearly half a century after the Institute started publishing such volumes. But Robson's successor D. R. Stoddart, whose editorship extended over six years (1977–83), put his stamp very firmly on the journal and stressed his convictions with considerable force in a series of reports given at successive Annual General Meetings. The issues for which he was responsible are so recent that their content will be familiar to all those members who—for all that is said to the contrary—read the papers published in *Transactions,* and an analysis of them is, therefore, unnecessary. Stoddart was a resolute defender of the principle of a mixture of articles based essentially on submissions by individual authors, and resisted all attempts to split the *Transactions* in any particular way or to compromise with any of the suggestions coming forward from members of the Council or from the IBG membership at large. When he handed over to M. W. Williams in January 1983 his colleague M. Blacksell, the Editor of *Area* wrote (Area 15, 1983, 70): ' Of all the Institute's officers in recent years none has been more spirited in defence of their record as of the IBG itself than the outgoing (it seems a more appropriate adjective than retiring) Editor of the *Transactions*, David Stoddart '.

It would seem appropriate to conclude this section on *Transactions* by making an attempt to assess the standing of the journal that has appeared, in a variety of forms, on a regular basis throughout almost the whole of the IBG's existence. Individual numbers of *Transactions* have, on occasions, been reviewed by various geographers, generally in very favourable terms. Thus R. J. Small, writing about no. 48 (1969) (*Geographical Journal,* 136, 1970, 644–6), referred to its variety ' in terms of geographical content ' and to the maintenance over the years of ' a uniformly high standard of scholarship and presentation ', and many would undoubtedly concur in the view that *Transactions* remain the most important and respected outlet for the results of research carried out by professional geographers in Britain. There are, however, some very different points of view. Some of these were expressed by K. M. Clayton (President-designate in 1983) and T. O'Riordan when they reported on a survey that they had carried out on ' the readership of *Transactions* and the role of the IBG ' (*Area* 9, 1977, 96–8). Reminding their readers that the IBG had begun ' as a radical youngster seeking to encourage and publish research ', they commented ' Members of its Council have persistently praised the Institute's prestige periodical, the *Transactions,* as an example of a sound geographical publication which unashamedly brings together a wide ranging array of articles written by an equally varied collection of geographers, thus making available to the profession the fruits of its research across the whole spectrum of geographical endeavour '. Nevertheless their conclusions were that ' British geographers do not appear to turn to the *Transactions* as a depository of geographical research. They are much more likely to subscribe to and to read other journals when seeking pertinent research and reviews in the fields of their research '.

This viewpoint has also been expressed by R. J. Johnston, now the Secretary of the IBG, though not at the time that he was writing in *Area* (12, 1980, 19). He suggested that ' as a general journal the *Transactions* of the IBG now has a very low utility for most members. It is expensive, relative to the members' subscription and to the costs of the specialist journals. In recent years it has published general issues, containing papers some of which may be of interest to and read by recipients, interspersed with theme issues which, by their very nature, are of interest to a small minority of members only. Increasingly it is a journal which is shelved by its purchasers immediately they have scanned the table of contents '. He went on to propose the scrapping of *Transactions*, with an expansion of *Area* (to six issues a year) to serve as ' an outlet for notes, news, and comments; short technical papers; the presidential address and obituaries; and reviews and review articles '.

The History of the IBG is hardly the place to discuss the differing points of view put forward by protagonists and opponents of *Transactions* in its present form, least of all when the author of the History was Editor of the *Transactions* for a longer period than any subsequent editor; but it is clear that the situation, academic and financial, has to be watched very closely, and certain aspects of the problem are dealt with in the final chapter where the future development of the IBG is considered.

The Newsletter

In 1964 the Council decided to encourage the Secretary, W. Kirk, in his initiative to publish, at least once a year, a Newsletter for the distribution of information and comment among the rapidly growing membership of the IBG. At the Annual General Meeting in 1964 he had floated the idea that ' should circumstances facilitate it ' he would circulate a newsletter of current IBG activities and ' pass on information received from other societies, commissions, research groups, *et al* '.

The first issue appeared in July 1964 with a foreword by Kirk stating that ' at the outset it is intended to be a regular feature of each July when members must be circulated in any case with preliminary details of the next Annual Conference, but if the demand increases more frequent Newsletters could be circulated '. Much of the content of the Newsletter would arise, the Secretary thought, from Council business and secretarial correspondence, but he felt that members should feel free to use it as a medium for transmission of their own views, items of general interest, notices, etc. His hope was that the Newsletter would contain ' all those views which affect the conduct of the Institute as a professional and research association ' and would also give wide publicity to the activities of ' study groups working under the aegis of or in close association with other Institutions '.

So the first issue included preliminary information about the Annual Conference to be held at Bristol in 1965, a summary of members' replies to the questionnaire circulated with S. H. Beaver's Presidential statement of February 1964, and an invitation to submit evidence to the University Grants Committee on libraries, together with miscellaneous notes. The second newsletter (July 1965) followed a similar pattern and included a statement on editorial policy (in which it was stated that it was hoped that the *Transactions* would in future ' include a higher proportion of papers dealing with topics and problems of general rather than local interest and embracing more fully the trends and current interests of British geography '). There was also a report on the recent acquisition of a central headquarters for the Institute in the home of the RGS.

No. 3 (July 1966) was noteworthy for the enlargement of a Reports and Correspondence section in which there appeared a letter from A. D. Cooper of Luton College of Technology on ' the professional status of British geography '. Cooper's plea—largely responded to in the following years—was ' for the Institute of British Geographers to drive out from its present fastness and give a professional lead to British geography '. Could the Institute, he asked ' shake itself and come to terms with the new demand for geography '? Otherwise, he suggested (perhaps somewhat controversially in the light of the recent rise in popularity of archaeology), ' the place of geographers in modern Britain will be similar to that of archaeology, interesting, sometimes significant, but mostly beyond the fringe '.

The publication of Cooper's letter to the Secretary for the consideration of the whole membership of the IBG was indicative of several new developments in both the subject and its professional organisation, and the replacement of the three ' Newsletters ' of 1964, 1965 and 1966, issued in typescript on A4 paper, by a booklet of 12 pages with a pale green cover at A5 size in 1967 seemed a natural development. In this number the Secretary wrote of the Institute as a professional association, noting both its achievements and the special difficulties under which geography laboured, and he appealed for comments and constructive suggestions for consideration by the Council and the next Annual Conference.

By 1968 there was a demand for extra issues, and Council recognised that other arrangements had to be made. It was decided that the Newsletter should be the responsibility of the newly created Editorial Board, and in future include ' various items that have normally been included in the *Transactions* '. During 1968 there were two issues of the Newsletter (no. 5 in March, no. 6 in September), and no. 6 was edited by two members of the Council and of the Editorial Board, J. A. Taylor and E. M. Yates.

Undoubtedly the Newsletter had been an outstanding success, the last issue alone having a remarkable range and variety of content spread over 63 pages. These included notes for the guidance of officers of formally constituted study groups; accounts of two of the oldest departments of geography in Britain both of which had celebrated the fiftieth anniversaries of the establishment of their honours schools—Liverpool (by R. W. Steel) and Aberystwyth (by E. G. Bowen); and a report by J. R. Tarrant of an extensive enquiry into the use of computers by geographers in different research fields. There were also articles on ' Geography in CNAA ' (by S. H. Beaver) and ' Geography and the polytechnics ' (by G. H. Gullett), both of which are significant pointers to the development of the

Institute in relation to sectors of higher education outside the universities in subsequent years. The final paper in this issue of the Newsletter, ' A preliminary contribution to the geographical analysis of a Pooh-scape ' was contributed by Llwynog Llwyd, who describes himself in a footnote as ' an exiled Celt who now finds himself, to his surprise and gratification, teaching in, and carrying the news of the Celtic resurgence to, an Antipodean University '. It had been sent to me as President at the time with a request that, if acceptable, it should be published anonymously; and I suspect that the identity of the author is still unknown to most members of the IBG.

Area

During 1968, Council decided to replace the Newsletter by a new publication in 1969 and appointed H. C. Prince as editor. The need for such a periodical, demonstrated as Kirk put it in his foreword by ' favourable reactions to the " Newsletter " ', was generally apparent and it was clear that there was a desire to see it appear with greater frequency and carry not only news but a variety of material of current interest to professional geographers.

The Editorial Board, together with the editor-elect, gave much thought to the format; and Prince was not attracted by the first title suggested, the ' Bulletin of the Institute of British Geographers '. Council had decided that abstracts of papers read at the annual conference, together with reports of discussions and symposia, should be published but the editor was given complete freedom, with certain financial restrictions, to design a new journal to appear four times a year.

Area has come to play so significant a part in the life of the IBG and thus of British geography that it is worth quoting both the Secretary's view that he believed Prince would produce ' an adventurous forward-looking quarterly that would provide British geographers with a vehicle for the exchange of ideas and news ', and also parts of the editorial of the first issue in January 1969. *Area,* it was said, ' welcomes for consideration short articles on subjects of scholarly interest to geographers '. It also serves as a medium for the expression of professional opinions on matters of public interest and as a channel for the communication of reports on the activities of members.

Its aim is to encourage free and impartial discussion of ideas, observations and techniques. ' During the past year ', the editorial stated, ' the Institute's Newsletter has increased in length and broadened in scope to take account of the many activities upon which geographers are currently engaged both individually and as members of research teams. To probe, to report and to examine the implications of work being done in these expanding fields of study a new periodical has been called into existence, under the title of *Area*. While continuing to serve as the main vehicle for reports and announcements of the Institute's activities, *Area* has wider aims '.

Area, the editor suggested, ' is not intended to provide yet another encapsulated definition of the subject, setting arbitrary limits to free-ranging inquiries. On the contrary, studies concerned with points, with central places, with lines, with networks, as well as with areas and with spatial relationships, are recognised as making equally important contributions to the advancement of knowledge about the earth's surface. Many other topics, not specifically concerned with area, but of vital interest to geographers, are being investigated at the margins of architecture, sociology, history, psychology, engineering, politics and mathematics. Nor is it intended to overlook techniques employed in other disciplines which are being applied with varying success to the solution of problems in geography. New hypotheses now being tested and methodological issues now being raised challenge basic assumptions made in studies of ecology, diffusion, innovation, industrial location, geomorphological processes, environmental perception and other questions. If *Area* is to be an adventurous forward-looking journal it cannot ignore these developments from whichever quarter they may originate '.

The editor hoped that *Area* would also ' serve as a forum for the exchange of informed opinion on matters of public interest. It is now widely acknowledged that the work of geographers may have an important bearing on questions of regional planning, transport policy, urban renewal, land utilisation, conservation and amenity. Geomorphologists, urban climatologists and medical geographers may make contributions to the solution of water-supply problems, to the design of urban areas, to the placing of buildings and open spaces, to the understanding of the origin and spread of diseases. Agricultural geographers may ask how factory farming or entry into Europe would affect land use in Britain. Others may examine the use that is made of the countryside for recreational purposes. Yet others may participate in discussions about the delimitation of local government boundaries, the effects of the increasing use of private motor cars and the movement of old people at the time of retirement '.

' As a house journal of the Institute, *Area* will announce some of the diverse activities of British Geographers. It may not always be the first to report news of appointments at the Department of Mines and Surveys or changes in the Phil.B. regulations at Camford or improvisations of equipment at the air photo laboratories at Evercreech or Captain Maconochie's birthday revels, but it will attempt to report the proceedings of meetings and conferences held by the Institute and its study groups. The work of research institutions, grant-awarding bodies, international and interdisciplinary organisations will be kept under review, and excerpts from the underground press of mimeographed papers will occasionally be brought to notice in a very limited way, it will provide correspondents with space for notes and queries, publicise some of the many new research topics and follow work in progress. It is the aim of *Area* to place on record such matters as may be of serious interest to geographers in a professional capacity '.

Finally Prince expressed the hope that by ' affording rapid communication to its readers and speedy publication to its authors, it is to be hoped that discussion and debate will be stimulated and new ideas will be generated and developed. If, in addition *Area* presents a bright and attractive image, it may enlist the attention of an audience beyond the profession. '

The first issue contained fifty-seven pages, and in addition to reports of the Conference and symposia, and lists of the officers and of the five existing study groups, there were several short articles including one on computer graphics by K. E. Rosing, a note on social science research in geography by M. Chisholm, an account of the work of the Centre for Environmental Studies and of the Countryside Commission, and a report on the 21st International Geographical Union Congress in India.

There could hardly have been a more auspicious moment for launching a new 'current affairs journal' for geographers. At the beginning of 1969, the Centre for Urban and Regional Studies was scarcely three years old; the Centre for Environmental Studies had just embarked on a programme of research; SSRC and NERC were both reorganising their procedures for considering research grants; the Countryside Commission had just replaced the National Parks Commission; the British National Committee for Geography was being reconstituted; and a host of geographical problems were being investigated by parliamentary committees. The editor of *Area* saw each of these events as both a challenge and an opportunity.

From the outset the contrast between *Area* and *Transactions* has been marked, and there has been virtually no overlap in the functions that the two journals perform. *Area* has concentrated on the publication of four main kinds of material: geographical and related research, discussion, reports of conferences and meetings, and news and information. The first type of material is, of course, also published by *Transactions* but the articles in *Area* have tended to be shorter and more ephemeral while the production process has been geared to a much more rapid turnover of manuscripts.

Area has provided a forum for lively debate both in the form of correspondence and in critiques of current issues, including at various times the Redcliffe-Maud report on local government reorganisation, the Wheatley report on Scottish local government, and the Roskill Commission on the siting of London's third airport; while J. W. R. Whitehand's article on the diffusion of quantitative methods from a Cambridge-Bristol axis aroused considerable interest and controversy.

Prince retired from the editorship of *Area* during his third year of office in order to take up a temporary academic appointment in the USA during a period of study leave from his post at University College London. In so doing he created a tradition by which the occupants of the editorial chair have changed at fairly frequent intervals. He believed—as have subsequent editors—that the fresh ideas that a new editor brings are important. Moreover, as all editors of *Area* point out, producing such a journal at frequent intervals is so time-consuming (the outgoing correspondence alone is well in excess of a thousand items per annum, and this is only a small part of the job) that it would be unreasonable to expect an honorary officer to undertake it for more than a few years.

Prince was succeeded by B. T. Robson, at that time a member of the staff of the Department of Geography in the University of Cambridge. With the very full co-operation of the printers, Henry Ling, he built on the foundations laid by Prince, and without any secretarial help he did much of the work himself. He chose cover designs in a different colour relating to the season of the year for each number with continuous pagination throughout each volume; several of the drawings in the text and on the covers were his own work. He saw the issue of the balance of the content of *Area* as vital. It had begun life in essence as a newsletter, and in his view, 'it always seemed important that it should try to achieve a fair balance between articles, on the one hand, and news reports and snippets on the other. ' In his experience *Area* attracted so much unsolicited article material once it had got into its swing that there was a real danger that, to quote his own words ' it could have become " just " another but smaller academic periodical. That would have been to deny its unique role, as I saw it, of being a professionally printed, relatively expensive house journal with a rapid turn-around. Hence the need to strike a balance between ephemera and substantive articles. '

Robson was also concerned with the importance of feed-back from the profession. Obviously it was reassuring to know that it *was* read; that, he has observed, must always be grist to an editor's ego. But the fact that it was read, allied with the rapid turn-around, meant that it offered an opportunity to develop genuine debate in its pages. It was this that he took most pains to try to cultivate: first, by introducing regular editorial or invited commentaries at the outset; secondly, by twisting some arms to get provocative pieces or reports such as those from Hugh Prince and David Smith on the 1971 AAG Conference; and thirdly, by introducing a Comment section to get printed debate and response about earlier articles or matters of moment.

Two years later, in 1974, Robson became Editor of the *Transactions*, and John Hall of Queen Mary College, London, was appointed Editor of *Area* in his place. *Area*, now five years old, was greatly appreciated by the members of the IBG who deluged the Editor with reports of study groups and of other Institute activities, with comments, and with short articles. Hall continued in the style and manner of his predecessors but he found it increasingly difficult to give to a lively publication that appeared on a regular and quite frequent basis the time and attention that were needed. Council was unwilling or unable—or perhaps had not yet appreciated the necessity—to find the money for assistance, editorial and secretarial, for the Editor of *Area* that it had recently made available to the Editor of *Transactions*. Despite these problems Hall succeeded in serving the membership admirably and being responsible for the production of fourteen issues of *Area*—a greater number than any previous editor of this publication. Moreover in 1974 he was persuaded to accept a further year in the editorial chair, notwithstanding the inadequacy of the support that was being given to him to do this work. That year proved to be a particularly busy one in his department, and he found it impossible to adhere to the rigid programme of publication established during previous years. There was a considerable accumulation of suitable material for publication in *Area*, and only then, and at long last, did Council recognise the urgency of the need for some help for the Editor. The beneficiary was, however, not Hall but his successor, J. W. R. Whitehand of Birmingham, who took over the editorial chair in July 1977. It is not every editor who receives an accolade from his successor but this is what Whitehand said of Hall in his first editorial, ' A change of drivers ' (*Area* 9, 161). *Area* was losing, he wrote, ' an Editor whose versatility and enthusiasm have extended to all aspects of the journal's production ', and under whose guidance *Area* had ' in considerable measure achieved the healthy maturity predicted by his distinguished predecessor, Dr Brian Robson '. He went on to refer to the administratively unwieldy nature of a ' single-handed editorial operator' which caused the loss of ' the speed, flexibility and immediacy which are crucial to its attractiveness as a forum for issues of the moment'. Whitehand welcomed the financing of part-time editorial and secretarial assistance which had become available to him in Birmingham as ' the editorial office moved out of the south-east triangle of the country for the first time'.

Hall, of whom a colleague has said, ' John did almost everything except the actual printing!', had undertaken what in his own words he described as ' a solo operation ' (' an editorial signing-off', *Area* 9, 160), but he rejoiced to know that his successor had ' already organised helpers', these now being available thanks to the new financial arrangements made by the Council. Hall himself gave editorial oversight to some of the work that had accumulated during his last months as Editor, and was responsible for volume 9, no.2, which appeared after, and not before, nos. 3 and 4 which were produced by Whitehand. There was a further catching up in 1978 with the publication in one year of five, instead of the usual four, issues of *Area*.

Whitehand was conscious of the way in which the very acute difficulties of the Editor of *Area* had not been appreciated by Council. Indeed it had not recognised the existence of the problem in any formal way for a very considerable time, even though it was one that had been building up over a period of several years. He took steps to ensure that there was no recurrence of the difficulties encountered by Hall by producing regular written reports for the consideration of the Council so that all members could appreciate the volume of material that was coming in and the size of the mammoth task that faced the editor. This was especially great because of the need for heavy editing since, as Whitehand puts it, ' the profession as a whole is not really adjusted to the pithy style that *Area* requires'. A paid part-time Editorial Assistant, with a small amount of secretarial help, largely solved the problem although the solution came, in his view, ' at least four years later than it should have done'.

For Whitehand the editing of *Area,* with copy-editing done by Susan Whitehand, his wife, became a ' way of life' between July 1977 and January 1980. With great resolution he tackled the backlog of papers so that volume 10, no. 3 (1978) included many of the articles submitted during 1975 and 1976 that would, under normal circumstances, have been printed in earlier volumes. He aimed to retain much of the original character of *Area* although during the difficult years when the accumulation of manuscripts was being dealt with, it was necessary to resort to various expediencies. He was particularly anxious to attract comments on articles and to seek out reports and other items. This resulted in a flood of material that was dealt with by increasing the number of pages per issue and shortening the average length of items. Referees he found were particularly helpful in terms of both speed and efficiency, so that it was possible to ' publish high priority items' within as little as three months of the receipt of the original manuscript. All in all, the journal then, as now, deserved the commendation of one geographer, now an officer of the Institute, who described *Area* as ' lively, well-read, relatively cheaply produced, and frequently published'.

This flourishing publication was taken over in 1980 by the present Editor,

Mark Blacksell, who continued the policies of his predecessor while at the same time introducing a number of new features which make *Area* even more indispensable to members of the Institute and to geographers generally. Whitehand, as a retiring Editor, had permitted himself an editorial comment in volume 9, no. 4 (273–4) on ' the silent majority ' in which he surveyed some of his findings from nearly three years in office with the comment that ' the majority of articles submitted for publication, at least to the Institute's two journals, are rejected '. Blacksell did not begin his reign as Editor with an editorial but significantly invited a colleague in the University of Exeter, J. B. Harley, to provide an extended commentary on the report of the Ordnance Survey Review Committee chaired by Sir David Serpell (*Area* 12, 1980, 1–8). A year later, however, he contributed a first page article (*Area* 13, 1981, 1) when he asked a very pertinent question under the heading ' A future in Britain or Europe? '. Noting that ' anniversaries are very much the vogue at present ' and citing among other things, the celebration by the RGS of its 150th birthday and the fact that the IBG was beginning to prepare for its Golden Jubilee, he asked whether the time was not appropriate for taking stock and ' given the prevailing spirit of the age, to ask whether an Institute of *British* geographers is the best way forward into the next century? '. Ought not the IBG, in its second fifty years, to take some very positive steps to broaden further its rather narrow national focus '. He was sure that with ' the groundwork that has been laid in the recent past ' ' the Institute is ideally placed to seize the initiative, and such a bold and imaginative move would give a new lease of life as it moves from maturity to old age '. Perhaps that forward look into the future may be regarded as the keynote of the present Editor's tenure of office, and successive issues of *Area* have alerted readers to many matters to which they should be giving earnest attention; and no doubt the same outlook will be characteristic of his successor, Robin Flowerdew, who takes over responsibility for *Area* from the beginning of 1984.

Special Publications

Compared with many disciplines, geography is poorly endowed with commercial publishers prepared to undertake the publication of research as distinct from student textbooks. Thus the role of the Institute in providing outlets for research monographs and collections of research papers has always been particularly important. From 1968 to 1979 the Institute did this by acting as its own publisher. But a major problem with this arrangement stemmed from the Institute's limited capability to promote sales outside its own membership. There was, therefore, only a slow return on a capital investment in each volume that was sizeable in relation to the Institute's total income. Thus, although many of the old series of Special Publications ultimately paid for themselves, sales were spread over many years. It was felt that if a commercial publisher could be persuaded to bear the risk a larger output would be possible with no burden on the Institute's resources. This was an important consideration in the negotiation of an agreement in 1979 with Academic Press to publish Special Publications on the Institute's behalf.

Volumes in the new series are already being published at nearly twice the rate of the old series. There are, however, alongside the gains, some unintended effects. Academic Press is understandably less than enthusiastic about publishing volumes that are likely to appeal to only a small readership, so that some freedom has been lost. If specialised research is to be a viable proposition for the Series it is necessary to reach specialists throughout the world, and this is already having an effect on the subject matter and authorship of volumes in preparation. There is, for example, an increased proportion of authors from overseas and from outside the discipline, and many of them are not members of the Institute.

The new arrangement has also increased the suceptibility of Special Publications to the exigencies of boom and slump in the book trade. Within eighteen months of the publication of the first volume in the new series, commercial constraints were limiting the number of proposals for volumes that could be accepted; and the fact that several worthy proposals for volumes in human geography have had to be rejected because of concern about their commercial viability in the present depressed state of the academic book trade will be reflected in the number and nature of the new titles in the Series that appear in the mid-1980s.

Furthermore, whatever the state of the market, it is doubtful whether under the present arrangements the needs of specialist researchers writing for predominantly British geographers will be met. Thus some of the types of manuscripts that were published in the *Transactions* series of monographs and, later, in the old series of Special Publications will be unlikely to find a place in the new series; and it is questionable whether study group publications, despite their rising numbers, will be able to fill entirely the gap in the Institute's publishing capability that this leaves.

Nevertheless, the prospects for the Series appear to be good. The standard of production of the volumes so far is high, and there has been little difficulty in attracting manuscripts of high quality. Major advantages over the old arrangements include world-wide advertising and distribution at no cost to the Institute, royalties to authors, an ' override ' royalty to the Institute, and the removal of the burden to the Institute of undertaking sub-editing and storage. The main task of the Editorial Board responsible for the administration of the new series is to capitalise on these assets while resisting the inevitable pressures to sacrifice academic excellence for marketability.

The IBG and its first publishers
From the very beginning the publication of work by geographers was regarded as, if not the sole, at least the supreme justification for the foundation of the IBG and it is, therefore, appropriate to record something of the special relationship that was forged between the IBG and its first publishers, the firm of George Philip and Son Ltd.

What had stimulated the original members to join together in the new enterprise that became the IBG was the need for additional outlets for publication, coupled with a sense of exasperation and frustration resulting from the difficulty of obtaining space for scholarly work in established periodicals such as the RGS's *Geographical Journal* and the GA's *Geography*. How right these feelings were, it is difficult to judge with the passage of time, but those concerned with the first beginnings of the Institute who are still alive are adamant about the reality of the situation; and certainly a perusal of the *Geographical Journal* and *Geography* in the early 1930s does not indicate that there was much acceptance of papers written by academic geographers, especially younger members of the profession who had not yet attained the rank of being a well-established senior author such as Sir Halford Mackinder or C. B. Fawcett.[7] Undoubtedly the younger geographers of the day considered the prospects of having their work published in the *Geographical Journal* to be very poor—particularly, it is said, if it were in human geography. D. R. Stoddart in his summary account of the history of the Institute in the special jubilee issue of *Transactions* (NS 8, 1983, 1–13) refers to the then Director and Secretary of the RGS, and Editor of the *Geographical Journal,* A. R. Hinks FRS, as 'formidable and frequently irascible' (Stoddart, 1983, 2), but quotes J. A. Steers (1982) and Alice Garnett (1983) as suggesting that Hinks's attitude was more a matter of maintaining academic standards than an aversion to any particular type of geography. Be that as it may, many academic geographers felt that the *Geographical Journal's* prime, if not exclusive, concern was for exploration and mountaineering, and their view was that the RGS was dominated, again in Stoddart's words (1982, 12), ' by aristocratic and military men of perhaps narrow sympathies'. Yet the Society's Council in its centenary year (1930) included several members with long university experience, with C. B. Fawcett, H. J. Fleure and Ll. Rodwell Jones as well as Sir Halford Mackinder, who was at the time a Vice-President of the RGS. Their influence upon editorial policy must, however, have been slight. In the two volumes for 1930 (volumes 75 and 76), for example, there are few contributions by recognisable academic geographers apart from Fawcett's paper already noted and a two-page note by E. G. R. Taylor on ' The missing draft project of Drake's voyage of 1577–80 ', and another by her on ' Samuel Purchas ', and a long paper by R. O. Buchanan on ' Hydro-electric power development in New Zealand '. The two volumes for 1933 (81 and 82), the year of foundation of the Institute, as Stoddart has pointed out (see p. 6), contained the usual ' characteristic papers ', though there are also academic contributions from, among others, H. C. Darby, A. C. O'Dell and E. C. Willatts—all of whom were relatively young men (25, 21 and 22 years of age respectively) at the time. What seems strange, with hindsight, is the fact that there was at no time a meeting between the officers of the RGS and those who were most concerned about publication outlets and who were particularly involved in the subsequent establishment of the new group that became the IBG.

What was most acutely felt, however, was the lack of any prospects for the publication of works of monograph length (30,000 words and upwards). These were not in general research theses, for there were relatively few of these written by the handful of geographers in university posts at the time; in any event the PhD, still a very new research degree in many British universities in the early 1930s was available to very few geographers—although several of the Institute's founder members (Alice Garnett, H. C. K. Henderson and Alice F. A. Mutton, among others) had doctorates. What is significant is that it was only after the

Second World War that the IBG decided, as a matter of policy, to publish short rather than long papers or monographs. All the pre-war publications were monographs, and there were not many of these. The Minutes are not always specific on the names and titles of the authors and how many were under consideration by the Council; but it is clear that very high, rigid standards were applied by the referees appointed by the Editorial Board and that the rate of rejection was also very high (a minute of January 1934 refers to three out of four rejections).

Even if scholarly writing was available, and ready for publication, there had to be the resources and the means for its production, and the infant IBG was very fortunate to have roused the interest, and the confidence, of one publishing firm, that of George Philip and Son Ltd. Indeed it would be hard to exaggerate the significance of the support given to the IBG by members of this long-established cartographic and publishing firm. George Philip had been famous for the preparation and publication of maps for many years ever since its establishment in Liverpool in 1834 and later in Fleet Street and in Willesden.[8] Its general interest in education, over and above the sale of atlases and maps in schools, colleges and universities, showed itself in the help that it gave to at least two important scholarly bodies, the Historical Association and the GA, and during the 1930s and for many years later the IBG was to benefit in the same way as these two organisations.

The IBG records are not clear as to where the initiative lay in bringing about, at an early stage, this fortunate liaison between the firm and the Institute. Several of the IBG's founder members would have been aware of the nature of the arrangements existing between George Philip and the GA, and possibly the Historical Association too; but the interest and enthusiasm of certain senior members of the firm may well have been the dominant influences in the persons of E. O. Giffard, the firm's Educational Liaison Officer, and E. Gordon Godfrey, who joined the firm in 1922 and who rose rapidly to become first a Director and later Managing Editor of the firm. From the outset these two gentlemen pressed the claims of the IBG for all the help that the firm, with its geographical interest, could give, and their pleas were heard sympathetically first by George Philip Senior, who died in 1937, and later by his son, George Philip Junior, who had read the Geographical Tripos at St Catharine's College, Cambridge between 1930 and 1933.

Even the Council's minutes do not give any indication of the nature of the arrangements worked out between the firm and the Institute. Was a subsidy involved? Were special rates charged? Was the publishing of IBG works done on particularly favourable terms? Or did the undertaking of printing and publishing by one and the same firm result in savings that were significant, indeed vital, at this stage in the Institute's history? Unfortunately all the geographers and others who could provide answers to these questions are no longer alive or do not recall the precise nature of the apparently unwritten understanding between publisher and learned society.

Whatever the basis of the arrangement, it is clear that the link with the firm of George Philip, and the trust shown in it by its directors, notably Giffard and Godfrey, was of tremendous value at the time. Could the IBG have survived without their help during the 1930s? Undoubtedly not, especially when it is realised that the Institute was embarking on a publishing programme—its essential *raison d'être*—on the basis of incredibly meagre resources; indeed these amounted to no more than subscriptions of a total membership that even at the outbreak of war in 1939 numbered less than 100 with an individual subscription of only £2 per annum. Yet between foundation in 1933 and the temporary cessation of its activities six and a half years later at the outbreak of war, the Institute published five monographs together with *The changing sea-level* by Henri Baulig, referred to above (pp. 14–16). In the single year, 1937, three publications appeared—Alice Garnett's *Insolation and relief: their bearing on the human geography of Alpine regions,* L. E. Tavener's *Land classification in Dorset* and Dorothy M. Doveton's The *human geography of Swaziland*. This was a remarkable achievement for so young and small an institution and was not surpassed until 1968. Unfortunately these volumes received very little publicity. The almost penniless IBG does not appear to have been able to advertise its existence or its wares to any extent, and reviews are few and far between. One reviewer (J. A. Steers, *Geographical Journal* 91, 1938, 63–4) congratulated both Miss Garnett and the Institute on the monograph *Insolation and relief* which he regarded as ' an instructive and careful piece of work of real value to the geographer and also to the agriculturist and ecologist '. But the *Geographical Journal's* reviewers of the monographs on Dorset (W. G. East) (90, 1937, 465–6) and Swaziland (W. Fitzgerald) (92, 1938, 273), although members of the Institute, made no specific reference to these works as being products of the IBG.

After the war George Philip fully maintained its backing for the Institute, and the officers of the immediate post-war years and during the 1950s knew, as no other group could, how real and disinterested was this support. It continued notwithstanding the Council's decision, taken only after very careful consideration (and in the light of a very real problem in post-war publishing with its inordinate delays), to have its printing done (as described on pp. 31–2) by the Alden Press of Oxford while the firm remained the Institute's publishers (as it did until 1968). Giffard continued to attend most Annual Conferences, as he did for the GA and the meetings of Section E (Geography) of the British Association for the Advancement of Science. Godfrey's interest and help showed itself in a different way. For more than ten years he regularly invited the executive officers of the Council—the Secretary, Treasurer and Editor—to an informal dinner, ostensibly at least for the discussion of the Institute's publishing programme, at the National Liberal Club. As one who was on many occasions a recipient of his hospitality, I came increasingly to value his friendship and his interest and advice, as well as the remarkable publishing experience that he had. However informal and jovial the dinner, we were called to order at some stage in the evening—usually just before one of us announced that he must leave quite soon to catch a late-evening train from Paddington, Euston or Liverpool Street—to deal with those items of IBG business that it was appropriate and helpful to discuss with the Managing Director of our publisher. Within three or four days he would circulate a record of our discussions, which always looked much more important in typescript than they had seemed in the immediate aftermath of an excellent dinner! Among Gordon Godfrey's many services to the Institute was the advice that he gave to the officers on matters of copyright of both text and maps (something that had been of special interest to him over many years), and these services were very properly recognised in 1960 when Council elected him to honorary membership of the Institute, while the interest in, and support for, the IBG continued right up to the time of his illness that led to his death in 1972. His son, Patrick, an Oxford geographer and now a Director of the firm, joined the IBG in 1951 as an ordinary member. His colleague, H. Fullard, who had helped editorially in the production of IBG publications from 1938 and became a member of the Institute in 1948, was present at the fiftieth anniversary celebrations in Edinburgh in January 1983.

In the turmoil of the printing and publishing world in the years immediately following the Second World War, the Institute benefited from the understanding attitude of its first publishers, George Philip and Son Ltd, and by the willing co-operation of the printers to whom it turned at the beginning of the 1950s. The development of the links with the Alden Press (Oxford) Ltd and the special role of W. J. Furneaux have been noted on pp. 31–2, 58, 61. The combined efforts of publishers, printers and the editor not only enabled the IBG to survive the trauma of the publishing world during those years and to re-establish its publishing schedule but it also provided the basis for the very considerable expansion of publication that characterised the Institute during the 1960s and even more so in the 1970s. Significantly the Alden Press continued to print *Transactions* until 1980 even though *Area* was printed elsewhere, and the firm's contribution to the wellbeing and prosperity of the IBG should be recorded alongside the Institute's indebtedness to the firm of George Philip for its unwavering support of the Institute during its early and difficult years as a learned society that put great store in its output of scholarly publication.

The first volume of *Area*, produced in 1969, was printed by the Curwen Press Ltd, of Plaistow, London E13, but Henry Ling Ltd of Dorset took over the work from 1970 and have remained the printers of *Area* ever since. Moreover since 1980 the firm has taken over responsibility for the printing of *Transactions*, retaining the special features of the series, of which the Institute is, with good reason, very proud. The IBG has been most fortunate in the service given to it by the firm and particularly in the personal interest and advice of Tony Kennett and George Hill. Those of us who had worked closely with the Alden Press were sorry when the break had to come as a result of a close scrutiny of the financial outlay required by all the IBG's publications, and the obvious economies made possible by the concentration of the now very considerable publication programme of the IBG in a single publishing unit. It is clear that Henry Ling Ltd, already with considerable experience of working with successive editors of *Area*, will continue in every way the tradition of co-operation and service that the IBG has profited from in its other publishers and printers.

Notes
1. This number appeared particularly late, and there were special circumstances that account for the delay, but other journals were experiencing similar difficulties. *The Geographical Journal*, for

example, began putting the month and year of publication on the cover alongside the date of the particular issue in 1946, and during the immediate post-war period there was a gap of some four months each time. It is relevant here to note that in fact the RGS published very few of the research memoirs planned, and one in particular was ' in the press ' for many months—partly, though not solely, the result of the same problems of the printing trade that affected the IBG in the immediate post-war years.

2. Miller, A. A. (1952) ' Three new climatic maps, 1951 ' *Transactions* 17, 15–20
3. Parry, J. T. (1960) ' The erosion surfaces of the south-western Lake District ', *Transactions* 28, 39–54. Figure 2, ' The drainage pattern and erosion surface remnants of the south-western Lake District ' faces p. 41
4. Kidson, C. (1960) ' The shingle complexes of Bridgwater Bay ', *Transactions* 28, 75–87. Figure 2 ' The shingle complexes of Bridgwater Bay ' is on pp. 76–7
5. The sole exception was in 1956 when I was involved in a move from Oxford to Liverpool, and was myself responsible for delays in dealing with page proofs that prevented the publication of the volume until March 1957. It is noteworthy that the Alden Press's record of punctuality was maintained even in 1959 when a printing strike of seven weeks' duration upset printing schedules throughout Britain.
6. *Transactions* 29, 1961, 142 (underline to Figure 5)
7. Fawcett at this time was much engaged in the publication of papers concerned with population both on a global scale and in the British Isles. His famous paper ' The extent of the cultivable land ' appeared in 1930 (*Geographical Journal,* 76, 504–09, and his ' Distribution of the urban population in Great Britain ' was published two years later, also in the *Geographical Journal,* 79, 100–16. The latter paper was an extension of ideas that appeared in 1929 in ' The balance of urban and rural populations ' (*Geography,* 15, 99–106).
8. *The story of the last 100 years: a history of George Philip and Son from 1834–1934* (London 1934) provides a very interesting and informative history of the firm.

VI

Annual Conferences

Despite the dominance of the quest for publication outlets in the thinking that brought the Institute into existence in the early 1930s, the yearly Conference, with the associated Annual General Meeting, has also always played an important part in the life of the IBG. In pre-war days the conference took place simultaneously with the Conference of the GA which was always held at the London School of Economics. At that time many members of the IBG were active members of the Association, a far higher proportion than is the case today. Numbers attending were usually quite small though they represented a considerable proportion of the membership. Great care was taken to prevent clashes with the major events in the GA programme, and the initial reaction to proposals for a residential conference away from London was, if not hostile, at least doubtful because clearly much store was laid on this meeting together once a year of many teachers of geography, whether in universities, training colleges or schools. Moreover, as explained on pages 12–13, the Association had shown much co-operation and good-will during the period when the IBG was being born, and H. J. Fleure, at that time one of the most senior professors of geography in Britain, and Honorary Secretary of the Association, was a member of the first IBG Council and was invariably positive and helpful in the kind of help—including possible assistance in the publishing field—that he hoped that the Association could give to the infant Institute.

Thus for the first decade and a half of the Institute's life (which included the years of the Second World War) there was never any significant move on the part of the officers to hold the conference anywhere other than in London, and to have it (as is common with many London-based conferences) non-residential in character. Following on three post-war conferences of the traditional type in the Januaries of 1946, 1947 and 1948, Council decided to stage a residential conference, on an experimental basis, in the University of Oxford, where the Bursar of Jesus College, J. N. L. Baker, the recently retired President of the IBG, offered the facilities of Jesus College, of which I—at the time Acting Secretary of the Institute in the absence in New Zealand of R. O. Buchanan—was also a member. At that time no one could have imagined that this was going to mean the end of regular London conferences.

In fact the Oxford conference of 1949 was so successful, both academically and socially, that there has never been any question since of whether or not the Annual Conference should be residential. With an attendance of 92 the participants not only outnumbered the total membership immediately before the war, but it represented a very high proportion of the current membership of about 160. This high conference turn-out has always been a feature of the IBG, so much so that L. D. Stamp (1966) stated that he did ' not know of any professional association which attracts such a large proportion of total membership to its annual conference ' (*Transactions* 1966, 40, 20).

Initially, the conferences were based on what has been called the ' golden triangle ' of (in alphabetical order) Cambridge, London and Oxford, Oxford 1949 being followed by Cambridge in 1950 with a still larger number in residence at St John's and St Catharine's Colleges (Figure 3). Plans for a London residential conference in the following year fell through (see p. 33) and the conference returned to Oxford, once again being housed at Jesus College and its near-neighbour Lincoln. In 1952 the Institute made history by going out of England for the first time, to the University College of Wales, Aberystwyth. Despite some early doubts as to the likely attendance in what to some members seemed a very remote location (and Aberystwyth is not the most readily accessible of the seven Constituent Institutions of the federal University of Wales), the conference proved to be one of the happiest and most successful held up to that time, no doubt in part because members could not ' drop in ' on the conference for short periods as had always happened in London and, to a less extent, in Oxford and Cambridge. Most of those who came to Aberystwyth arrived at the beginning and stayed to the end, with a high proportion of those attending travelling by the limited rail services to Aberystwyth. It is a commentary on those times that relatively few members of the Institute owned cars. It is also interesting to realise that in those pre-Beeching days there were still reasonable rail services from most parts of Britain to Aberystwyth although even then, so far as I can recall, there were no trains on Sunday between Aberystwyth and Shrewsbury, at least during the winter months.

By 1952, therefore, IBG residential meetings were well established and there was no longer any question of a reversion to the old type of meeting in London. There was, however, a strong case for another London conference of a residential nature (and attempts had been made to hold one in 1951), partly to emphasise that the Institute still saw many of its interests as complementary to those of the members of the GA. The timing of the Bedford College Conference in 1953 was carefully arranged so that it was possible for members to attend both the IBG meeting and part, at least, of the GA's conference. It also ensured a much larger attendance of IBG members than was usual at the Annual Lecture arranged each year by the RGS. On these occasions the RGS acted as host and provided a sumptuous tea, with the GA and the IBG acting as equal partners. Many of the more senior members of the Institute will recall what might be described as an academic sermon delivered by H. C. Darby (1953), at the time Professor of Geography at University College London, on ' The relations of history and geography ' (*Transactions* 19, 1–11) to a very large and responsive audience of geographers from all three societies gathered in the hall at the RGS's

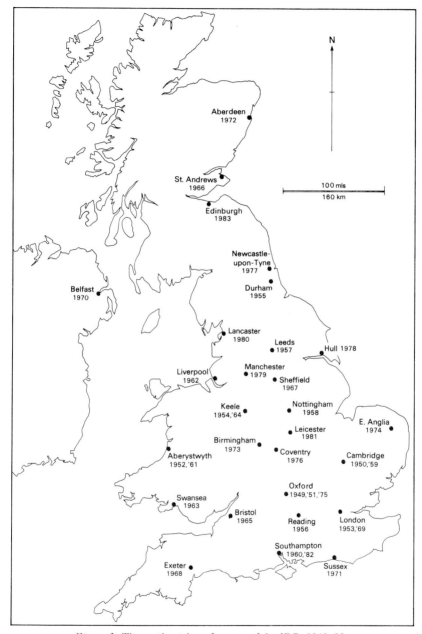

Figure 3. The residential conferences of the IBG, 1949–83.

house in Kensington Gore where, many years later, the offices of the Institute were to be established.

The success of these conferences encouraged a number of universities and colleges to offer to act as hosts to the IBG, including Keele where the University College of North Staffordshire had been established for only a very short time though its Department of Geography had already proved itself to be one of the best and most active of the College's foundation departments. Keele was selected as the venue for the 1954 conference, and thereafter the IBG spread itself ever more widely—Durham in 1955, Reading in 1956, Leeds in 1957, Nottingham in 1958. The places to which the IBG has gone over the years are indicated in Fig. 3, and it is unnecessary to refer to each and every conference. But it is interesting to observe the scatter of venues and to note that the conference has been three times to both Scotland (St Andrews 1966, Aberdeen 1972, Edinburgh 1983) and Wales (Aberystwyth 1952 and 1961, Swansea 1963) and once to Northern Ireland (Belfast 1970). To date only one conference has been held in an institution other than a university—that of 1976 which was based on Coventry (Lanchester) Polytechnic. Since residential conferences were introduced in 1949 there have been three in Oxford (1949, 1951, 1975) and two each in Aberystwyth (1952, 1961), Cambridge (1950, 1959), London (1957, 1969) and Southampton (1960, 1982). Durham (1955) will have its second conference in 1984.

During the 1950s, at a time when there was considerable expansion in certain universities, it was sometimes necessary for an individual university to state that, while keen to host a conference, it would not want the Institute to come before a stated date, by which time it was assumed that a particular lecture room or a new hall of residence or some other new development had been completed. There are numerous references to these matters in the Council minutes of this period and little local difficulties revealed themselves from time to time, and on one occasion almost a last-minute switch of venue had to be made; but conferences have taken place year after year with ever-growing numbers and more and more complexity, and, it would seem, with steadily increasing success. At the last London meeting in 1969 a thousand members were known to have attended at least part of the conference, and in centres elsewhere, where a much higher proportion of the members stays in halls of residence, numbers in excess of 800 have been achieved in several universities.

All conferences, and the host university or polytechnic and its department of geography or environmental science, are different and are enjoyed by members for a wide variety of reasons. Council is very conscious of the problems posed by size, and geography staffs must quake when they hear suggestions that they might be hosts for a forthcoming conference. But despite all the difficulties, and the heavy demands inevitably made by such large and complex gatherings, it would appear that the IBG conference is regarded as among the prestigious meetings that universities like to attract, and invariably the host university or college is happy to provide a reception, and at the Annual Dinner the University has usually been represented by its Vice-Chancellor or Principal.

The organisation of an IBG conference is inevitably elaborate, and Council has given thought to the problems that arise by the issuing of guide lines for the use of the local committee and its secretary and, in recent years by the appointment of one of its members to act as Conference Secretary.[1] Thereby liaison at every stage with the host university is assured and the programme is built up with maximum local flexibility combined with overall Council control. The bulk of the burden falls upon the local Secretary and his colleagues, normally in the department of geography, and invariably they have risen to the challenges of a large conference and a huge diversity of arrangements within a highly complex programme. To date nearly all conferences have proved financially viable, and costings have been made on the assumption that they will be self-financing and, so far, no conference has needed financial support from outside.

The Presidents and their addresses

The Presidents of the IBG have interpreted their roles in a variety of ways but all of them have played an especially important part in the Annual Conference which, at least since the office became an annual appointment, comes at the end of the presidential year and is the occasion for the delivery of the presidential address.

Rodwell Jones chaired the inaugural meeting in 1933 but the first President was C. B. Fawcett (1933–7). He was succeeded by R. N. Rudmose Brown (1937–9). J. N. L. Baker was elected President in 1939 and remained in office through the dormant years of the IBG during the Second World War. In the light of the comments that were often made in the early years by critics of the IBG—and perhaps particularly by those who were looking for reasons for not joining this new professional association—it is worth noting the geographical scatter of leaders of the Institute during the first decade and a half of its existence: Edinburgh, London, Sheffield and Oxford. Indeed the suggestion that the IBG was ever London-based and London-dominated does not deserve investigation since it is so clearly untrue and unwarranted. If the London membership was particularly active and supportive in the early days, it was only the consequence of the size of the geographical community within Greater London and the relative ease with which members could come to meetings, the majority of which were held somewhere in London during this period apart from occasional meetings called during the annual conferences of the British Association for the Advancement of Science.

No presidential addresses were expected of the first presidents although Baker read a paper on ' Geography and politics: the geographical doctrine of balance ' which was given pride of place, as a communication from the President, in the *Transactions* published in 1947 (*Transactions*, 13, 1947, 1–15). But, according to Buchanan (*Transactions*, 20, 1954, 1), Baker's full-scale address ' he explicitly refused to call a presidential address '. In it there were numerous references to the thoughts of one of British geography's great pioneers, Sir Halford Mackinder, but at the same time Baker developed, in a manner appropriate to a President of a learned society, some of his own philosophical ideas.

Baker's successor, A. Austin Miller, gave an address prepared at the request of the Council on ' The dissection and analysis of maps ' (*Transactions*, 14, 1949, 1–13). In it he expressly stated that ' I do not wish the form of my address to be regarded in any way as setting a precedent to bind the long line of Presidents '; and he went on to suggest ' that a Presidential Address, unlike the majority of papers that are read by members of the Institute, should not be in the form of some original investigation; rather I regard it as an opportunity to pass in review some aspect of our subject in a critical but, I hope, constructive frame of mind '. This statement by an early President of the Institute is interesting, especially as it established, by and large, the pattern of all the many presidential addresses that have been delivered subsequently.

Miller's views were noted and acted upon by his successor, S. W. Wooldridge, who addressed the Institute with his ' Reflections on regional geography in teaching and research ' (*Transactions*, 16, 1950, 1–11). It was a hard-hitting, provocative and forthright statement that was heard with admiration and considerable approval by the audience at the Annual Conference held in Cambridge in January 1950. Those of us with genuine research interests overseas—myself among them—were amused rather than annoyed by his oft-quoted references to ' the cult, or rather the disease, of what I would call " otherwheritis " '. This, he thought of as a real peril to the well-being of geography, since at best he saw it as an expression of ' a genuine and natural wanderlust, whether spiritual or sporting in its motive ', and at its worst, it could, he alleged, ' lead to a species of egotistic, impressionistic geography, a congerie of travellers' tales, agreeably titillating, no doubt, to the stifled imagination of strap-hanging town-dwellers, but making no claim whatever to scholarship ' (*ibid.*, p. 9). He may have been mistaken in his view that ' the human geography of Somerset is more interesting and in many ways more significant than that of, say, Somaliland '; and while all of us could agree that the physical difficulties of studying Somerset were much less, many of us did not believe that the intellectual difficulties presented by a study of Somerset were ' incomparably greater ' than they were in Somaliland (p. 9). But the President was a man of great stature—physical as well as mental—and the members present respected what he had to say whether or not they concurred in his views on many matters; though as a younger geographer (D. R. Stoddart) has recently put it in *Transactions* NS 8, 1983, 5): ' It is difficult to imagine a president of comparable style today—or an audience which would meekly accept such strictures '.

The office of President was at that time held for two years so that a presidential address appeared in the programme only every other year, usually during the conference at which the President handed over his duties to his successor. There was, therefore, no address in 1951, but A. G. Ogilvie, who had been involved as a geographer working in Scotland in the discussions about the nature of the Institute at an early stage in its establishment and, as noted on page 27, had played a very significant part in the development of the new association, delivered his address on ' the time element in geography ' (*Transactions*, 18, 1952, 1–15) at the Annual Conference in January 1952 in Aberystwyth. At the Annual General Meeting in the previous year a former President, J. N. L. Baker, had proposed that the President, after the expiry of Ogilvie's two-year term of office, should hold office for one year instead of two. In his view the time had come to have a new President each year with the enlarged membership of the IBG and with the considerable increase in the number of senior and experienced academic geographers with the ability to provide the Institute with presidential leadership. The first to take office for a single year under the revised constitution was R. O. Buchanan. No one knew more about the inner workings of the Institute than he did, because of his long association with the IBG, for most of the time as an office-bearer—as Assistant Secretary (1935–8), as Secretary (1939–50), as an Ordinary Member of Council (1951) and then as President in 1952. As indicated elsewhere, Buchanan's influence in the IBG was very real throughout the whole of that period, not least for the invariable soundness of his judgment and by his location in central London where so much of the Institute's activity was concentrated and where the majority of Council's decisions were taken (Wise, 1983)[2]. Very appropriately his address, given in the University of Keele in January 1954, was entitled ' The IBG: retrospect and prospect ' (*Transactions*, 20, 1954, 1–14). It remains still an invaluable, and largely first-hand, account of the early years of the Institute by one of the IBG's outstanding protagonists.

The next President was Wilfred Smith whose address on ' The location of industry ', read at the Durham conference of 1955, broke much new ground and indicated for the first time to some geographers the possibilities of a far more rigid, indeed quantitative (though Smith did not use that word), approach to their studies in economic geography. Smith, like Ogilvie, died suddenly not many months after his period in office as President, and his presidential address serves, rather as does Ogilvie's, as a statement of his thinking right at the end of a distinguished career, all of it spent in the service of the University of Liverpool, of which he himself was a graduate, one of the many who became university geographers during P. M. Roxby's long tenure of the John Rankin Chair of Geography in that university.

From 1954 onwards there has been a president each year and a presidential address has always been delivered apart from 1960, when W. G. East was on study leave in the USA and so could not read his lecture on ' the geography of land-locked states ' (*Transactions*, 28, 1960, 1–22), and 1982 when illness prevented R. S. Waters from preparing an address and being present at the conference. A full list of Presidential Addresses and details of their publication is given in Appendix F.

The decision to make the presidency an annual office was unanimous at the time though subsequently it was questioned and, on several occasions, alternatives were aired by Presidents and/or debated by Council. Some suggested that a mere twelve months as President gave the individual little opportunity of learning much of the workings of the IBG or of appreciating the nature of the appointment, and no chance whatsoever of influencing, let alone determining, Institute policy. Only occasionally had the new President had recent experience of membership of the Council as an officer or as an ordinary member. Buchanan's remarkable record in office prior to his election as President was unique though Smith had been an Ordinary Member of Council in 1952 and 1953 immediately before becoming President in 1954.

There was some truth in the suggestion that presidents were at a disadvantage under the new arrangements, and it is significant that this coincided with a period of consolidation in the IBG's history when the other offices were occupied by their holders for considerably longer than has been the case in more recent years. There were reasons for this—the offices were onerous and virtually no assistance was provided by the IBG and perhaps there was less 'kudos' about these appointments in the still relatively small and not particularly influential Institute than is true of the much larger and more highly organised IBG of today. Moreover it seemed that the membership at large appeared to assume that an officer would continue until such time as he actively sought relief for one reason or another. Whatever the reasons for this situation, the fact is that during the 1950s continuity was provided by the Officers as a body, and they were well qualified to give advice to a President who was relatively inexperienced in IBG ways.

An analysis of the presidential addresses given annually for many years is no part of the history of the IBG, though it would be an interesting, though perhaps not particularly revealing, study for a research worker. But a few very general remarks about the nature of the presidents may not be inappropriate.

The President of the Institute of British Geographers in its Jubilee year, 1983, the thirty-seventh to hold office, is J. W. House. He is the holder of one of the geography chairs that bears the name of a distinguished geographer or of a generous benefactor, the Halford Mackinder Professor of Geography in the University of Oxford. This chair commemorates one of the great pioneers of British geography without whose efforts the Institute, and many other geographical activities in Britain, could never have come into being and, as noted above (p. 4), a Vice-President of the RGS at the time of the foundation of the IBG.

The majority of his predecessors have been, like House, Professors of Geography in different universities in the United Kingdom. Most of them have been senior people though several of them have been quite young in years although experienced in geographical affairs and in their involvement in the concerns of both the IBG and of geographers generally. Indeed among the youngest ever elected to the presidency were three of the early Presidents (Baker, who was only 46 in 1939, Miller 47 and Wooldridge 49) while in more recent years only two have been under the age of 50 at the time of their election (Gregory 47 and Chisholm 48).

To date there have been two exceptions, both Fellows of Colleges in Oxford and Cambridge respectively and both of them very active Officers in the Institute before succeeding to the Presidency—J. N. L. Baker and B. H. Farmer. Baker, President from 1939 to 1947 and for long the *doyen* of geographers at Oxford (where he was Reader in Historical Geography and a very active Fellow and Bursar of Jesus College) played a very significant part in the affairs of the Institute from its inception and, as shown on pp. 27–8, it was through his faith in its future, along with that of other members such as Buchanan, that the Institute had a rebirth after the end of the Second World War. The other non-professorial President, Farmer, was like Baker, a Reader in Geography and a Fellow of St John's College, Cambridge. He had been Assistant Secretary (i.e. Treasurer) from 1952 to 1956, and Editor from 1961 to 1966. A Cambridge colleague of his, and a Fellow of Trinity College, W. V. Lewis, would have become President in 1962 but for his tragic death in a road accident in the USA at a time when he was Vice-President of the Institute[3]. As with Baker and Farmer, he had been active in the Institute's affairs for a long time, and served as Assistant Secretary, with responsibility for financial matters, between 1946 and 1948.

There has so far been only one election of a President from a Polytechnic— J. W. Birch, President in 1976. But Birch had had a long career in universities before he went as Director of the Bristol Polytechnic in 1975, notably as Professor of Geography in the University of Leeds, to which he came after some years as Professor of Geography in the University of Toronto, Canada.

Only one of the Presidents of the Institute has so far been a woman—Alice Garnett, President in 1966. She had been associated with the Institute from the beginning, and her monograph, *Insolation and relief*, was among the first to be published by the Institute in the 1930s. Her memories of the early days of the Institute have been published in the special Jubilee issue of *Transactions* (8, 1983, 27–35), and as Secretary of the GA for many years she watched with great understanding the simultaneous growth of the two complementary organisations, the GA and the IBG.

Under the present constitution it is known that the Senior Vice-President, K. M. Clayton, will succeed House at the Annual General Meeting in the University of Durham in January 1984 and that he in turn will be followed by G. M. Howe, the present Junior Vice-President, for 1985. As a result of a recent postal ballot conducted for the office of Junior Vice-President for 1984, it has been determined that the President in 1986 will be R. Lawton.

Note

1. R. U. Cooke was the first Conference Secretary appointed and he served from 1974 to 1976. He was followed by I. B. Thompson (1976–7), Joan M. Kenworthy (1977–9), J. G. Cruikshank (1979–81), J. H. Johnson (1981–3) and R. J. Rice (1983–)
2. Wise, M. J. (1983) 'Three Founder Members of the IBG: R. Ogilvie Buchanan, Sir Dudley Stamp, S. W. Wooldridge, a personal tribute' *Transactions* NS, 8, 41–54
3. Professor A. C. O'Dell was another Vice-President who died (on 17 June 1966) before succeeding to the Presidency of the IBG (p. 149)

VII

Study Groups

Study groups have come to play an increasingly important role in the organisation of the Institute during the last twenty years—indeed so much so that, as indicated above (p. 40), they now determine in large measure the form of the Annual Conference and, in the view of some members, they constitute something of a divisive element within the IBG as a whole. Their activities have undoubtedly reduced the number of plenary or general sessions that are now arranged and form the focus of attention of many members to such an extent that their participation in the conference in general becomes minimal. The view that the influence of study groups is largely deleterious may be an extreme one, but that it exists at all is indicative of the great success of many of the study groups and of the influence that they have upon the progress of the subject.

Initially, when membership was small and when, perhaps, most geographers were generalists rather than specialists, all conference sessions were open to all and attended by most. Indeed in those early days the focus of IBG activity had, of necessity, to be the business meeting, the Annual General Meeting, attached to which was the reading of such research and other papers as were offered by members. There were rarely sufficient to permit specific grouping of papers related to similar themes. Thus at the last conference before the Second World War—and packed into a limited period at a convenient point in the rather more ambitious programme of the Annual Conference of the GA—there were papers on the profile and valley forms of the River Trent (K. C. Boswell), the Czechoslovak crisis (Hilda Ormsby), population distribution in Luxembourg (K. C. Edwards), medieval towns in West-Central Europe (R. E. Dickinson), the historical geography of rural settlement in south-west Scotland (J. H. G. Lebon) and transport and industry in South Wales (S. H. Beaver)—a mixed bag by any standards; while there was a joint session with the GA and the Economic History Society which asked the question ' How should economic historians make use of British regional geography? '

A similar pattern was followed with the resumption of activities after the war with papers being grouped whenever possible. Thus at the annual conference at the RGS in 1948 my paper on ' Some geographical problems of land use in British West Africa ' followed R. J. Harrison Church's paper ' The case for colonial geography ' (*Transactions* 14, 1949, 27–42 and 15–25 respectively); but most of those attending the meeting were in the audience, just as those of us who were not particularly knowledgeable in, say, physical geography invariably, and indeed without question, attended lectures given by physical geography colleagues. Perhaps it helped us to be better and more rounded geographers. Certainly it prevented the geographers of those years from being as narrow as is now the case even with the youngest members of the Institute—indeed perhaps it is the student members of the Institute who are particularly specialised in their interests and their knowledge. It is symbolic of those times that the theme chosen by one of the great Presidents of the early years of the IBG, S. W. Wooldridge, an outstanding geomorphologist (as indicated by his contribution in the IBG monograph with D. L. Linton, *Surface, structure and scenery in south-east England* (1939)) and also the author of a noted essay on Anglo-Saxon settlement in *An Historical Geography of England before A.D. 1800* (edited H. C. Darby), chose as the theme of his presidential address in 1950 ' Reflections on regional geography in teaching and research ' (*Transactions* 16, 1950, 1–11).

Yet despite the catholicity of many members in their geographical interests and understanding in the early days of the development of the subject as a university discipline and of the growth of the IBG, the signs of the need for more specialised sessions and for better and more deeply informed discussion of themes appeared early on. Undoubtedly these tendencies were encouraged by the establishment of residential conferences that made possible the calling together of *ad hoc* groups of members with special interests. The increase in membership also led to the presentation of more papers at annual meetings and, if all offered were accepted, the programme had to include concurrent sessions.

In 1954 G. T. Warwick suggested that in arranging the next conference programme ' the attempt might be made to arrange sessions devoted to symposia '. It was decided that ' while this might not be practicable, the Secretary should encourage the submission of papers on related topics to permit readily of grouping '. At the Leeds conference of 1957 for the first time simultaneous sessions were arranged; and a year later what was described in the Council minutes as an ' experiment ' was repeated, ' though not necessarily for sound academic reasons but because it meant that three more papers would be accommodated than would otherwise have been possible '. It was also proposed to introduce a new feature at the conference—an evening of group discussions on a number of topics.

These developments paved the way for the creation within the Institute of research or study groups and in 1960 J. W. Birch raised the possibility of research committees with specific fields of enquiry being set up. He was invited to prepare a memorandum to which the Council later gave ready agreement to the idea in principle. The Annual General Meeting welcomed a proposal for the establishment of research groups within the Institute under the authority and surveillance of Council; and Council ' agreed to keep the conditions governing their operations as liberal and flexible as possible '. Birch was appointed convener of the first group constituted in order to undertake research on the mapping of farming types and related studies. It held a separate meeting during the Liverpool conference in 1962, and organised other activities elsewhere; yet, surprisingly, although this may have been the first group to be formed in this way as a result of the Council's new thinking on the matter, it does not appear to have received 'official' recognition by Council until 1968 when it was described as 'an active group'.

The geomorphologists had banded themselves together in the British Universities Geomorphological Research Group (BUGRG), an informal group brought together by D. L. Linton following an article by R. S. Waters (1958) on morphological mapping in *Geography* (43, 10–17). In 1961 this became the British Geographical Research Group, the word 'university' being dropped from the name for the sake of euphony. It was immediately known as the BGRG, a title that it has maintained ever since. But it was not specifically a group of university teachers and research workers; E. M. Bridges, for example, at that time working for the Agricultural Research Council, was from the outset one of its most active members.

Some members, mindful of the ineffectiveness of certain of the international commissions set up by the International Geographical Union over the years, were dubious of the likely outcome of this initiative within the IBG. But it soon became obvious that this new movement was the appropriate way of identifying the common interests of specialist geographers at a time when the rapidly grow- ing membership of the Institute and the size of the attendance at conferences made it increasingly difficult for newcomers to the profession to identify those with similar interests within the subject. Council's early decision to support groups by a subvention from central funds on a *per capita* basis undoubtedly helped them financially; but much more important have been the energy and enthusiasm of the officers of the individual groups, coupled with the ready response of the membership at large. Members, generally, felt, it seemed, that in these new developments the Institute was offering something that they wanted and needed.

In the years that followed Council positively encouraged these developments and actively helped any groups of members whose mutual interests suggested that there was value in their working more closely together on an inter-university basis under the auspices of the IBG; though there is perhaps a hint of suspicion in the Council's decision at the Swansea meeting in 1963 that there should be 'a member of the Council . . . present at each discussion group during the con- ference'. Among the groups formed or considered were those concerned with statistical techniques (later described as quantitative methods), population studies, urban geography, the geographical terminology of the agricultural land- scape, and the 1851 Census data on occupations. Several of these were approved by Council and did some very good work and made themselves responsible for the organisation of conferences and symposia and for the publication of papers. The BGRG, for example, arranged a successful field meeting in Devon for dis- cussions on denudation chronology, and the Population Studies Group, under its convener, A. J. Hunt, was responsible for the 1961 Census Atlas of Great Britain which was later published under the auspices of the IBG as publication no. 43 (*Population Maps of the British Isles, 1961*, 1968).

This increase in group activity gave rise to various problems in relation to the administration of the Institute, and Council decided in 1968 to establish a working party ' to examine the entire issue and consequences of study group organisation '. The working party met on two occasions, and at the second meeting representatives of active Study Groups were invited to participate in discussion on the relationships of Study Group administration with the central administration of the Institute.

Council accepted its report and agreed that £30 should be made available forthwith to each of the Urban Geography, Population Geography, Terminology of the Agrarian Landscape, and Statistical Techniques Study Groups while that on Types of Farming, as noted above, was deemed to be ' an active group '. Each group was to have a Chairman, a Secretary/Treasurer and a small committee that would be responsible to the Council of the IBG. Those who were specialists in cognate disciplines who wished to participate in the deliberations of the Study Groups and who were not members of the IBG could be regarded as ' official visitors ' but Council would maintain a watching brief on the non-IBG component in the membership of Study Groups. There were to be annual reports to the Council and each member of the Institute was given an option, for a trial period of two years from October 1968, to ' declare an interest ' in a particular group which was then to be allocated the sum of five shillings per ' interested member ' per annum out of general IBG funds. More financial help could be given by Council if it was requested, more especially for groups with a small membership. The central office would, as far as possible, provide limited secretarial and clerical help such as the addressing of envelopes and the duplication of typescripts. Council agreed that discussion of Study Group activities would become a regular item on Council agenda, and that representatives of the Groups would be invited to attend such meetings if matters of importance to any particular group were being discussed.

The decision to give members an option on the study group to which he or she wished to belong was warmly welcomed, and it had the effect of ensuring that at least a fair proportion of the total membership expressed preferences for participation in particular groups; and in 1973–4 it was decided that two (instead of one) study/research groups should be allowable free of charge and thereafter charged at the rate of £1 per group each member.

These financial arrangements were welcomed by all the groups then in existence apart from the BGRG which was presented with a dilemma. Hitherto that group had enjoyed, and valued, its independence, financial and otherwise. The IBG was offering a considerable financial inducement through subvention from central funds; and since most members of BGRG were geographers many were also members of the IBG. Thus to many in the group it seemed foolish to reject this offer of assistance, especially as there was always the possibility that a rival concern might be started within the IBG so that research effort would be diluted. Yet all members of the group were understandably anxious to retain its independence, and they saw that to become fully absorbed within the Institute would have posed some difficulties for the minority of non-geographer members who would not want to join the IBG (from the beginning there were always geologists and civil engineers who had shown interest in the Group's work, and the interdisciplinary nature of the group has undoubtedly been a source of much of its strength). There were both pros and cons to be considered. The Officers of the IBG were conscious of the marked contrast between the comparative affluence of the BGRG and the poverty of many of the other Study Groups, while strong views were held by some whose interest in environmental sciences made them recognise the special problem of those who were not trained as geographers but who nevertheless wanted to work closely with geographers in the study of geomorphological problems.

It was thought by some that the late D. L. Linton, a moving spirit in the BGRG from the beginning, would have wished to see the Group wholly incorporated within the Institute; but the reality of the difficulties of such a step were appreciated on both sides, and much turned on the co-operative approach adopted by the group's officers at the time in their full and frank discussions with the officers of the IBG. Eventually the Committee of the BGRG decided to recommend to its membership that the group should become affiliated to the IBG as a study group. Safeguards were insisted upon for the Group in so far as its membership and its publications were concerned. With assurances from the IBG regarding the autonomy of the Group and its policies, the decision to become a study group was taken in 1970.

This affiliation seems to have resulted in a very happy association and a particularly fruitful one in terms of publications. The *Transactions* have continued to carry geomorphological articles and there has been a plethora of material from the BGRG including 26 Technical Bulletins; 10 sponsored conference volumes; 4 IBG special publications (*Slopes, form and process*, 1971; *Polar geomorphology*, 1972; *Fluvial processes in instrumented watersheds*, 1974; and *Progress in geomorphology*, 1974); 4 *Geographical Magazine* series; 4 research monographs; a bibliography of geomorphology; a register of research; and two new series, ' Up-dating Geomorphology' and ' Classic Landforms', as well as the ' house magazine ', *Geophemera*. These very considerable achievements were appropriately celebrated by the Group in 1982, the twenty-first anniversary of its establishment, at a buffet supper at which several of the founder members were present. A paper read at that time by C. Embleton, ' Twenty-one years of British geomorphology ', has recently been published in *Progress in physical geography* 7, 1983, 361–83.

At the Annual General Meeting of 1969 the Secretary was able to report in the following terms:

' The Study Groups had completed a successful year. They were now beginning to play a most important part in the affairs of the Institute, arranging meetings not only at the Annual Conference but during the year and thus providing an element of continuity of contact among members of like interests. Projects of co-operative research organised by the Groups could well lead to publication of theme volumes by the Institute. The Groups also provided valuable links with other academic and governmental institutions, as was evidenced by the formation of a Geography Advisory Panel to the Registrar General as a result of submissions put forward by the Population and Urban Study Groups .'

Today it is, as noted above, the study groups that really determine the framework for the programme of the Annual Conference, and a very high proportion of the meetings taking place are those convened by study groups and attended, in large part, by the members of those groups. There is no doubt that the use of study groups as focal points for the organising of conferences is the most effective and systematic way of producing a programme that is both attractive and comprehensive. The danger is that the study groups will hog the programme, and an increasing characteristic of Annual Conferences today is the general lack of plenary sessions when the whole membership comes together. Indeed, in the overcrowded programmes of recent years it has sometimes been necessary for meetings of study groups or committees to be called concurrently with plenary sessions, though this is discouraged by the local conference secretary and is done only of necessity.

The sixteen Study Groups recognised and active today are listed in Appendix G, and reports from all of them have been published in recent issues of *Area* (for example 14, 1982, 78–92; 14, 1982, 322–32). Some groups have gone further. The Quantitative Methods Study Group, for example, has drawn attention to the role that it has played since its formation in 1964 (with incorporation in the IBG as a Study Group in 1968) as the vehicle for increasing international awareness of British work in quantitative and theoretical geography with contributions by several members of the group to *European progress in spatial analysis*, edited by R. J. Bennett, the Study Group's chairman (Bennett, 1981) and to *Quantitative geography: a British view*, edited by Bennett and N. Wrigley (Bennett and Wrigley, 1981).[1]

Safeguards have been introduced to prevent an excessive proliferation of study groups. Thus a request to Council for recognition must be supported in writing by a minimum of forty members. It would seem that Council has invariably granted all that has been asked, in that the minutes nowhere record rejection, though some suggestions have caused hesitation, even suspicion. In passing it may be recorded that one of those raising some doubts in the minds of a few members of the Institute is the latest to be established—the Women and Geography Study Group. But whatever hesitations may have been expressed in certain quarters, it is interesting to read the report in *Area* of the meetings of the Group held in Edinburgh in January 1983 (*Area*, 15, 82–3). The topic ' Recession, work and the family ' is said to have ' attracted a far larger audience than even the most optimistic members of the Committee had envisaged ' to what the report describes as ' a crowded, but not unpleasantly fuggy ' atmosphere after the chill of single study bedrooms '.

All the study groups are concerned with areas of study within geography apart from the Higher Education Learning Study Group established in 1981, significantly at a time when geography's place in the field of education called for special attention and when the Institute's role in participating positively and forcibly in the national debates on the effects of the cuts in higher education provision was, and still is, of particular importance. Very properly the IBG had voiced its anxieties, alongside those of similar bodies such as the GA, and Council initiated a session on ' The impending crisis in geography in higher education ' during the Southampton conference in 1982. The existence of the Study Group has undoubtedly helped to focus the strongly held views of members on the deleterious effect of Government policy on higher education in general—in the public sector as much as in universities—and on the state and prospects of geography in particular.

Study Groups are, therefore, by no means confined to the purely academic, and sometimes highly specialist, interests of members; and they have a key role to play in the future development of the subject and of the Institute just as they have played a dominant part in the growth and strengthening of the IBG during the past two decades. As M. Blacksell (1982) wrote in his report in *Area*: ' There is no question but that the vigorous growth of the Study Groups over the past decade . . . has added enormously to the scope and depth of research within the Institute. They in their turn appear to be responding very positively to the more active interest that the IBG Council is now taking in their affairs. While the Institute is certainly more than a collection of Study Groups, it would be immeasurably poorer without them ' (*Area*, 14, 67).

Note

1. Bennett, R. J. (ed.) (1981) *European progress in spatial analysis* (London)
   Bennett, R.J. and Wrigley, N. (eds) (1981) *Quantitative geography: a British view* (Henley-on-Thames).

VIII

International seminars

'The international seminar programme has become a major IBG activity', the retiring Honorary Secretary of the Institute, R. Lawton, wrote in 1976 (*Area*, 8, 121), and this statement remains equally true today. The beginnings were modest, however, and many difficulties were encountered in the early days. The international dimension of the IBG showed itself from the start with Henri Baulig, a leading French geographer, Professor of Geography at the Sorbonne, being the author of one of the Institute's first publications (*The changing sea-level*, 1936), and with the institution before the Second World War of discussions for the exchange of publications between the membership of the very young and small IBG and of the considerably larger and longer-established Association of American Geographers.

After the War geographical societies on the continent of Europe, as in Britain, needed a period for recovery and consolidation, and it is, therefore, hardly surprising that no formal links were established for some years. As a member of Council A. F. Martin had asked in 1953, on the basis of conversations that he had had in Paris with Jean Dresch, for the encouragement of the development of contacts with the members of the Association des Géographes Français, and the German publication *Erdkunde* approached the Institute in the same year with a view to advertising its publications in the *Transactions*. There was, however, no follow-up; indeed the *Transactions* has never had any advertisements in contrast to *Area* which carries a limited number, mainly from publishers of geographical books.

The venture in international relations represented by the first Anglo-Polish seminar of 1959 broke 'new and fertile ground for the Institute' in the words of the then Honorary Secretary, A. E. Smailes (*Transactions, 1959*, 26, vi). The significance of this seminar and of the further seminars with Poland that followed, and their influence in encouraging a whole series of bilateral meetings, were assessed by Lawton (1976) in a review in *Area* (' The international seminar programme of the Institute of British Geographers ', *Area*, 8, 121–6). He suggested that the extensive activities developed with an ever-widening range of contacts with different countries, mainly though not exclusively in Europe, were ' probably unique among British scientific societies, if not internationally '. Much has always depended upon the enthusiasm and perseverance of a relatively small group of geographers who had personal contacts with geography and geographers in the countries concerned in these seminars. But equally important has been the collaboration and support of individual British universities (who have acted as hosts) and of bodies such as the British Council, the RGS, and the Great Britain/East Europe Centre; not however, and perhaps a little surprisingly so, of The Royal Society, even though this is the body which, through the British National Committee for Geography, is the channel for links with the International Geographical Union which organises, every fourth year, the International Geographical Congress.

In other countries the links have been established with a variety of institutes or academies. Thus the first seminar of all, that with Polish geographers in 1959 on ' Problems of applied geography ', stemmed from an invitation extended to the IBG by S. M. Leszczycki, as the Director of the Institute of Geography in the Polish Academy of Sciences. It was held under the auspices of UNESCO with the support of the British Council. Twelve IBG members participated in the seminar at Nieborow under the leadership of K. C. Edwards. A return visit was held in Britain, at Keele, in 1962 with seventeen British geographers led by S. H. Beaver. The seminar was principally concerned with problems of industrial development and urbanisation. Illness prevented Beaver from participating in the third Anglo/Polish seminar on ' Techniques in geography ' held in Baranow Sandomierski in 1967, and R. H. Osborne led the party of thirteen British geographers. He also acted as host for the Fourth Anglo/Polish seminar on ' Geographical aspects of urban-rural interaction ' when twenty British and twelve Polish geographers spent a week in his own university at Nottingham in 1970.

The fifth and sixth seminars with Polish geographers were arranged in 1974 and 1977. The former met in Poland at Torun with the theme of ' Applied physical geography ' and with E. H. Brown as the leader of a British group of ten. The 1977 seminar, concerned with ' the relevance of studies of contemporary environments to those of Quaternary times ', was held in Sheffield during the INQUA meeting organised by R. S. Waters.

After 1970 the IBG's international seminar programme grew rapidly with the organisation of seminars with geographers in India (1972 and 1975), in the Federal Republic of Germany (1973 and 1975) as well as with Romania (1972), Hungary (1974 and 1977), Yugoslavia and Bulgaria. Efforts were also made to organise meetings with geographers in the USSR and Czechoslovakia. But no attempt is made to deal in detail with the numerous seminars and symposia organised by many individuals, in Britain and abroad, or to give references to the accounts published in *Area* and elsewhere, such as T. H. Elkins' review of the third British-German symposium held in Bonn and Bochum in May 1978 (*Area* 10, 283–4). They have all been, in the words of one participant, ' most successful—and enjoyable—in broadening academic interests in methodology and current developments in the countries involved and in promoting friendships '.

Appendix H gives as complete a list of international seminars held to date as is possible to glean from the far-from-complete records of the IBG. The decline in activity during the 1980s reflects, one trusts, no more than the effect of recession in Britain and elsewhere and is in no sense an indication that there is a diminution in the will to meet and to collaborate with geographers in other countries in Europe or in the Commonwealth. Noteworthy, too, is the development of closer ties with geographers in the USA, while an especially successful seminar in historical geography was held in Canada in September 1975 under the joint auspices of the Canadian Association of Geographers and of the IBG (represented in this instance by the Historical Geography Study Group). There have also been initiatives shown by other groups or by individuals, such as the British/North American seminar on outdoor recreation which was partly funded by the SSRC and in which J. T. Coppock played a leading role. The most recent (August 1983), and apparently very successful, meeting to discuss ' Strategies for regional industrial diversification and change ' was held in Canada at Calgary, organised jointly by members of the Canadian Association of Geographers and of the IBG's Industrial Activity and Area Development Study Group.

By 1970 the development of these international links led to a Council discussion on the desirability of appointing a seminar officer and the Secretary, W. Kirk, was asked to draw up ' Notes for guidance of organisers of foreign seminars '. They refer to the work of a Foreign Secretary, described as the liaison officer between Council and the appointed organisers of seminars, and they stress that it is Institute policy that each seminar should be self-financing (with special arrangements where there are currency difficulties, as with Poland). It was decided, however, that for the present ' no special seminar officer would be appointed. '

By 1974, with the further proliferation of these activities, an External Relations Committee was set up by Council when it decided to conduct a review of the development and methods of organisation of the Institute's international seminar programme. The new committee had delegated to it responsibility for the ' formulation of policy and taking of initiatives concerning the Institute's . . . relationships with geographical organisations at home and abroad. ' Procedures were codified, as far as was possible, and guide-lines laid down for organisers of seminars in a paper adopted by Council in May 1975. In practice, as Lawton pointed out in his paper, the organisation of international seminars was largely the concern of the conference organiser together with the Secretary and the Treasurer, representatives (invariably geographers) of the host institutions, and the participants in the seminar who often included the President or a Vice-President. Council has always been very closely involved in the negotiations preceding the issuing of an invitation and in the subsequent determination of the programme, and it has always received a report and any resolutions from the seminar upon its completion.

A further development in 1982 was the appointment of P. J. Taylor as Overseas Seminars Secretary ' to co-ordinate proposals and to ensure that the rules are applied and to take proposals for seminars to the Council '. A proposal for seminars should come from a member of the Institute (or group of members), who have already made initial contacts in the partner country; and it should identify a theme for the seminar, a venue, a timetable, and a leader of the delegation. The Institute's role is to encourage seminars, and participation in them by a wide selection of the membership. The rules are set out in full in *Area* 15 (1983), 65–6, and their publication indicates not only the IBG's continuing commitment to the holding of such seminars but also its determination to emphasise the international dimension of the Institute of British Geographers in its development of close contacts with European countries, the USA and different parts of the Commonwealth.

International relationships of the IBG are, then, seen at all stages as being in the mainstream of the Institute's activities. This is surely essential, particularly in a subject such as geography, though some involvement in Commonwealth affairs and in European collaboration (long before membership of the EEC made it fashionable or commendable) is not as widespread in British learned societies as might be expected; indeed some of them are almost notoriously parochial in their interests, and the example set by the IBG is commendable, especially as there are countless obstacles to be overcome in the development of international relations, in geography as in all other academic disciplines. Funding is a particular problem where there are no earmarked sources of money for this specific and highly desirable objective, and industry is not disposed to assist geographers in the manner in which it frequently supports physical scientists. The Great Britain/East Europe Centre has been especially helpful in the sponsoring of links with Romania and Hungary, and it would certainly assist in the same way, if effective contacts could be established, with Bulgaria and Czechoslovakia. Ironically the special problems always seem to relate to our immediate neighbours in Western Europe, though here the IBG has benefited through the participation by some of its members in ventures such as the Franco-British geographical conference on human geography in 1975, funded by the Social Science Research Council,[1] and the meeting arranged in association with the Centre National de Recherche Scientifique (CNRS) in Lyon in the following year. For a period a French geographer, Philippe Pinchemel, served on the SSRC's Human Geography Committee, while some of the IBG's Study Groups (Historical Geography and Quantitative Methods) have encouraged the development of research contacts in Europe through the organisation of meetings in Strasbourg (1978), Cambridge (1980) and Munich (1980).

Note

1. This Conference held at the Royal Geographical Society in London on 8–10 April 1975 included eleven participants from each country. The papers, edited by J. I. Clarke and P. Pinchemel, were published as *Human geography in France and Britain* (Social Science Research Council, London, 1976)

IX

Field meetings

Field-work was, from the beginning, a major interest of the members of the IBG and thus of the Institute itself. This is very understandable in that inter-war geography—and indeed much geography in the 1980s as well—saw field-work as an integral part of the subject and vital in the training of students of geography. In many pre-war university courses work in the field was compulsory, and it was moreover an activity in which most members of staff participated; and if the work done was not particularly analytical but more of what is sometimes described as a ' look see ' nature at least it was undertaken on foot or on bicycles so that observations made were at first-hand and at close quarters, and in some detail. Coaches were used sparingly, and there were of course, no minibuses; nor were there many field centres as there are in so many places today.

It is hardly surprising, therefore, to find the IBG Council, at only its third meeting, held in the Collegiate School, Leicester, on 8 September 1933 suggesting that arrangements be made for an excursion led by S. W. Wooldridge in the Chilterns on the Sunday of the meeting that was being planned for January 1934, and for many of the IBG's subsequent conferences the tradition of a field day, in which a majority of the members attending participated, was maintained.

An obvious link for geographers with a special concern for field-work and a willingness to attend field meetings was with the meetings of Section E of the British Association. The weekends (both Saturday and Sunday) were in any event devoted to excursions, and often the first afternoon was given over to a geographical tour of the area in which the meetings were being held. It was natural, therefore, for Council to explore the possibilities of IBG field meetings being arranged for three or four days immediately before or after the British Association week. D. L. Linton, at a Council meeting in January 1936 suggested that ' a two- or three-day meeting, for excursions only, immediately before the meetings of the British Association, was both feasible and desirable, and on the motion of Mr. Steers and Mr. Crowe it was agreed to arrange a three-day excursion meeting in the Lake District for September 6, 7 and 8, 1936. '

Appendix I lists those field meetings held under IBG auspices between 1936 and 1963 with such supplementary information as can be culled from the Minutes of Council during that period. Long before the costs of travel and accommodation became as heavy as they have during recent years, there were difficulties—partly finding suitable centres with the appropriate living and other facilities, and partly because of the commitments of individuals at the time of the year proposed (usually September). The Council Minutes often record a disappointing response to circular notices about projected field meetings, and this despite the fact that only a dozen members appear to have been regarded as a viable size for the type of programme proposed. Nevertheless several successful meetings were held during the 1930s, and the inclusion of field-work in the Institute's range of activities seemed to be well-established.

Thus the possibility of a field programme was included in the discussions in the Council at one of its very early post-war meetings (6 February 1946) when it considered its plans for a revival of IBG activities. S. W. Wooldridge suggested a summer field-meeting based on Oxford which he would lead, assisted if possible by Dr. K. S. Sandford for a study of the Thames terraces. Plans were in fact abandoned because of the difficulty of finding accommodation. Nevertheless despite accommodation problems everywhere, and the difficulty of making suitable transport arrangements, a renewed effort to restore field meetings was made in the following year, and a Scottish field excursion, based on a University of Glasgow hall of residence and led by A. Stevens, followed the first post-war meeting of the British Association held in Dundee. In the following year (1948) S. W. Wooldridge led a field party that was accommodated at the Field Studies Council's centre at Juniper Hall, near Leatherhead, at the end of the Brighton meeting of the British Association, and D. L. Linton organised a field meeting in Sheffield in 1949 following the British Association week in Newcastle upon Tyne. But in 1950, there was little support for a meeting in Nottingham that K. C. Edwards had undertaken to organise in the summer when the British Association met at Birmingham, and plans for field work at Aberdeen in 1951 after the Edinburgh British Association week similarly foundered. Council indeed wondered whether it might be appropriate to dissociate IBG field work from the British Association meeting to overcome some of the difficulties encountered by members. Nevertheless there was a partial tie-up still in both 1952 and 1953 when some very successful field excursions were held in Ireland. That of 1952 was centred in Galway and followed the British Association meeting in Belfast and was led by A. Farrington of the Royal Irish Academy and organised by a member of the Council, Dora K. Smee (whose earlier research had been based in Ireland).[1] The 1953 tour was based on Dublin and followed the Liverpool meeting of the British Association and was again led by Farrington and J. P. Haughton of Trinity College, Dublin. But nothing came of plans for a Forest of Dean field-week to follow the Oxford meeting of the British Association in 1954 and there is no discussion recorded in the Minutes of any proposals for field excursions in 1955 and 1956. However in 1957 when the British Association went to Dublin, and in the light of the experience of the Irish excursions earlier on, Council agreed in principle to take the opportunity to revive its summer field meetings by organising one in Ireland; and the Recorder of Section E. (M. J. Wise) was encouraged to collaborate with Haughton of Trinity and Farrington in the organisation of a joint IBG/British Association field meeting.

The field-work based on Cork and Kenmare attracted 34 participants of whom, the Minutes record, 'about half were members of the IBG', including the President (R. H. Kinvig). Thereafter, however, there is no record of any field meetings taking place, or even being discussed by Council, until 1962 when Council considered suggestions for meetings on denudation chronology and for the investigation of problems relating to research on the 1961 census. The physical geographers met in Devon under the leadership of C. Kidson but there is no record of the census research workers holding a formal gathering. Significantly the Devon meeting was largely organised by a study group (the British Geomorphological Research Group), not by the IBG as such, and this started a new trend in the Institute—the planning of such occasions not for general field-work but for the very specific objectives of particular study groups. The Council in January 1962 welcomed such field meetings and seminars ' as a means of widening the scope of Institute activities now that membership was increasing so much. '

It is appropriate also to record the change in attitude to the organisation of field-work and field excursions as part of the annual conferences. So long as plenary sessions were common, with the membership of the conference of manageable proportions, it was customary to invite the Head of the host Department of Geography, or one of his colleagues, to give an introductory lecture (often on the first evening) on the area in which the conference was being held. On occasions there would be supplementary lectures on related aspects of the area, some of which might be illustrated in the field later in the conference. Whole days might be devoted to field-work, in which nearly everyone took part, with no formal sessions until the evening when a lecture might be given or the Annual General Meeting held. These occasions were appreciated by the membership at large, especially when the conference was taking place in an area that was new to most of those attending—perhaps particularly in Northern Ireland, Scotland or Wales. The only occasion when all the field excursions arranged had to be cancelled because of weather conditions was at Swansea in 1963. In recent years, with the growth in size of the Institute, the increased activity of study groups, and the proliferation of concurrent sessions, the lectures on the local area and the associated field excursions have largely disappeared. This is regretted by some members but the majority recognises the difficulty of making the necessary provision for them in a conference programme that is already impossibly full. A limited number of excursions is normally arranged and very successfully executed but relatively few members take advantage of what is generally regarded as ' an optional extra '. Such changes in emphasis are no doubt inevitable in the new circumstances of the much expanded and greatly strengthened fifty-year-old IBG. Older members of the Institute may perhaps be permitted a certain nostalgia as they talk of the camaraderie of conferences in the past where many friendships were first made and developed in the field. But possibly the same sense of comradeship emerges from the feeling of identity that undoubtedly has been engendered during the 'seventies and 'eighties by the remarkable development of the IBG's Study Groups.

Note

1. The earlier editions of Stamp, L. D. and Beaver, S. H. (1933 and later editions), *The British Isles: a geographic and economic survey* were, in the words of the senior author, L. D. Stamp (preface, ix), ' greatly enriched by a special study of the ports and commerce of Ireland by Dr. D. K. Smee of the University of London, Bedford College ' (chap. xxxi, 658–86)

X

Relationships with other bodies and public participation

The IBG in its early stages thought little beyond the desirability of having good geographical research published and, as a young institution, it avoided participation in the discussion of public affairs. It looked upon the RGS as the old-established body that had traditionally been the spokesman for geography in the national scene while in educational matters the GA had a particular role to play. Moreover in these early days it lacked the numerical strength and the professional expertise that mark it so much in the 1980s and which make it a formidable body by any standards. The situation fifty years ago was very different especially as the RGS and the GA had viewed with some suspicion the birth of a new group of geographers (pp. 7–10). The infant and almost penniless IBG had to be circumspect in its relationship with these other bodies and indeed it appears to have been very reluctant to involve itself in anything that was not directly connected with the research needs that had brought the Institute into being. Thus when in 1936 the Institute was asked by a member to investigate the opportunities that existed for facilitating travel and exchange lectureships for members of university geography staffs, the request was turned down by Council on the grounds that this 'raised issues that lay outside the fields of competence of the Institute'.

Nevertheless, very early in its history (indeed at two Council meetings during 1934) it made representations, largely at the instigation of Eva G. R. Taylor, to the Director of the British Museum about the housing of the map collections of the Museum. A letter was sent asking that a larger and better equipped map room should be provided together with a comprehensive catalogue. Funds were not immediately available (the mid-1930s were not so unlike the 1980s, at least in this respect) but in due course the map collection was housed, staffed and organised very effectively, and the wishes of geographers, expressed through the Institute, may have had a significant influence.

Less successful was the Institute's plea to the Ministry of Agriculture and Fisheries to reprieve the Fifth (Relief) edition of the Ordnance Survey one-inch map which it had been decided to discontinue in 1937. Yet certain concessions of special value to geographers were obtained, and several of the President's suggestions, put forward on behalf of the membership of the IBG as a whole to the Departmental Committee set up by the Ministry in 1936 to consider the revision of Ordnance Survey maps and to review the scales and styles in which they should be issued to the public, appear to have been accepted (Buchanan, 1954, *Transactions* 20, 12–13).

Shortly before the outbreak of war L. D. Stamp was invited to gather together a group of geographers to bring together, in cartographic form, some of the background information required for the Barlow Commission on the distribution of the industrial population. But because Stamp was going to be in India for several months, and because of the urgency of the request, E. G. R. Taylor was asked to take over the work from him. The group of geographers who collaborated with her—mostly young and nearly all members of the IBG—helped in the production of the maps that were published in the *Geographical Journal* (Taylor, 1938). Partly arising from this work, and a few months later, in association with the British Association for the Advancement of Science (Section E), Taylor developed her plans for a national atlas on which she reported in a discussion at the RGS on 4 December 1939 (Taylor, 1940)[1]. These were significant forward steps for geography at the time but what is important to note is that it was the RGS that brought them together—and presumably provided a limited amount of finance—not the new and still infant professional body, the IBG.

Over the years the IBG has made remarkable advances from the modest stand that it was able to take on some issues affecting geographers in pre-war years, as noted above (p. 15), and the somewhat tentative requests that it had to make for appropriate representation on bodies such as the National Committee for Geography (first raised at a Council meeting in 1946), to its present position of considerable strength. It is unnecessary to trace the progress of its efforts in detail or to note the frustrations as well as the successes as it has moved to a situation where it enjoys at least equal status with its related societies such as the RGS and the GA in England and Wales or the RSGS in Scotland. But a few examples will help to show what was gradually accomplished.

The change in formal recognition is illustrated particularly well by the National Committee for Geography, a body that is organised administratively by The Royal Society. It now has adequate representation from all the main societies, and is no longer dominated, as it once was, by the RGS and representatives of what were regarded as appropriate Government departments. Moreover the chairmanship is now filled by a geographer whereas for many years it was always regarded by The Royal Society as essential that its chairman should be a Fellow of The Royal Society even if—as was invariably the case—he was not a geographer. Thus the leader of a British delegation to any Congress of the International Geographical Union, was always a distinguished scientist, perhaps with some knowledge of geography, but he was not a geographer. This often acted against British interests in geography at the international level, and those of us who were members of the British delegation to the Stockholm Congress of 1960 will long remember the leader's puzzled looks at the references to the IBG during a meeting which culminated in his asking, ' What does IBG stand for? '

The Council has on many occasions stressed the need for the closest collaboration with other geographical societies, in Britain and overseas, and has gone to great lengths to prevent unhealthy or wasteful competition between them. In the early years the linking of IBG activities with the Annual Conference of the GA in London and with the annual meeting of the British Association ensured that geographers generally were aware of what different groups were doing for their subject. The RGS provided much appreciated hospitality, especially in the difficult years immediately following the Second World War, by asking the Institute to hold its meetings there in 1948 and with its standing invitation to the Council to make use of the RGS's Council Room for its meetings whenever convenient, and above all by the lead that it gave in planning the joint lectures given each January in the lecture hall in Kensington Gore under the combined auspices of the RGS, the GA and the IBG. These lectures, attended by several hundred geographers from all three societies, became a significant event in the geographical calendar. Particularly noteworthy from the IBG's point of view were the large gatherings of geographers for these lectures during the Institute's two residential conferences in London. H. C. Darby addressed a very large meeting in January 1953 ' On the relations of geography and history ', a much read lecture that appeared in *Transactions* 1953, 19, 1–11, and in January 1969 J. R. James, formerly Chief Planner in the University of Housing and Local Government but at the time Professor of Planning in the University of Sheffield, spoke on ' Regions and regional planning ' to what the report in *Area* on the IBG conference described as ' a record attendance at the joint meeting ' (1, 1969, 19). It had been feared that the development of residential conferences normally held out of London (Chapter VI) would break the link with the GA Conference, and clearly it did affect the attendance at the GA of university geographers, including those living in London. Efforts were made by both the IBG and the GA to avoid a clash, and even an overlap, of dates, and suggestions were made that London-based geographers might provide hospitality for visitors to encourage those from universities elsewhere to continue their support for the GA and its associated publishers' exhibition. But over the years the tradition has almost been forgotten, especially as the university membership of the GA constitutes only a relatively small part of the Association's total of more than 8,000 subscribers; while since 1976, the GA has, for a variety of reasons, moved its conference dates from early January to the Easter vacation and in recent years the IBG has persuaded many publishers who regularly display their products at the Association's conference to join in what has proved to be a very successful and much patronised exhibition of books mounted at the conference centre of the year. Changed circumstances at different times call for new initiatives and new measures, and far from there being any deleterious competition between the Association and the Institute, the distinctive roles of the two organisations are seen very clearly. The one is concerned with geography in education and the other is dedicated to geographical research and problems of teaching in higher education, and this suggests a wide range of collaborative ventures to which the Councils of both bodies are giving increasing attention (see pp. 132–3). In these discussions the RGS is also involved, and the climate of opinion for co-operation and mutual support between the various geographical societies must be more favourable today than it has ever been.

This recognition of the place that the Institute rightly holds in academic and national life has been built up gradually, as the development of its history has demonstrated in earlier chapters. Progress was particularly marked from about 1960 onwards. At that time the Institute was given representation on the Map Users' Committee of the Ordnance Survey, and in close collaboration with a number of other bodies, including the fairly newly-established Society of University Cartographers, pressure was brought to bear on those responsible for granting recognition to, among others, cartographers in university departments of geography. A joint committee, on which the Institute was represented, was established for the ONC (Ordinary National Certificate) and HNC (Higher National Certificate) awards in Cartography, Planning and Surveying.

This period in the mid-1960s was very significant for higher education, especially though not exclusively through the publication of the Robbins Committee report in 1963, and the Institute was affected by the new developments in a variety of ways. Apart from the creation of several new universities, some of the Colleges of Advanced Technology were given university status (Salford and Strathclyde are examples) while from 1965 onwards polytechnics were designated so that eventually there were 30 such institutions in England and Wales besides the 'Central Institutions' in Scotland. The new thrust in higher education meant that a whole new cohort of young people was exposed to the possibilities of continuing their studies while those already established in posts in universities and comparable institutions had the great satisfaction of watching this long-overdue expansion in educational provision take place. So far as geography was concerned, the impact was patchy. Some of the new universities, indeed a majority of them, introduced no geography, at least under that name—a somewhat surprising fact in view of the very large numbers of young people who were taking the subject at Advanced Level. Some of the polytechnics developed geography, and most of them recruited a number of geographers, though not always with that description and in some cases they were scattered throughout the institution in a variety of departments. But their employment was indicative of the range of interests recognised in the subject, which at the time was going through the so-called 'revolution' associated with the development of quantitative methods and a more theoretical approach to the subject. To this transformation of geography the Institute collectively and many of its members individually made major contributions, though it is not appropriate in the history of the IBG to attempt to assess these. From the point of view of the Institute the significance of the growth in the number of academics employed in institutions of higher education is that many of the newly appointed members of staff joined the IBG mainly because of their shared interest in the discussion and publication of research although in a few instances it may have been true, as has been said, that it was in the hope of eventually securing an appointment in a university rather than in a polytechnic. Certainly the non-university element in the IBG increased very considerably during the years when membership was still growing quite rapidly, although it was some time before polytechnic geographers were represented directly on the Council by one of their own members, just as at an earlier period it had taken some years for there to be Council representation of geographers in Government departments and other establishments outside the university sector[2]. Indeed not until 1971 was there such representation when J. C. Goodridge of Plymouth Polytechnic was elected to serve for three years. More recently T. C. Kennea served as a member of Council, and between 1978 and 1981 was Treasurer, though at the time of his election he was on the staff of the Social Science Research Council and Secretary of the Council's Human Geography and Planning sub-committee, prior to his appointment to Kingston Polytechnic.

In the post-Robbins period the Institute responded positively in a variety of ways. Thus in 1964 it took advantage of the opportunity to make a submission to the UGC Committee on Libraries (the Parry Committee), in which it underlined the special problems of material for undergraduate teaching and post-graduate study in geography, including the need for bringing together books and periodicals alongside maps, atlases and air photography. Four years later there was a submission to the National Libraries Committee, in which the Institute described itself as ' a learned society and professional association with a member-ship of over one thousand professional geographers employed in University, Technical College, Training College and Government service ', and similar points were made about the special needs of geographers with a plea for the development, within the framework of the National Libraries, of ' a Map Centre with truly comprehensive cover in materials depicting the surface of the earth '. This, it was suggested, would be ' a great contribution to international study of human utilisation of the earth's surface. ' It was also thought that, particularly for the collection of the data from the censuses of overseas countries, there was a strong case for ' the establishment of a national repository with facilities for consultation on inter-library loan ' for ' mapping and study of world population by geographers, demographers and other social scientists '.

In 1970 the Institute sent to the Minister of Housing and Local Government some preliminary observations on the Redcliffe-Maud Report on Local Govern-ment (*Report of the Royal Commission on Local Government of England, 1966–69*, Cmnd. 1970). The document was intended not to influence political decisions but ' to indicate the professional interest of geographers in the implementation of the general principles recommended by the Commission. ' The Secretary in his covering letter made the point that ' geographers in different parts of the country, with expert local knowledge on, for example, the nature of city regions and boundaries of urban fields, could contribute to the successful reform of the areal arrangements for local governments '. The document was ' a token of the Institute's concern in a matter that has . . . a strong geographical base to it. ' The submission has an interesting reference to the work of C. B. Fawcett, the Insti-tute's first President between 1933 and 1937, in the following sentences: ' It is worthy of note that the establishment of a provincial framework was fore-shadowed by the work of C. B. Fawcett in *The Provinces of England* as early as 1919. What Fawcett saw as true and applicable in the early part of the century applies even more strongly in the present day '.

During the year 1965 both NERC and SSRC were constituted by the Govern-ment, and geographers generally had to establish their relationships with these bodies. The IBG had a role to play on their behalf in a variety of ways. Physical geography had its battles with the NERC, and climatologists in particular had a hard task in convincing the Council's first chairman, Sir Graham Sutton, formerly Director-General of the Meteorological Office, of the scientific validity of their research. But NERC was a very significant step forward in the organisation of scientific research especially in the disciplines such as geography concerned with aspects of the natural environment, and geographers increasingly took advantage of the new opportunities provided for them.

The Heyworth Committee's Report on Social Studies was published in 1965 (HMSO, Cmnd. 2660) after two years of study which included consideration of written evidence submitted by the RGS and by the IBG. The Report was reviewed by L. P. Kirwan (1965), then the Director and Secretary of the RGS (*Geographical Journal, 131*, 373–5), and he stressed that the Committee had concerned itself particularly with what it regarded as 'the traditional social sciences' while recognising that there were a number of 'related disciplines', including law, architecture, history and geography. Geography, in the view of the Committee, was a discipline 'where difficulty in developing the social side has been encountered, and the growth in the students has not so far been accompanied by a corresponding expansion of research in social geography'. The Report also noted the great importance of training in mathematics and statistics and suggested that in future 'no student in the field of social studies should graduate without a good working knowledge of statistics'. Kirwan used the publication of the Report as an opportunity for drawing attention to the division of interest in geography between the NERC and the SSRC, and also the anomalous relationship of geography to the two National Academies in Britain—The Royal Society and The British Academy.

In fact the Committee did not see geography, even human geography, as forming an integral part of the proposed SSRC, and geographers were very concerned about this, especially as there appeared to be some danger of 'falling between two stools' through not being the prime responsibility of either the NERC or the SSRC. Action was, therefore, taken by a group of individuals without waiting for the weighty, and perhaps somewhat prolonged, consideration by the Councils of the various geographical societies; and although there was some criticism of their intervention at the time, especially at the annual conference of the Heads of Departments of Geography later in the year, it was generally recognised that the appropriate steps had been taken—and taken quickly—to establish the position of human geography in relation to the SSRC at an early stage in its existence. A small group of human geographers arranged to meet Michael Young, the then Chairman of SSRC, consisting of Emrys Jones, J. W. House, R. Lawton and myself. We approached him as individuals and in no sense was it an initiative of the IBG but all of us were active members of the Institute, and we felt able to assure the Chairman of the SSRC that we believed that we were speaking on behalf of professional geographers generally. Somewhat to our surprise—and delight—he immediately responded to our plea and suggested that within a matter of weeks we should prepare a report on the activities of geographers in relation to SSRC interests. House undertook to do this but almost immediately realised that pressure of other commitments would prevent him from keeping to the very tight time-scale laid down by the SSRC, and M. D. I. Chisholm, who had not been in the unofficial delegation and was at that time in the University of Bristol, was asked to undertake the work. In a remarkably short time, and during a summer vacation, much information was collected from many different departments of geography, and the nature of the report convinced the Chairman of the validity of the case that had been presented to him. It was agreed that a human geography sub-committee should be established, which SSRC then combined with a new committee for planning in the interests of administrative efficiency and the first chairman of the Human Geography and Planning Committee was Chisholm, the co-ordinator of the review of the activities of British human geographers.

Not all developments within the SSRC in subsequent years have been to the liking of geographers. They have, for example, been much exercised by the disappearance of subject committees, such as Human Geography and Planning, and their replacement by committees covering a wider range of disciplines. Moreover as a group they are unlikely to welcome the still more recent change in the SSRC's title whereby in future it will be known as the Economic and Social Research Council (ESRC), though it remains to be seen whether this is merely a change of name or will be reflected in any significant change of policy or emphasis. Geographers sit as members of the Council as they have done during most of the Council's history, while (of much greater significance from the point of view of geographers generally) the Environment and Planning Committee is chaired by a professor of geography, B. T. Robson, whose IBG credentials are impeccable, for there are few who are better informed about its affairs, he having been a member of Council continuously from 1970 to 1976 while Editor of *Area* for three years and then of *Transactions* for a further three years. Indeed to date he is the only member who has served the Institute and its members in both editorial capacities, and, as shown on pages 64–5 has played an important part in the moulding of the Institute's publications policy to meet the needs and the challenges of recent years. The legitimate concern of geographers with the work of the Council and with the changes in policy and approach resulting from recession and financial constraints, coupled with the Government's attitude towards research in the social sciences, has been reflected in the pages of *Area*,[3] and this medium for the communication of new developments and new ideas, the exchange of views, and the expression of the anxieties of geographers, is in itself a justification for the regular quarterly publication of a journal such as *Area*. It is indicative too, of the increasingly professional involvement by geographers in public affairs, largely through the organisation provided by the Institute.

Despite the recognition of the subject professionally and in academic circles, both nationally and internationally, to an extent that could never have been anticipated at the time of the IBG's foundation, geography and geographers continue to face many problems, some of them exacerbated by the cut-back in the resources available for higher education in recent years and the intensified competition between disciplines for the limited resources available. In the interests of both self-preservation and the continued progress of the subject, and in the light of the ever-escalating costs of running a learned society, the various geographical societies, notably the GA, the IBG and the RGS, have been looking again—with perhaps more urgency than previously—at the possibilities of closer co-operation with a view to avoiding duplication of effort and cutting overheads and strengthening the support for the subject.

The shared interests and the common concerns of the IBG and the GA are particularly helped at the present time by the fact that the Institute's Secretary, R. J. Johnston, and one of the Association's Joint Secretaries, B. E. Coates, are colleagues in the Department of Geography in the University of Sheffield. The headquarters of the GA have, since 1948, been based on a house in Fulwood Road which is rented from the University which has, in many ways, shown itself to be very well disposed towards the aims and objectives of the Association. Moreover many members of the IBG are either members of the GA nationally or of local branches of the Association, a great number of which are in cities and towns with universities or polytechnics (even if the proportion is much less than it was in the early days of the IBG); and the similarities, as well as the differences, between the two organisations are well known and widely recognised.

Co-operation with the RGS is encouraged, as has been suggested in various places in this history, by the siting of the IBG's central office for the past eighteen years in the RGS's building in Kensington Gore. An important forward step was taken in 1981, while M. J. Wise was President of the RGS, when some IBG Council members met with members of the Council of the RGS to discuss greater collaboration. On 14 May 1981 the IBG Council gave its support to the concept of a ' Council of British Geographers ' to consist of the officers of both societies, meeting perhaps twice a year, with the agenda and organisation determined alternately by each society. It was agreed that the officers of the IBG for this purpose should be the President, the Secretary, the Treasurer and one of the Editors. The situation was summarised by the Secretary in a note in *Area* (13, 1981, 256) in which he explained that the possibilities of a closer association between the two bodies centred upon administrative organisation and methods; increased use of RGS facilities by members of the IBG; joint meetings and publications; and the possibilities of a federal structure involving both societies. The first three were based on economic needs and attempts to increase and improve the services to IBG members, but the last touched on broader points. It was emphasised that the special need for a ' Council of British Geographers ' arose from the necessity for a group to hold a watching brief on matters of national concern to geographers that were no longer considered by the British National Committee for Geography, which now concentrated solely on international matters. Members were invited to communicate their views on whether they wanted to maintain the present character and methods of operation of the Institute; whether they wished the Council actively to pursue the possibilities of co-operation under the first three items; and whether they wanted the Council to work out in detail the nature of a federal structure that could be considered at an Annual General Meeting[4].

While there has not been much reaction on the part of members generally to these proposals—probably indicating in a tacit manner confidence in the steps taken by the Council (which with 16 members from 12 different institutions may be regarded as reasonably representative of the IBG as a whole)—the prospects for close working together in matters of mutual concern would appear to be good. From the IBG's point of view the satisfying aspect of the situation in which the Institute now finds itself is that it has in recent years been fully consulted on most appropriate occasions; and it is generally regarded as the representative body for academic geographers, not only those engaged in higher education but also those geographers professionally employed in the Civil Service and by local government as well as in industry, commerce and related activities. Equally gratifying is the recognition of the qualities or the expertise—or both—of geographers by the positions of importance and influence that many individual members of the IBG occupy in academic life and in the public service.

Notes

1. See note 1 on p. 38
2. J. R. James, while Deputy Chief Planner of the Ministry of Housing and Local Government, was a member of Council in 1960 and 1961. Helen M. Wallis, Superintendent of the Map Library of the British Museum, was a member of Council between 1970 and 1972, and E. C. Willatts, for many years Principal Planner, Department of the Environment, served on the Council between 1971 and 1973
3. For example, Robson, B. T. (1981) ' SSRC and postgraduate training ' *Area* 13, 131–6. Robson, B. T. (1982) ' SSRC: David as Goliath ', *Area* 14, 61–4. Smith, D. M. (1981) ' SSRC rules: a critique of the new postgraduate training scheme ', *Area* 13, 263–7. Smith, D. M. (1983) ' SSRC and the demise of human geography ', *Area* 14, 42–4
   See also: Gregson, N. and Mohan, J. (1983) ' Training in human geography ', *Area* 15, 45–7. Cosgrove, D., Duncan, S. S., Massey, D. and Sayer, A. (1983) ' Changing geography and writing a Ph.D. ', *Area* 15, 47–51
4. While this volume has been in press detailed negotiations have been continuing between the IBG and the RGS about ways and means of increasing collaboration

XI

Administrative organisation

Council, with its Officers, has always been central to the administrative organisation of the IBG. Indeed this is still so, despite the great growth in membership and the proliferation of its activities during recent years and even with the establishment of an office in London and the appointment of an administrative assistant. Council still dominates the working of the Institute, and there has been resistance to the appointment of a general purposes committee or a small executive, although the Officers have always acted in this capacity, however unofficially, between meetings of the Council which normally take place four times a year, two of these being held during the Annual Conference, at the beginning and at the end.

In the early days of the IBG the work of the Institute was indeed the work of its Officers. But for their labours and enthusiasm, the new organisation could never have succeeded, and it is significant how often the same names appear and re-appear in the lists of those participating in IBG activities, whether as officers and members of Council, as lecturers at conferences or as authors. Much communication was by word of mouth and by the occasional letter (see p. 20). Operating very much on a shoe-string, as the economic circumstances of the time made inevitable, it was the deliberate policy of the Council that its meetings should coincide, whenever possible, with meetings of other geographical bodies such as the GA Annual Conference in London or the summer meeting of Section E (Geography) of the British Association for the Advancement of Science.

For a long time the IBG paid no expenses to members of its Council. It had little or no money in any event, and rail fares and overnight accommodation were relatively cheap; but university salaries were also very low. The minute book suggests that there was never any discussion about the payment of expenses in pre-war years. After the war, the work-load for Officers increased considerably. University departments helped a great deal with typing although Officers were generally responsible for their own filing, and even their typing was given a very low priority and always with an element of ' grace and favour '. The Annual Conferences, once they had become residential, produced a considerable burden on a particular department though this was only for a limited time and occurred only very occasionally. In those days university secretaries were normally attached to departmental heads rather than to departments (perhaps some mem-

bers feel that this is still the case!), and when IBG Officers were not departmental heads, difficulties arose. Council agreed in November 1948 that some
secretarial assistance might be paid for by the Institute in the light of Buchanan's
observations that ' too much of the Secretary's time was occupied with the handwriting of letters . . . so that the record preserved in the files of the Institute was
not as complete as could be desired '. He suggested ' some paid part-time steno-
graphers' assistance would improve the position considerably, and that £25 per
annum should be adequate for the purpose. ' After discussion Council increased
the sum suggested to £30 per annum.

In 1952 it was agreed that members of the Council should be free to claim
expenses up to a total (for *all* members of the Council) of £20 per annum (the
implication of the resolution was perhaps that it was hoped that they would not
in fact submit claims!). Three years later, as recounted on p. 34, Council
decided that it would pay the travelling expenses of Council members together
with 25 shillings a night for subsistence; and in 1956 it was agreed that £150
should be made available, for all the Officers, for such secretarial and other
expenses as they incurred in the carrying out of their work for the Institute.

It is worth recording how the Institute operated, with minimal resources,
during the 1950s, partly because it helps to explain why there was no major
expansion of the Institute's activities at this time, in contrast to what happened
a decade later. While I was Editor my wife, assisted by our children (two of
them subsequently became geography graduates despite this early experience of
geography's professional organisation!) regularly put together bundles of *Transactions* for postage to departments in different universities or for transport to an
Annual Conference where individuals with cars (there were not all those many
in that category in those days!) would be invited to take them away for distribution in their own departments. My wife, herself a geographer, helped me with
the details of the preparation of diagrams for submission to the printer and read
all the proofs, and in particular spent time trying to introduce consistency into
the references quoted by authors. It never occurred to me to take a taxi from
the School of Geography on the east side of Oxford to the Alden Press on the
west side beyond the railway station; nearly always, as Bill Furneaux has
reminded me recently, I arrived on a bicycle with a basket full of maps of all
shapes and sizes.

As editor it was important that I retained copies of all letters and reports sent
to referees and authors, but much of the other correspondence was, as at an
earlier period in the Institute's existence, handwritten. This was particularly true
of the short (and not always particularly legible) notes from B. H. Farmer written
when he was Assistant Secretary and responsible for the Institute's finances. His
method of work was to allow IBG letters to accumulate for a few days before
dealing with them in a short space of time, usually at a weekend, as his filing
tray began to overflow. Subscriptions were recorded in a large ledger, still available in the IBG Office for inspection, in which the entries are in the handwriting
of the succession of individuals who looked after the Institute's financial affairs
at different periods.

Farmer had temporarily vacated the Assistant Secretary's post when he left

Cambridge for Ceylon (now Sri Lanka) for a period of study leave in 1955 and then resigned his office because of his heavy involvement with the work of the Ceylon Land Commission even after his return to England. Thus H. C. K. Henderson, who had stood in for him initially on a temporary basis, became Assistant Secretary in 1956, an office which he retained until 1967 when he was elected President (although in 1962 the office was redesignated as Treasurer without, however, any change of function). With the increasing size of the membership of the IBG, and with a growth in the sales of publications (both volumes and offprints), Henderson needed assistance in his IBG work. For the accounts he was given help by Jean Eames, at that time senior technician in the Department of Geography at Birkbeck College. For a long period she assisted on a voluntary basis, while she gained the experience that made her the obvious, indeed the only, choice when the Institute at long last decided to appoint an Administrative Assistant, and eventually she took over the Central Office when it was first established in the house of the RGS at 1 Kensington Gore in 1965. The Secretary's correspondence also increased in volume throughout this period but was for the most part handled in the office of University College London until Smailes moved to the Chair of Geography and Headship of the Department at Queen Mary College where he was able to use the secretarial and other resources available to a professor. But the lack of such assistance became a very real problem when Smailes was succeeded in the secretary's office by G. North, a lecturer in the Department of Geography at Manchester, although North's resignation from the post after a relatively short period in office (under two years) was precipitated more by the demands made upon him within his University through his appointment to the Wardenship of one of its halls of residence, St. Anselm.

The informality and the essentially *ad hoc* nature of the Institute's administrative arrangements clearly could not continue indefinitely, especially with the outburst of new activity resulting from the upsurge of membership, and indeed the ferment in the university world as a whole, in the 1960s. The long-serving officers of the 1950s (four of us served for a total of 28 years in that period) gave way to newer officers who had a higher expectancy of secretarial and other assistance and who began talking seriously about the possibility of the establishment of a Central Office for the IBG. This was in line with discussions that were going on at the time for a centralised British Institute of Geographical Research which, it was assumed, would be based upon London, and probably sited at the RGS.

Prior to her appointment as the Institute's first Administrative Assistant, Jean Eames worked, as she herself has described it, ' spare time ' for the IBG for nine years (from 1956 to 1965), for not only did she assist ' Doc '—H. C. K. Henderson—in the systematic keeping of the Institute's accounts but she also organised the handling of the stocks of publications, and the sale of offprints as well as of complete volumes, and ensured that there were adequate supplies of publications for sale at Annual Conferences (this at a time when there were many new members who were anxious to purchase back numbers to extend the runs of IBG publications that they possessed). She, and others who became IBG members later but were at this time Birkbeck 'mature students' (to use the modern terminology), together with some members of the staff recall how there were bulk deliveries of *Transactions* by the Alden Press and packages for delivery to university departments were then made up, nearly always late at night, or at least not much before 9 p.m., after the completion of the evening's lectures. Much use was made of the University of London's inter-college postal service for the distribution of *Transactions* within the University (though it is reported that certain members resented the fact that their volumes were not sent to their home addresses, notwithstanding the obvious saving of cost). It is not inappropriate to record in this history of the IBG the Institute's indebtedness both to the wives and families of officers at all periods in its development and to the students of Birkbeck College who, probably without realising it, were making a substantial contribution to the progress of the Institute at a time when finances were still limited and when voluntary work of this nature was absolutely essential for its survival.

The Department of Geography at Birkbeck College—then housed not as it is now in Gresse Street but in the main building of the College in Malet Street, almost immediately adjacent to Senate House—became very much the administrative centre of the Institute. Not only was one of the IBG's three executive officers a senior member of the staff (Henderson) but he was given much help by his colleagues, notably Eila M. J. Campbell and J. Davis, as well as by Jean Eames and many of his part-time students; and Birkbeck, with University College London, were centres for the University of London's Inter-Collegiate Lectures, most of which were arranged for Fridays. Thus the Secretary at the time, A. E. Smailes, regularly met his colleagues and could readily discuss, no doubt among other things, IBG business, while I found it a very convenient department to visit from Euston Station, the destination of the many journeys that I made between Liverpool and London. Moreover in the Bloomsbury area on a Friday there would be other University of London geographers, most of them active IBG members, and including some past presidents (R. O. Buchanan and S. W. Wooldridge) and several who later became presidents (including J. H. Bird, E. H. Brown, H. C. Darby, W. R. Mead and M. J. Wise) or occupied other offices in the IBG (such as C. E. Everard). Much Institute business was, therefore, discussed, if not decided, within the confines or in the vicinity of Birkbeck College at this period. Ideally the administrative headquarters for the IBG would have been established in Birkbeck but no accommodation of the right size at the right rental was available. Indeed the College was described as 'bursting at the seams' and was seeking for itself accommodation outside the original college and in due course moved the Department of Geography with other departments to the building in Gresse Street where it still is.

Council discussions about the desirability of having a headquarters in London with full-time staff employed by the Institute appear to have been wide-ranging and, at times, confused. It was recognised that the person appointed, whatever his or her title, would be of limited direct assistance to either the Secretary or the Editor but would ease the burdens of the Treasurer very considerably through the work done centrally for the collection of subscriptions, the sale of publications and the other financial transactions in which the Institute was involved. A new appointment would, furthermore, be of general assistance to the Institute as a whole. The Administrative Assistant would be responsible for minute-taking, the production of notices for Council and for the distribution of material for annual conferences apart from what was produced in the host Department of Geography. It was clearly going to be a very significant forward step in the interests of the administrative efficiency of the IBG, but the search for suitable accommodation proved much more difficult than had been anticipated, especially as initially it appeared that no room was going to be available in the RGS's house. Central London (particularly Bloomsbury), Potters Bar, Finchley and other suburban locations were considered—even Watford, with its good suburban and main line rail links—all without success, when the RGS (through the good offices of L. D. Stamp, President of the IBG in 1956 and President of the RGS between 1963 and 1966) found that it could after all offer house room. The RGS was able to offer favourable terms to the Institute and if some may have had hesitations about this closer link-up with the Society, these proved to be more apparent than real. The IBG office is separate and distinct, like the offices of *The Geographical Magazine* above it and other offices elsewhere in the building such as those used by the Institute of Navigation; but it benefits from the proximity to other services which have always been made readily available to the Institute if appropriate arrangements are made beforehand. Because of its geographical position, the office has not become a Mecca for geographers in central London, as Birkbeck College seemed to be on occasions, but it is a point of reference and a postal address. Its location does mean that it is visited by relatively few geographers, and usually only by those with specific business to transact or by occasional visitors who have gone to Kensington to attend meetings of the RGS or to use its library. (In fact the overlap of membership between the IBG and the RGS is surprisingly small). There would have been many advantages had it been possible for the IBG's headquarters to be located elsewhere, perhaps particularly in the university quarter where there are large departments of geography including those at University College London, Birkbeck, the London School of Economics and the School of Oriental and African Studies, but the establishment of a central office can be regarded as a considerable success and the Institute had a ' presence ' in West London immediately adjacent to the RGS. The office is manned as fully as possible and a limited amount of part-time help is given, particularly at times of peak activity, notably for the distribution of publications. But inevitably there are times when no-one is in the office so that the telephone cannot be answered, especially when Council meetings are arranged out of London or at the time of the Annual Conference when the administrative assistant is absent from her post for two or three days at a time.

The establishment of an office in London provided room for the storing of the considerable stocks of the *Transactions*, which the Alden Press found increasingly difficult to keep in its Oxford warehouse, and of the Institute's other publications. But it also made possible the development of a sales centre, from which publications could be sold directly to the public on a much greater scale than had ever been possible before. Indeed the necessity for the appointment of an

Administrative Assistant was closely tied up with Council's decision in the early 1960s to go all out for library, as well as other, subscriptions. Jean Eames recalls the build-up over the years of this side of the Institute's activities—an aspect of which most members were wholly oblivious though indirectly they all benefited through the new financial stability that it gave the Institute which enabled it to advance, among other things, its publications programme. The volume of work involved in the circularisation of libraries throughout the Commonwealth, indeed throughout the world, was tremendous, and it was essential that orders for publications were dealt with in a systematic manner, without the disturbance and interruption of the often conflicting demands on time of anyone employed in a university department of geography. The sales of offprints were also considerable, and it was necessary for someone to give undivided attention to this part of the IBG's activity. In these ways the Institute received considerably greater funding, without an excessive increase in the size of the subscription, during the 1960s, and some indication of the importance of this side of the IBG's business is provided by the number of library subscriptions existing in 1983. The latest accounts show how large the sales of publications have become and what an invaluable source of finance for the Institute they have become. There is no harm, however, in reminding ourselves of the significance of the devotion of our founder members who started this sales policy, albeit in a very modest way, back in the 1930s.

The great majority of Council meetings have always been held in London, in many respects the most accessible of all places in the United Kingdom even for those who live at a great distance from it. But the Council has quite often met in the university where the next conference is to be held so that members of the Council can see the setting of the conference and be informed on the spot by members of the local committee responsible. There is no doubt that the organisation of conferences has been helped considerably by their involvement in this way, while it has also enabled members of Council to see at first-hand other universities and other departments of geography. Normally two Council meetings are held during the Annual Conference, one immediately before the conference begins and the other at the end of the conference when matters raised at the Institute's Annual General Meeting can be considered.

Jean Eames served for eight years in the office and resigned only because of her mother's poor health which made it difficult for Jean to be involved every day in travel from Potters Bar to Kensington. At the Annual General Meeting held in the University of East Anglia on 6 January 1974 honorary membership of the Institute was conferred on her, at the same time as the honour was given to four former Presidents of the IBG—K. C. Edwards, B. H. Farmer, A. E. Smailes and R. W. Steel—and to a founder member who had throughout her career been a stalwart and generous supporter of the Institute, Dora K. Smee. To mark Jean's retirement from the post of Administrative Assistant she was presented with a cheque, and the President (J. T. Coppock)—in the words of the minutes—' expressed the great gratitude of all members to Miss Eames's devoted and loyal service to the Institute '.

It is unlikely that anyone will ever give the same kind of service, over so long a period, to the Institute as Jean Eames has; but the IBG has been fortunate in those who have followed her in the office—Lucinda Barnard (who became Mrs. Gough-Cooper) (1973–75), Wendy Greenwood (1975–82) and the present administrative assistant, Alison Hind, who joined the Institute in the autumn of 1982. The central office has become even more indispensable with the growth in the Institute's financial resources and in generally increased activity, particularly that generated by the study groups. Thus the work load has grown steadily especially as headquarters takes responsibility for much of the administrative work associated with the study groups. The success of the Treasurers in expanding the sales programme of the Institute has also meant more business in the office at headquarters, and part-time help has been obtained to assist in the sending out of material. One of these helpers, Esmé Diamond, has in fact served regularly in the office for more than ten years.

At the Keele meeting in January 1964, nearly twenty years ago, S. H. Beaver when President raised the question of the desirability of the Institute having a permanent address and also the possibility of the appointment of not only ' a paid assistant secretary, even if for the present only part-time '. He saw another solution too—a permanent Director of the Institute—' perhaps a retired Professor if one could be found conveniently located to the site of the headquarters. Such a Director might combine (as Mr. Kirwan does at the RGS) the functions of Secretary and Editor, and thus make more effective use of the paid assistant and relieve another over-burdened academic from what is in fact probably a more arduous job than that of the Secretary '.

He went on to say: ' I believe that our destiny is aimed rather higher than the mere publication of excerpts from PhD theses, and I hope that we shall not hesitate to do whatever is proper for improving the status and public image of the Institute as *the* highest geographical authority in the country '.

In fact at that time the outcome of these discussions about a headquarters and the necessary associated staffing—and in the light of the financial circumstances of the mid-1960s, was the establishment of the office in the house of the RGS and Jean Eames's move from Birkbeck to Kensington. But talk about further developments, in the Council and among the membership at large, continued and in a sense intensified as the Institute grew in size and complexity. Moreover a very different attitude towards growth was showing itself, the change in approach being exemplified by these two extracts from minute books in 1963 and 1971. At the Council meeting of 4 January 1963 18 new members (including a future editor of *Area*, now the member responsible for the Institute's Special Publications) and 30 student members were elected, and the resignation of three members noted. But the subsequent minute records that ' Concern was expressed over the rapid growth of Institute membership and Council took note of the added need to scrutinise application '. Eight years later, however, the Treasurer reports at the Annual General Meeting of 6 January 1971 with obvious satisfaction that ' a record 300 new members joined during the year '. Such an expansion, and not only growth in the membership figures, clearly called for the strengthening and perhaps the streamlining of the Institute's central administrative organisation; and very careful thought was given to the various alternative possibilities.

In the light of what happened subsequently it is unnecessary to record all the details of the discussions relating to a new headquarters appointment. A relevant factor in the decision not to proceed with the appointment of an Executive Officer, at the salary that such a post would make essential, may well have been the slowing down of membership (Fig. 1). As Lawton reported at the Annual General Meeting of 5 January 1976 as he was about to relinquish the Secretaryship after four years in office, IBG membership had grown from 815 in 1964 (the year of the Robbins Report) to 1800 in 1973. The 1819 members of September 1975 suggested, he thought, that ' we may well have reached something of a plateau '. Indeed he believed that the Institute would ' have to work hard to retain the present level of membership. ' His report continued:

' I had hoped, at the beginning of my term of office, to see the Institute grow to a position where it could afford at least a part-time executive secretary before I ended my term of office. This is clearly now not possible in the immediate future. But I hope it is an objective that will not be lost sight of. The membership of what claims to be a leading professional, as well as an academic, organisation (albeit in a limited sense) has a right to expect access to a growing and very varied range of information involving professional geographers. It is difficult, under present circumstances, for honorary officers and Council to be aware of and able to act quickly on all matters over which the IBG ought to express a view. The Institute has become more involved in what can generally be described as " External Affairs ". It has received great help from Study Groups and individual members who serve on *ad hoc* committees, organise seminars or represent the Institute on various national bodies, but we need to continue to expand this aspect of our work in a positive way. It may be that the question—which we have discussed from time to time—of enlarging the size of Council (and, perhaps, slightly increasing the term of office of its members) would help to cope with the increasing amount of business and give greater opportunity for members to serve. But I am sure that extra administrative staff will be needed in the not-too-distant future, whatever the structure of Council. '

Lawton's successor, D. Thomas, shared his views and in October 1976 Council agreed that two Honorary Research Liaison Officers should be appointed to undertake two main tasks: (i) to explore the need for research liaison with outside bodies, both public and private, to assess whether such liaison needed further development and by what means, and to report back to Council at the earliest opportunity; (ii) as far as possible, given the circumstances, to meet the need revealed by establishing external links with outside bodies.

Members of Council felt ' that one task, which might come at a later stage, would be the listing, perhaps through study groups, of the research interests of members '. It was also felt that the appointment of two such officers might pave the way for a salaried executive officer. It was agreed that J. T. Coppock and R. U. Cooke should be invited to serve as the two officers and should be co-opted to the Institute's External Relations Committee; and at a later meeting the two Officers expressed their view that ' the appointment of an Executive Officer was the only practicable and desirable solution to the problems of external liaison '.

During 1977 members were asked to ' examine closely the desirability of some sort of Executive Director ', having been told that no decision had been taken as to the salary level of such an appointment though ' all discussion so far had

assumed that any officer would be an academic geographer.' At the Annual
General Meeting, held in the University of Hull on 5 January 1978, members
had before them a report that had been previously circulated, prepared by the
Secretary on behalf of Council and recommending the appointment of a salaried
Executive Officer. But, as recorded elsewhere (pp. 49–50), the Council's recommendation was rejected, albeit by a narrow majority; and so, after fifty years
the Institute still finds itself without the senior executive officer that many regard
as essential and for which the necessary resources had been accumulated, at least
to finance the post for a reasonably long experimental period. The problem of
proper staffing is not one that will go away by neglecting it—though it must
be admitted that some of the protagonists for the appointment are less convinced
now that they see a period during which membership of the IBG seems unlikely
to increase substantially with the inevitable consequences on the scale of the
financial resources available for this, and any other, development. But even with
no growth the intricacy and complexity of the work of the Institute remain, and
place a very heavy burden upon all the Officers, and perhaps particularly on
the Secretary, who to date has always been a senior member of a university
department of geography. Undoubtedly the appointment of an Executive Officer
would be very costly, and it might be difficult to find the right man or woman.
Apart from the statement of the Council, already noted, that it had been assumed
that the person appointed would be an academic geographer, there is little doubt
that the general opinion of Institute members would be that the officer should
not be an academic manqué, someone who had 'failed to make the grade' in
ordinary university or polytechnic life, nor should it be a retired member of, say,
the Civil Service or the Armed Forces. Equally it might not be appropriate to
appoint someone who had taken 'early retirement', for whatever reason, from
an institution of higher education, and there would clearly be difficulties if the
person concerned was seconded for a period of years from a tenured university
or polytechnic appointment. Thus the Institute faces a real problem in the coming years if it is to continue to grow in the way in which it has over its first
fifty years. As this history of the IBG shows, it has survived through many years
of considerable difficulty and latterly has gone from strength to strength, with
ever-increasing influence and esteem, and it has established itself as a very successful 'publishing co-operative' yet with a payroll of minimal proportions. The
further development of its central administration is a problem and a prospect
that will need to be 'teased' over very carefully by officers in the future, and
it will certainly demand the close attention of members if they are to be given
the service that they can reasonably expect of a professional organisation such
as the IBG.

PART THREE

THE IBG: TODAY AND TOMORROW

XII

Today

In the previous chapters an attempt has been made to trace the beginnings of the IBG and its subsequent development and to emphasise the special activities that make the Institute of 1983 what it is, for its members, in academic life, and in the world of learned societies. In the early days the question-mark hanging over the infant society was whether it would survive at all. The post-war years saw its revival, and during the 1950s there was considerable consolidation. This period prepared the Institute for the large expansion that was possible during the 1960s with the extension of higher education as recommended by the Robbins Committee and characterised by the establishment of several new universities and the designation of the polytechnics, and the comparative affluence of those years. During the early 1970s there was a further period of consolidation when membership continued to grow for several years while there was a remarkable diversification of the Institute's activities. But by the end of the 1970s, the IBG found itself living in a rather different economic climate where higher education, in both the university and the public sectors, was under considerable threat, and where many of the high hopes of the immediate post-Robbins period were frustrated.

The nature of the demands made upon the officers of the Institute at these different periods in its development is reflected in the differences in the length of service given to the IBG by its officers. As indicated in earlier chapters, a comparatively small number of members played a dominant role in the Institute's affairs in the early stages, notably R. O. Buchanan, who was an officer for twenty of the Institute's first twenty-one years. During the years of consolidation after the Second World War there was for some time relatively little change among the officers, many of whom served for considerably more years than is now generally the case. More recently, however, with the increasing size of the membership and the remarkable proliferation in the work done by the IBG, the officers have changed fairly frequently (the normal span of office is three years), though there are a number of exceptions (see Appendices D and E). These years have, as has been shown, been marked by a growing professionalism with the Institute having an increasing, and very welcome, impact upon public life.

It is not easy to assess the position of the IBG today as a learned society and as a professional body. It has, very rightly, shown itself to be much concerned with the effect of the cuts in higher education, and while it may not have been as vocal as some other subject groups have been, nevertheless it has on a number of occasions acted as a pressure group where the impact on the welfare of geography, and of those who profess it, has been seen to be deleterious. Indeed it is likely that in the coming years the IBG may have to be still more active in the defence of the discipline if the subject is to fulfil its role in higher education in all its varied forms. Happily the discipline for which the IBG has a special responsibility, geography, can now be regarded—and not only by its protagonists—as a strong subject, one that has developed in ways and to an extent that can never have been foreseen by the pioneer geographers who founded the Institute half a century ago. There have, of course, been strains and stresses within the subject, and much of what has happened in recent years has been, in the view of some, more revolutionary than evolutionary. But since these trends are very familiar to most, if not all, readers, it has not been my intention to dwell on these aspects of the development of the subject, vital though they undoubtedly are to the history of geography as a discipline though only indirectly to the history of the IBG as an institution.

Among the activities of the IBG discussed, special emphasis has been placed upon the publication of research undertaken by its members since this has always been fundamental to the existence of the Institute. In earlier years field-work carried out by members was significant, while in the post-war years the building-up of international contacts was important. The active encouragement of study groups has been almost entirely the work of the last two decades, and it is during the same period that what has been described as public participation by the IBG has developed very markedly. For such an expanding and inevitably complex organisation as the IBG has become, there must be a good administrative base, and the evolution and extension of this over many years has, therefore, been treated in some detail.

There are, of course, many other facets of the IBG today. No-one now—not even the Secretary or the Administrative Assistant—can claim to have within his or her grasp the whole workings of a very lively group of more than 1,800 professional geographers. In this history it has not been possible to devote separate sections to all of the Institute's activities but this is not because they are unimportant or have but little impact on the well-being of the institution as a whole.

Little has been said, for example, except incidentally, about the concern rightly shown by the Institute for those who, for one reason and another, are disadvantaged. This includes, at the present time, those young people in Britain who find themselves denied a place in a university, a polytechnic or an institute of higher education as a direct result of the cuts imposed upon higher education, although it must, of course, be admitted that IBG members have a vested interest in this situation in terms of the security of their own posts. More altruistic is the practical sympathy shown by members for universities overseas that have been affected by political circumstances beyond their control. In 1971, for example, there was an appeal for books for the rebuilding of the library of the University of Nigeria at Nsukka following its destruction by fire at the end of the Nigerian Civil War. In 1972, the President, B. H. Farmer, encouraged members to help the universities in Bangladesh at Dacca and Rajshahi to replace books and maps destroyed in the Indo-Pakistan war. Former members of the staff of the Department of Geography at Makerere University, Uganda, have been active in encouraging members to help with the restocking of the Makerere Library, and there has been a generous response. In several cases, the Institute itself has presented stocks of its publications for libraries that lacked them and had not the foreign exchange to acquire them by purchase.

The Institute also caters for the needs of members in other ways besides the publication of research and the organisation of the activities described in earlier chapters. Thus over the years there have been arrangements with the Association of American Geographers for the purchase on behalf of individual members of its publications—a scheme that, somewhat surprisingly perhaps, has been taken up by only a small minority of the membership. A Book Club was started in 1978 under the enthusiastic guidance of first R. J. Johnston and more recently R. Bradshaw. Despite some ups and downs, it still continues to provide a useful service to members faced with ever-increasing book prices.

Finance has always been an important concern of the IBG and it can never afford to be ignored. But no attempt has been made to analyse the policies of successive Treasurers, since what is of greatest importance at any particular time are the current reserves and their availability, or otherwise, for the special purposes of the Institute. What matters for the IBG today is not, therefore, the financial vicissitudes from year to year over the past half-century but the state of the balance sheet presented by the Treasurer at the last Annual General Meeting.

There has been massive development in the financial resources of the IBG since the early days when the membership and their payment of subscriptions was recorded in a single ledger, along with the limited number of other financial transactions in which the IBG was involved. As resources have increased, chiefly through the enlarged membership and the larger subscription rates (and latterly with very considerably increased publication sales), the work of the Treasurer has become highly complex. From the beginning, all those responsible for finance have naturally sought to make as much money as possible for the Institute and its work. Where Treasurers have differed is in their attitude towards the accumulation of these resources. All have had the wholly laudable objective of husbanding them as carefully as possible; but some have wanted to accumulate reserves as a cushion against unforeseen eventualities while others have looked upon such moneys as an encouragement, and an opportunity, to embark on new ventures. No-one has wanted the IBG to be merely a viable concern in financial terms; all have agreed that it should be able to play a very active role in national life as well as an established and growing learned society. Today it is vital that the Institute should have comfortable reserves, in order to ensure that the society would be in a position to take worthwhile initiatives to further the discipline and to represent its interests in the world at large. A long line of excellent Treasurers has served the IBG very well indeed, and their work has generally been welcomed by those members present at AGMs who have seen their officers as taking a right and proper care of the IBG's finances.

Inflation has affected the Institute very seriously during recent years, as have the increased costs of, among other things, Council's travel and subsistence expenses, the upkeep of a central office in London, and larger bills for printing and publishing. The accumulated resources and reserves of today make the sums of earlier years seem minute and even derisory. But, as Treasurer after Treasurer has emphasised, there is a need for constant vigilance and caution, and a healthy balance must never be taken as a licence for profligate expenditure. On the face of it, the resources of the IBG appear now to be quite considerable—certainly they are what many similar learned societies would be very glad to possess. But it is important that members' subscriptions should be maintained at a level that anticipates the effects of inflation and of increased costs, and not be determined only after the draught of increased expenditure has been reflected in the latest balance sheet. Indeed it is argued by some that the annual subscription is still too low, for it appears that it is considerably less than that of several comparable societies. Perhaps the membership at large agrees with this view since there were no dissenting voices raised—not at least at the AGM in Edinburgh in January 1983—when a substantial increase in the subscription was agreed. It is true (as the graph of membership in Figure 1 makes clear) that there has been a decline in membership in recent years, and that the decline is particularly marked when there is a subscription increase; but, as indicated elsewhere (p. 18), this is largely reflected in the decline in student membership, which is hardly surprising at a time when there are fewer research grants available even for very good students. There is, moreover, an understandable hesitation by student members to seek full membership until they are firmly established in their professional careers, and a distressingly large number of younger and excellently trained geographers now find themselves unemployed after the completion of their postgraduate studies.

Lack of employment and limited career opportunities, and the inadequacy of support for good research, are only some of the many problems faced by geography and higher education today. Nevertheless the IBG would seem to be in good heart, financially and in other ways. This was very apparent at the 50th anniversary annual conference in Edinburgh where, as the Editor of *Area* put it (Blacksell, 1983, 68–9): ' The Golden Jubilee Year of the IBG was celebrated in fine style ' with more than 600 participants (that is, about one-third of the total membership). ' Reflecting on past achievements was, however, only one aspect of the deliberations; there was also ample evidence of the growing esteem in which the Institute and its work are held in the wide range of outside guests and speakers who felt it worthwhile attending the Conference. In his speech at the Annual Dinner the Secretary of State for Scotland, George Younger, was obviously impressed by the many different ways in which geographical research was being used in the work of his Department, indicating that not only is our work relevant, but increasingly is being seen to be relevant. It is clear that over the past decade the discipline has moved from a position on the fringes of public and private policy-making to one where its active engagement is taken for granted. As alway some of the most impressive features of the Institute's involvement was the broad scope of the fields of geographical enquiry covered by the various sessions '.

These comments are as appropriate an assessment as one could have of the state of the IBG in its jubilee year, for the Edinburgh conference underlined in so many ways the great progress that geography as a discipline and the Institute as an organisation have made in the past fifty years.

XIII

Tomorrow

It would hardly be appropriate for a history of the IBG during its first fifty years to attempt any survey of the possible developments of the next fifty years; but having looked closely at the generally very healthy state of the organisation today it is perhaps legitimate to give some consideration to what the Institute is likely to be, and to do, in the immediate future.

The IBG today is, it would seem, basically what its members make it and what they would want it to be. Council may not always appear to be particularly responsive to the wishes of members, and the comments and complaints, along with many constructive suggestions, are expressed quite frequently, and sometimes forcibly, in the pages of *Area,* and at Annual General Meetings, or informally during Annual Conferences, meetings of study groups, and in departmental common rooms throughout Britain. But if there is dissatisfaction among members about what Council is doing, it rarely sustains itself sufficiently and in a positive enough manner to bring about significant changes in the organisation of the activities of the IBG. Council appears to represent reasonably well at least a great many of the different strands that constitute the 1800-member strong Institute of 1983. What a recent Officer has said about conferences could equally be applied to the activities of the Institute generally: ' there seems a general contentment with the mixture provided by the Council in its annual conferences, and there is always sufficient choice of alternative programmes that no member could possibly feel that there was nothing in it for him or for her '. Thus, by and large, Council seems to serve the membership by the varied provision of activities and services for which it is responsible, and the members generally are supportive and appreciative in their reaction to what they find available to them.

To consider at all adequately the various options that face the IBG today, and to rehearse the arguments for and against the different policies that might be followed during the 1980s, is impossible for someone who is not a member of the Council and so has not been present at any of the discussions of recent years. But correspondence with several of the current officers suggests that, while there may be considerable differences in viewpoint, there is remarkably little divergence in their appreciation of the long-term objectives of the Institute. While some see the IBG as still being essentially a ' publishing co-operative ', others feel that, now that the Special Publications series is the concern of a commercial publisher, it would be logical to have all the Institute's publications issued in this way. That view sees the IBG as more of a club designed for those involved in tertiary level teaching and research in geography, with the Annual Conference as one of its principal activities. Members holding these views would, one suspects, want to see a shift away from the authority of Council towards a loose federation of study groups that might become increasingly ' autonomous-minded '. Yet inevitably the cooperative, the club, the federation, or however we care to define or to see the IBG of the 1980s, must have a central office, not only to organise its considerable publications programme and promotions exercise but also to co-ordinate, and even to monitor, the Institute's multifarious activities, much of it generated by individuals scattered through many different institutions of higher education in all parts of Britain. In such a situation Council's role must be that of a watchdog as it seeks to provide an efficient and effective central organisation and an economical and valuable range of publications and as it encourages both the teaching and research activities of geographers. Council must also endeavour to preserve the Institute as a forum for discussion among academic geographers, through its publications and conferences and in other ways, and it must keep alert to the need for a modification of its activities and structures in response to changing demands.

Of paramount importance is the creation and maintenance of a sound financial base for the Institute, and there is some confidence that a healthy financial picture will emerge during the next two or three years, partly as a result of the 1983 increase in the subscription rate and partly as a consequence of a recently agreed and completely new policy for the pricing of the Institute's journals. Reserves should not, however, be allowed to become too great since this can so easily encourage complacency on the part of members—as indeed may have happened at times during the 1970s.

Resources are there to be used, but individual members of the Council, and different groups of members within the Institute, undoubtedly have widely divergent views as to what should be the Institute's priorities in the spending of its moneys. Nevertheless there are many areas where there must be general agreement about the desirability of certain expenditures. Many members would undoubtedly subscribe to more generous funding for genuine research initiatives proposed by the more active study groups; but how much, and how such developments should be organised, are big issues. There are other possibilities, too, that demand careful attention. Should some of the larger and more active groups be encouraged, even forced, to look elsewhere for financial support—from the research councils or from trusts or industry? Should there be more flexibility within the study group structure with more inter-group activity, along with the short-term formation (and subsequent dissolution) of problem-oriented working parties? Such projects, it is thought, might well attract outside funding to supplement the at present quite inadequate grants (only £2500 per annum) available from the Council for study group activity.

Overseas seminars are clearly vital to the well-being of the IBG and should be very actively encouraged for this is one of the ways in which the existence of the IBG will become better-known than it is at present, not only among our

European neighbours but throughout the Commonwealth and other parts of the English-speaking world, notably in the USA. Ought there to be much closer collaboration with geographical groups in other countries, and with an organisation such as the Commonwealth Geographical Bureau which has arranged a number of seminars in different parts of the Commonwealth since its foundation in 1968, with much support from British geographers? Much greater financial support from the Council would be essential for such an enlarged international programme, without in any way reducing the requests made, as at present, to other funding bodies. Council has already agreed in principle that finance should be made available for any seminar that is likely to produce substantial results, but at present such support is largely nominal since little more than £200-300 would be forthcoming for any one venture.

Most important of all at the present time, it is essential that considerable resources should be used for the promotion of the interests of geography. A more active policy to improve the discipline's public image and its representation to government, industry and commerce, and in national and international affairs generally, would be warmly welcomed throughout the profession. The steps taken for closer collaboration with the RGS and the GA are undoubtedly in the right direction; but until recently they have not taken any of the societies very far along the road of real co-operation (with significant gains in the more effective use of their financial and other resources). As one officer has expressed it: ' modest sums spent on this aspect could prove an invaluable long-term investment, although it all hinges on getting the right strategy aimed at the right people '—and, maybe, at the right time. Indeed that time may have been reached during the latter part of 1983 with the announcement of a formal link between the IBG and its sister societies, the RGS and the GA, so that they may jointly do more to promote the subject as part of the essential basis of education in the UK.

The emergence of the IBG of the early ' eighties,—with its many study groups, its two successful international journals, a viable Special Publications series, an attractive and well-supported Annual Conference, and a considerable number of worthwhile smaller meetings—occurred during a period of relative academic prosperity. These years were marked in the Institute by considerable financial progress thanks to good management by the Council and the skill and devotion of successive Treasurers. In the less easy times into which the IBG has moved Council must maintain vitality among geographers by continuing to provide a stimulating environment and by investing particularly in those ventures that will be of benefit to a high proportion of the membership. Good financial management must continue—and there must be careful stimulation of study group activity and a wise and balanced publications policy; and its officers must be encouraged to take, whenever possible, a firm and positive line in representing the views of the Institute and its members as a collectivity of professionals who are entitled to express themselves forcibly and with expert knowledge on many matters that affect our national life. This indeed was what the Council did, on behalf of the IBG as a whole, in its very forthright submission to Lord Rothschild when he prepared his report on the future of the Social Science Research Council for the Secretary of State for Education and Science.

Above all, the IBG must present a united front, not in a methodological sense but in organisational and administrative terms. Much has changed in the subject, whose scope, content and even objectives are so different from what they were, yet geography retains some very firm foundations and a central and solid core that assures it a future that will be both stable and progressive. However divergent our interests and views may be upon academic matters within geography (and they are considerable), geographers must have a sense of belonging, a feeling of community, as indicated by their membership of the active, virile and outgoing organisation that most members perceive the Institute to be. In the words of the President, J. W. House, 'The IBG will flourish in the measure that geography as a subject prospers and retains a measure of coherence as it evolves. The IBG's positive role is to see that both processes are furthered, and, in so doing, to protect, defend and advance the interests of all geographers professionally involved in tertiary and higher education'.

One of the great geographers of the twentieth century, Sir Dudley Stamp—President of the Institute in 1956, and also President of the RGS (1963–66), the GA (1950), Section E of the British Association (1949), and the International Geographical Union (1952–56)—wrote, not long before his sudden death in 1966, 'I venture to suggest few professional associations have been as successful as the Institute of British Geographers' (*Transactions,* 40, 1966, 20). The Institute has, in the words of one of its present officers, 'been fortunate to have officers, councillors, conference organisers, editors and employees who have served it well, and the work of the study groups indicates the great depth of talent on which it will draw in the future. It has a firm base, a solid record of achievement, and the potential to serve academic geographers well for the next fifty years.' The Institute, in common with all British universities and polytechnics and higher education generally, is passing through difficult times, but we geographers are, as M. J. Wise has pointed out (*Transactions* NS 8, 1983, 54), 'fortunate in the inheritance that we derived from the generation which included the founders of our Institute. The best tribute that we can pay to their work is through an intensification of our own efforts for the Institute, and, through the Institute, for the study and application of geography'.

PLATES

Charles Bungay Fawcett
1933–7

Robert Neal Rudmose Brown
1937–9

John Norman Leonard Baker
1939–46
Secretary/Treasurer 1936–8

Arthur Austin Miller
1947–8
Secretary/Treasurer 1933–5

Sidney William Wooldridge
1949–50

Alan Grant Ogilvie
1951–2

Plate 1. The Presidents of the IBG, 1933–52

Robert Ogilvie Buchanan
1953
Assistant Secretary 1935–8
Secretary 1939–50

Wilfred Smith
1954

James Alfred Steers
1955

Laurence Dudley Stamp
1956

Robert Henry Kinvig
1957

Emrys George Bowen
1958

Plate 2. The Presidents of the IBG, 1953–8

William Gordon East
1959

Kenneth Charles Edwards
1960

Henry Clifford Darby
1961

David Leslie Linton
1962

Stanley Henry Beaver
1963

Percy Robert Crowe
1964

Plate 3. The Presidents of the IBG, 1959–64

Ronald Francis Peel
1965

Alice Garnett
1966

Harry Cyril Knapp Henderson
1967
Assistant Secretary 1957–61
Treasurer 1961–6

Robert Walter Steel
1968
Assistant Secretary 1949–51
Editor 1952–60

Emyr Estyn Evans
1969

Arthur Eltringham Smailes
1970
Secretary 1951–61

Plate 4. The Presidents of the IBG, 1965–70

William Richard Mead
1971

Bertram Hughes Farmer
1972
Assistant Secretary 1952–6
Editor 1961–6

John Terence Coppock
1973

Michael John Wise
1974

Stanley Gregory
1975

Jack William Birch
1976

Plate 5. The Presidents of the IBG, 1971–6

William Kirk
1977
Secretary 1964–71

Eric Herbert Brown
1978

Michael Donald Inglis Chisholm
1979

James Harold Bird
1980

Ronald Sidney Waters
1981

James Wreford Watson
1982

Plate 6. The Presidents of the IBG, 1977–82

John William House
President 1983

Ronald John Johnston
Secretary 1982–

David Antony Pinder
Treasurer 1982–

Michael Williams
Editor, Transactions 1983–

Andrew Mark Yates Blacksell
Editor, Area 1980–3

Plate 7. The Officers of the IBG, 1983

Geoffrey North
Secretary 1962–3

Richard Lawton
Secretary 1972–5

David Thomas
Secretary 1976–8

John Charles Doornkamp
Secretary 1979–81

Keith Martin Clayton
Treasurer 1967–71
President-elect 1984

Derek Robin Diamond
Treasurer 1972–7

Plate 8. The Officers of the IBG (I)

Trevor David Kennea
Treasurer 1978–80

Peter Randell Baker
Treasurer 1981–2

Clifford Embleton
Assistant Editor 1965–7
Editor, Transactions 1967–72

Robert John Price
Editor, Transactions 1973

Brian Turnbull Robson
Editor, Area 1971–3
Editor, Transactions 1974–6

David Ross Stoddart
Editor, Transactions 1977–82

Plate 9. The Officers of the IBG (II)

Hugh Counsell Prince
Editor, Area 1967–70

John Martin Hall
Editor, Area 1974–7

Jeremy William Richard Whitehand
Editor, Area 1977–9

Plate 10A. The Officers of the IBG (III)

Ernest Gordon Godfrey
(George Philip and Son, Ltd)

William John Furneaux
(Alden Press (Oxford) Ltd)

Plate 10B. The publishers of the IBG

Jean Eames
1965–73

Lucinda Gough-Cooper
1973–5

Wendy Greenwood
1975–82

Alison Kathleen Hind
1982–

Plate 11A. The Administrative Assistants of the IBG, 1965–83

William Vaughan Lewis
Assistant Secretary 1946–9
Vice-President 1961

Andrew Charles O'Dell
Vice-President 1965–6

Plate 11B. Vice-Presidents who died before taking up the office of President

APPENDICES

Appendix A

The Constitution of the IBG

The constitution of the IBG has been discussed—and amended—on many occasions, as is proper in a newly-established organisation that is vigorous and on-going and is ready to adapt itself to new opportunities and changing circumstances. It would have been appropriate perhaps to reproduce the first constitution, that agreed in 1933, together with the current constitution that incorporates a series of amendments over a number of years, agreed at the Annual General Meeting held in Edinburgh in January 1983. Unfortunately there appears to be no record of the first constitution though the Minute books of Annual General Meetings have references to a draft constitution presented in January 1933 which was referred to a drafting committee (consisting of C. B. Fawcett, Ll. Rodwell Jones and S. W. Wooldridge). This committee 'was recommended to get in touch with J. F. N. Green of the Colonial Office for advice and assistance on technical and legal matters'. It brought a revised version to the second Annual General Meeting of the IBG held in January 1934.

Many of the amendments of the early years referred to categories of membership and to voting procedures which for some years until 1951 required a postal ballot of all members (with at least two-thirds of those voting being the minimum necessary for the adoption of an amendment). The constitution that emerged from the discussions of the Council at that time resulted in the constitution approved unanimously by the Annual General Meeting in January 1952 which the minutes note was 'in the interests of the official organisation of the Institute's affairs', and 'took into account consequences of the post-war expansion of the Institute to a size that had not been envisaged when its constitution was drawn up'.

Since this was the first occasion when the constitution was printed in the *Transactions*, it is reproduced here from *Transactions 1952*, 1953, vii–viii.

CONSTITUTION (1952)

1. NAME.   The Society shall be called 'The Institute of British Geographers'.

2. OBJECTS.   The objects of the Institute shall be the study, discussion and advancement of Geography, especially by the holding of meetings which shall be open to the general public as well as to members of the Institute, and by the publication of papers and documents (hereinafter called 'The Transactions of the Institute').

3. MEMBERSHIP.

A.   The Institute shall consist of Ordinary, Honorary and Student members. Ordinary and Student members shall be elected by the Council following written nomination by two Ordinary Members.

Student Membership shall:

i.   be limited to full-time research students of geography at Universities in the United Kingdom.

ii.   be at half the current membership fee for Ordinary members.

iii.   entitle the member to read papers and submit work with a view to publication and to receive publications of the Institute, but shall not entitle him to receive other publications merely distributed by the Institute to Ordinary members.

B. i.   Subject to the provisions of paragraph (ii) hereof, each member shall be entitled to receive one copy of the Transactions of the Institute published by the Institute for any year of his membership.

ii.   No member other than an Honorary member shall be entitled to receive any such Transactions unless his subscription for the year as for which the same shall be published shall have been paid at the date of publication.

iii.   No Ordinary member shall be entitled to receive publications merely distributed by the Institute to Ordinary members unless his subscription for the then current year shall have been paid at the date of distribution.

iv.   Any person (member or non-member) may be supplied with any publications of the Institute on such terms as the Council may from time to time determine.

v.   Any member in arrear with his annual subscription shall not be entitled to make nominations or to take part in any meeting except as a member of the general public.

4.   ANNUAL GENERAL MEETING. There shall be an Annual General Meeting to consider business, of which at least four weeks' notice shall be given.

5.   FINANCE. The annual subscription shall be determined from time to time by the Annual General Meeting and shall thereupon be notified to all members.

6.   COMPOSITION OF THE COUNCIL. The business of the Institute shall be conducted by a Council consisting of a President, a Vice-President, an Honorary Secretary-Treasurer, an Honorary Assistant Secretary, and an Honorary Editor, together with six Ordinary members. The President shall hold office for one year and shall not be eligible for immediate re-election. The Vice-President shall hold office for one year and shall then succeed to the Presidency. The Honorary Secretary-Treasurer, the Honorary Assistant Secretary, and the Honorary Editor shall each hold office for three years and shall be eligible for re-election. Ordinary members of Council shall hold office for two years, three retiring at the end of each year, and shall not be eligible for immediate re-election as Ordinary members.

7.   ELECTION TO THE COUNCIL. The Council shall nominate annually at least three members of the Institute to serve as members of Council in place of the retiring members, and shall circulate its nominations at least four weeks before the Annual General Meeting. Members of the Institute shall have the right to propose additional names at the Annual General Meeting. Such proposals shall be made in writing, with the names of the proposer and seconder, and shall be handed to the Chairman at the begin-

ning of the business meeting. If the number of nominations exceeds the number of vacancies, election shall be by ballot at the Annual General Meeting.

8. FUNCTIONS OF THE COUNCIL. The Council shall conduct the affairs of the Institute. The Officers of the Institute shall perform such duties as the Council may assign to them.

9. ALTERATIONS TO THE CONSTITUTION. Any proposed alterations shall be sent in writing to the Secretary over the signatures of at least seven members, not less than eight weeks before the Annual General Meeting, and shall be circulated to all members not less than four weeks before this Meeting. The proposed alteration shall be put before this Meeting. Members may vote in person at the meeting or may transmit their votes in writing to the Secretary beforehand. The proposed alteration shall become operative if approved by two-thirds of the votes cast.

CONSTITUTION (1983)

Incorporating amendments passed at the Annual General Meetings held at:

University College of Wales, Aberystwyth	5 January 1952
University of Liverpool	6 January 1961
University of Sheffield	5 January 1967
University of Exeter	4 January 1968
University of East Anglia	5 January 1974
University of Oxford	5 January 1975
University of Lancaster	3 January 1980
University of Southampton	6 January 1982
University of Edinburgh	6 January 1983

1. NAME. The Society shall be called ' The Institute of British Geographers '.

2. OBJECTS. The objects of the Institute shall be the study, discussion and advancement of Geography, especially by the holding of meetings which shall be open to the general public as well as to members of the Institute, and by the publication of papers and documents (hereinafter called ' The Transactions of the Institute ').

3. MEMBERSHIP.
   A. The Institute shall consist of Ordinary, Student, Honorary, Senior, Joint and Associate Members.

   i. *Ordinary Members* shall be elected by Council following written nomination by two Ordinary Members. They shall comprise persons likely to further the objects of the Institute, and, subject to the provisions of Section (B) hereof, shall have full rights to attend and vote at meetings, hold office in the Institute, submit papers for reading and work for publications, and receive publications of the Institute.

ii.   *Student Members* shall be elected by the Council following written nomination by two Ordinary members. Student members shall be those registered full-time for a higher degree at any recognised institution of further or higher education. Subject to the provisions of Section (B) hereof, they shall be entitled to attend and vote at meetings, including the Annual General Meeting, to submit papers for reading and work for publications, and to receive publications of the Institute, but not to hold Office in the Institute. At the termination of their membership, student members may apply to Council for election to ordinary membership.

iii.   *Honorary Membership* shall be bestowed by the Council as a special mark of honour to particular individuals for long and notable service to the Institute. Their rights shall be the same as those of Ordinary Members.

iv.   *Senior Membership* shall be granted by the Council, to Ordinary Members of long standing upon retirement from their professional employment. Their rights shall be the same as those of Ordinary Members.

v.   *Joint Membership* shall be available to husband and wife when both are Members of the Institute. Only one copy of the Institute's publications and of other distributed publications shall be supplied but in all other respects they shall both have the privileges of Ordinary Members.

vi.   *Associate Membership*. Any individual who is a member of an Institute Study Group and not already a member of the Institute shall be designated an Associate Member. Any individual associated with a recognised institution of higher or further education as a teacher, researcher or registered postgraduate in geography shall not be eligible for Associate Membership. Associate members shall have no voting rights and shall not receive publications.

B. i.   Ordinary Members shall pay the full annual subscription; Student Members shall pay half the Ordinary annual subscription; Honorary Members shall not be required to pay a subscription; the subscription for Senior Membership shall be less than that for Ordinary Membership and shall be determined from time to time by the Council in relation to the price of publications produced by the Institute; with Joint Membership one shall pay a subscription at the Ordinary Membership rate, the other at Senior Membership rate.

ii.   No member, other than an Honorary Member, shall be entitled to receive publications of the Institute nor publications distributed by the Institute unless his subscription for the year in which the same shall be published shall have been paid at the date of publication.

iii.   Subject to the provisions of paragraph (ii) hereof, each member shall be entitled to receive one copy of the *Transactions* published by the Institute for any year of his membership.

iv.   Any member in arrears with his annual subscription shall not be entitled to receive publications, to make nominations for elections or to take part in any meeting of the Institute except as a member of the general public.

v. Any person (member or non-member) may be supplied with any publication of the Institute on such terms as the Council may from time to time determine.

4. ANNUAL GENERAL MEETING. There shall be an Annual General Meeting to consider business, of which at least four weeks' notice shall be given.

5. FINANCE. The annual subscription shall be determined from time to time by the Annual General Meeting and shall thereupon be notified to all Members. The financial year of the Institute shall run from 1st October to 30th September the following year.

6. COMPOSITION OF THE COUNCIL. The business of the Institute shall be conducted by a Council consisting of a President, two Vice-Presidents, an Honorary Secretary, an Honorary Treasurer, an Honorary Editor of *Transactions* and an Honorary Editor of *Area* together with nine Ordinary Members. The President shall hold Office for one year and shall not be eligible for immediate re-election. A Vice-President shall hold office for two years and shall then succeed to the Presidency. The Honorary Secretary, the Honorary Treasurer and the Honorary Editor of *Area* shall each hold office for three years, and the Honorary Editor of *Transactions* shall hold office for five years. Each shall be eligible for re-election. Ordinary members of Council shall hold office for three years, three retiring at the end of each year, and shall not be eligible for immediate re-election as Ordinary members.

7. ELECTION OF OFFICERS AND COUNCIL MEMBERS. The Council shall annually ensure that at least one member of the Institute is nominated for each vacancy, whether occasioned by retirement or otherwise. The membership will be invited to submit nominations to Council. Such nominations must be made in writing and must give names of the proposer and seconder, and must be received by the Administrative Assistant by the date specified in the invitation, for which the minimum notice will be four weeks. For all vacancies for which there is more than one candidate, a postal ballot of all members will then be held, using the Single Transferable Vote or Alternative Vote, as appropriate. The minimum period for the ballot will be four weeks. The results of the election will be declared at the AGM.

8. FUNCTIONS OF THE COUNCIL. The Council shall conduct the affairs of the Institute. The Officers of the Institute shall perform such duties as the Council may assign to them.

9. ALTERATIONS TO THE CONSTITUTION. Any proposed alterations shall be sent in writing to the Secretary over the signatures of at least seven members, not less than eight weeks before the Annual General Meeting, and shall be circulated to all members not less than four weeks before this Meeting. The proposed alteration shall be put before this Meeting. Members may vote in person at the meeting or may transmit their votes in writing to the Secretary beforehand. The proposed alterations shall become operative if approved by two-thirds of the votes cast.

Appendix B

Papers circulated to British geographers in 1932

ENCLOSURE 1

The following report, drawn up by the Committee[1] appointed in January 1932, was presented at a meeting of geographers held in York on 2 September 1932. In its present form it incorporates the amendments approved by this meeting.

1. OBJECTS IN VIEW

A. MEETINGS

a Reading and full discussion of papers at a meeting to be held in January.

b Short visits to various Schools of Geography and to localities offering opportunities for work in the field.

c An annual business meeting to be held either in the Autumn (at the British Association Centre for the year) or in January in London.

B. PUBLICATION

It is recommended that independent publication of research shall be instituted, ultimately it is hoped in the form of memoirs, but that in the meantime publication of shorter communications shall be undertaken, either independently or in existing journals, with or without financial assistance from the Institute.

2. MEMBERSHIP

It is recommended that all members of the present staffs of the Geography Departments of Universities and University Colleges shall be entitled to join as original members, but that subsequent membership shall be by election.

3. FINANCE

It is recommended that a sum of 10/6d be paid by members of the Institute at the beginning of the first year and that in this and succeeding years the total subscription or guarantee shall not exceed £3.

4. CONSTITUTION

a Composition of Council.

It is recommended that the business of the Institute shall be conducted by a Council, consisting of a President, an honorary secretary, an honorary treasurer, together with six other members. It is suggested that the President shall hold office for two years and shall be eligible for re-election. The Secretary and Treasurer shall hold office for three years and shall be eligible for re-election. Members of Council shall serve for two years, three retiring at the end of each year.

b Election to Council.

It is recommended that nominations for officers and members of Council signed by proposer and seconder shall be in the hands of the Secretary not less than six weeks before the annual business meeting. The Council will review the nominations and may add further names to the list, which shall be circulated to all members at least two weeks before the meeting. If the number of nominations exceeds the number of vacancies election shall be by ballot.

c Functions of the Council.

The Council shall conduct the affairs of the Institute. It shall appoint an editorial board, the members of which shall not necessarily be members of Council and who shall retire in rotation, the first retirement taking place after three years.

The officers of the Institute shall perform such duties as may be required of them by the Council.

5. OTHER RECOMMENDATIONS

It is recommended:

a That notice of any proposed alteration to the constitution shall be circulated to all members not less than six weeks before the Annual business meeting. The proposed alteration shall be put before this meeting and adopted if not less than two-thirds of the votes cast are in its favour.

b That members in arrears with their annual subscription shall not be entitled to receive publications, to make nominations or to vote at any meeting whatsoever.

6. TITLE

It is recommended that the title ' The Institute of British Geographers ' be adopted.

It should be pointed out that the foregoing recommendations are not to be regarded as necessarily in final form in respect of either substance or wording. They were approved by the Meeting at York subject to slight emendations which have been incorporated in the above draft, but the Council will no doubt review them in detail and submit a revised draft of Constitution and rules to the annual business meeting at a later date.

ENCLOSURE 2

STATEMENT

It may be recalled that the possibility of obtaining an additional outlet for advanced work in Geography has been considered by academic workers at various times in the past, notably by the late Prof. A. J. Herbertson and Dr. G. G. Chisholm whose plans were interrupted by the outbreak of war in 1914. The exchange of opinion and enquiry which have led to the promulgation of the present scheme have been in progress during the last two years. At a general meeting of University Geographers held in London in January 1932, a University ' group ' was constituted and a Committee was appointed to make recommendations as to the constitution and functions of the body. This committee reported to a well attended and representative meeting held at York in September. The recommendations were adopted with slight emendation by the meeting and a copy of the emended report is enclosed. The meeting at York also appointed an inaugural Committee to make arrangements for a meeting in January at which officers and council should be elected. The following gentlemen have served on the inaugural committee: Dr. P. W. Bryan, Prof. H. J. Fleure, Prof. C. D. Forde, Prof. Rodwell Jones, Dr. H. A. Matthews, Prof. A. G. Ogilvie, Mr. J. A. Steers and Dr. S. W. Wooldridge.

The Committee desire to emphasise the need of general and widespread support if the Institute is to discharge effectively the functions it has in view. In the matter of publication, investigations at an earlier stage showed that a considerable body of unpublished research work exists and the need for finding some outlet for this may fairly be deemed urgent. The Committee wish to make it clear that the proposed activities of the Institute, both in the matter of meetings and publication, are not in any sense to be regarded as competing with those of other geographical bodies and journals, but rather as supplementary. It has been rendered quite clear that the large and increasing volume of geographical work is such that existing journals cannot publish it all in view of their own essential and legitimate traditions and their prior commitments. The work envisaged by the Institute will not damage, but may reasonably be considered to assist, the other Geographical bodies of the country and a maintenance of cordial relations with them is an essential condition of success.

While the several preparatory Committees have kept the important matter of publication prominently in view, they have worked also to secure more frequent meetings of research geographers and have borne in mind the great need of securing means for the reading and discussion of papers, for which there is at present but limited scope.

Note

1. The following served as members of the Committee: J. N. L. Baker, C. B. Fawcett, H. J. Fleure, A. Garnett, A. G. Ogilvie, P. M. Roxby, J. A. Steers and S. W. Wooldridge.

Appendix C

Original or Founder Members of the IBG

A list of the ' original ' members of the IBG, containing seventy-three names, was published in 1935 on page ix of *Transactions* 1 and 2, and this list is reproduced below. Strictly speaking, these were not all original or founder members. The first record of the size of the membership occurs in the minutes of Council for 30 April 1933 and stands at thirty-nine. During 1933 the Institute welcomed further members without election though not all those recorded as being elected during that year are included in the published list (Vaughan Cornish, E. Lynam, D. J. Smetham and Miss C. A. Simpson). After 10 January 1934 applicants had to be nominated and then elected by Council.

Despite many enquiries it has not been possible to trace G. D. B. Gray and Miss B. M. Tunstall. Eighteen of the members listed are still alive, and three (S. J. K. Baker, D. D. E. Rodgers and J. A. Steers) attended the fiftieth anniversary celebrations of the IBG in the University of Edinburgh in January 1983.

Name	Date	Name	Date
Baker, J. N. L.	1893–1971	Huggins, K. H.	1908–
Baker, S. J. K.	1907–	Jervis, W. W.	1892–1959
Beaver, S. H.	1907–	Jones, Ll. Rodwell	1881–1947
Boswell, Miss K. C.	1889–1952	Kimble, G. H. T.	1908–
Bowen, E. G.	1900–1983	Kinvig, R. H.	1893–1969
Bowen, G.	1910–	Kirkaldy, J. F.	1908–
Brown, R. N. Rudmose	1879–1957	Lebon, J. H. G.	1909–1969
Bryan, P. W.	1885–1968	Lewis, W. S.	1893–1947
Buchanan, R. O.	1894–1981	Lewis, W. V.	1907–1961
Cons, G. J.	1893–1960	Linton, D. L.	1906–1971
Crowe, P. R.	1904–1980	MacMunn, Miss N. E.	1874–1967
Davies, E.	1908–	McPherson, A. W.	1907–1946
Dickinson, R. E.	1905–1981	Mann, Mrs. M. R.	1898–1950
East, W. G.	1902–	Matthews, H. A.	1899–1943
Edwards, K. C.	1904–1982	Miller, A. A.	1900–1968
Evans, E. E.	1905–	Newbigin, Dr. M. I.	1869–1934
Fairhurst, H.	1908–	O'Dell, A. C.	1909–1966
Fawcett, C. B.	1883–1952	Ogilvie, A. G.	1887–1954
Fitzgerald, W.	1898–1949	Ormsby, Dr. Hilda	1877–1973
Fleure, H. J.	1877–1969	Pelham, R. A.	1903–1981
Fogg, W.	1899–1965	Rishbeth, O. H. T.	1885–1942
Forde, C. D.	1902–1973	Rodgers, D. D. E.	1909–
Garnett, Miss A.	1903–	Roxby, P. M.	1880–1947
Geddes, A.	1895–1968	Scarfe, N. V.	1908–
Gray, G. D. B.		Smailes, A. E.	1911–
Green, F. H. W.	1911–1983	Smee, Dr. Dora K.	1898–1982
Gullick, C. F. W. R.	1907–1981	Smith, W.	1903–1955
Henderson, H. C. K.	1903–1983	Stamp, L. D.	1898–1966
Hinks, A. R.	1873–1945	Steers, J. A.	1899–
Hosgood, Miss B.	1890–1953	Stevens, A.	1886–1965

Swainson, Miss B. M.	1980–	Unstead, J. F.	1876–1965
Swinnerton, H. H.	1875–1966	Varley, W. J.	1904–1976
Sylvester, Miss D.	1906–	Williams, D. T.	1897–1963
Taylor, Dr. Eva G. R.	1879–1966	Williamson, A. V.	1897–1965
Timberlake, Miss E. M.	1904–	Wood, H. J.	1904–1952
Trueman, A. E.	1894–1956	Wooldridge, S. W.	1900–1963
Tunstall. Miss B. M.			

Appendix D

The Officers of the IBG, 1933–83

Year	President	Vice-President(s)	Secretary	Treasurer/ Assistant Secretary	Editor Transactions	Assistant Editor Transactions	Editor Area
1933–34	C. B. Fawcett		A. A. Miller	H. A. Matthews			
1935	C. B. Fawcett		A. A. Miller	R. O. Buchanan			
1936	C. B. Fawcett		J. N. L. Baker	R. O. Buchanan			
1937	R. N. Rudmose Brown		J. N. L. Baker	R. O. Buchanan			
1938	R. N. Rudmose Brown		J. N. L. Baker	R. O. Buchanan			
1939–46	J. N. L. Baker		R. O. Buchanan	W. V. Lewis			
1947	A. A. Miller		R. O. Buchanan	W. V. Lewis			
1948	A. A. Miller		R. O. Buchanan	W. V. Lewis			
1949	S. W. Wooldridge		R. O. Buchanan	R. W. Steel			
1950	S. W. Wooldridge		R. O. Buchanan	R. W. Steel			
1951	A. G. Ogilvie		A. E. Smailes	R. W. Steel			
1952	A. G. Ogilvie		A. E. Smailes	R. W. Steel			
1953	R. O. Buchanan	W. Smith	A. E. Smailes	B. H. Farmer	R. W. Steel		
1954	W. Smith	J. A. Steers	A. E. Smailes	B. H. Farmer	R. W. Steel		
1955	J. A. Steers	L. D. Stamp	A. E. Smailes	B. H. Farmer	R. W. Steel		
1956	L. D. Stamp	R. H. Kinvig	A. E. Smailes	B. H. Farmer/	R. W. Steel		
1957	R. H. Kinvig	E. G. Bowen	A. E. Smailes	H. C. K. Henderson	R. W. Steel		
1958	E. G. Bowen	W. G. East	A. E. Smailes	H. C. K. Henderson	R. W. Steel		
1959	W. G. East	K. C. Edwards	A. E. Smailes	H. C. K. Henderson	R. W. Steel		
1960	K. C. Edwards	H. C. Darby	A. E. Smailes	H. C. K. Henderson	R. W. Steel		
1961	H. C. Darby	W. V. Lewis¹, D. L. Linton	A. E. Smailes	H. C. K. Henderson	B. H. Farmer		
1962	D. L. Linton	S. H. Beaver, P. R. Crowe	G. North	H. C. K. Henderson	B. H. Farmer		

1963	S. H. Beaver	P. R. Crowe, R. F. Peel	G. North	H. C. K. Henderson	B. H. Farmer		
1964	P. R. Crowe	R. F. Peel, Alice Garnett	W. Kirk	H. C. K. Henderson	B. H. Farmer		
1965	R. F. Peel	Alice Garnett, A. C. O'Dell	W. Kirk	H. C. K. Henderson	B. H. Farmer	C. Embleton	
1966	Alice Garnett	A. C. O'Dell², R. W. Steel	W. Kirk	H. C. K. Henderson	B. H. Farmer	C. Embleton	
1967	H. C. K. Henderson	R. W. Steel, E. E. Evans	W. Kirk	K. M. Clayton	C. Embleton	J. T. Coppock	
1968	R. W. Steel	E. E. Evans, A. E. Smailes	W. Kirk	K. M. Clayton	C. Embleton	J. T. Coppock	
1969	E. E. Evans	A. E. Smailes, W. R. Mead	W. Kirk	K. M. Clayton	C. Embleton	J. T. Coppock	H. C. Prince
1970	A. E. Smailes	W. R. Mead, B. H. Farmer	W. Kirk	K. M. Clayton	C. Embleton	J. T. Coppock	H. C. Prince
1971	W. R. Mead	B. H. Farmer, J. T. Coppock	W. Kirk	K. M. Clayton	R. J. Price	C. E. Everard	B. T. Robson
1972	B. H. Farmer	J. T. Coppock, M. J. Wise	R. Lawton	D. R. Diamond	R. J. Price	C. E. Everard	B. T. Robson
1973	J. T. Coppock	M. J. Wise, S. Gregory	R. Lawton	D. R. Diamond	R. J. Price	J. A. Patmore	B. T. Robson
1974	M. J. Wise	S. Gregory, J. W. Birch	R. Lawton	D. R. Diamond	B. T. Robson		J. M. Hall
1975	S. Gregory	J. W. Birch, W. Kirk	R. Lawton	D. R. Diamond	B. T. Robson		J. M. Hall
1976	J. W. Birch	W. Kirk, E. H. Brown	D. Thomas	D. R. Diamond	B. T. Robson		J. M. Hall
1977	W. Kirk	E. H. Brown, M. D. I. Chisholm	D. Thomas	D. R. Diamond	D. R. Stoddart		J. M. Hall/
1978	E. H. Brown	M. D. I. Chisholm, J. H. Bird	D. Thomas	T. C. Kennea	D. R. Stoddart		J. W. R. Whitehand
1979	M. D. I. Chisholm	J. H. Bird, J. W. Watson	J. C. Doornkamp	T. C. Kennea	D. R. Stoddart		J. W. R. Whitehand
1980	J. H. Bird	R. S. Waters, J. W. Watson	J. C. Doornkamp	T. C. Kennea	D. R. Stoddart		M. Blacksell
1981	R. S. Waters	J. W. Watson, J. W. House	J. C. Doornkamp	P. R. Baker	D. R. Stoddart		M. Blacksell
1982	J. W. Watson	J. W. House, K. M. Clayton	R. J. Johnston	P. R. Baker	D. R. Stoddart		M. Blacksell
1983	J. W. House	K. M. Clayton, G. M. Howe	R. J. Johnston	D. A. Pinder	M. Williams		M. Blacksell

¹ W. V. Lewis was killed in a road accident in the USA on [8] June 1961 and D. L. Linton was elected as a Vice-President to fill his place on the Council and to succeed H. C. Darby as President in 1962.

² A. C. O'Dell died on 17 June 1966 and H. C. K. Henderson agreed to take his place and become President in 1967. Henderson had been a member of the Council from 1957 to 1962 as Assistant Secretary and then as Treasurer when the office was re-designated to accord with the functions of the holder of the appointment.

Appendix E

Ordinary Members of the Council of the IBG 1933–83

1933–34   J. N. L. Baker, R. O. Buchanan, H. J. Fleure, Ll. Rodwell Jones, P. M. Roxby, S. W. Wooldridge

1935   J. N. L. Baker, P. R. Crowe, H. J. Fleure, P. M. Roxby, R. N. Rudmose Brown, S. W. Wooldridge

1936   P. R. Crowe, R. H. Kinvig, D. L. Linton, Hilda R. Ormsby, R. N. Rudmose Brown, J. A. Steers

1937   K. C. Edwards, C. B. Fawcett, R. H. Kinvig, D. L. Linton, Hilda R. Ormsby, A. V. Williamson

1938   K. C. Edwards, C. B. Fawcett, W. Fitzgerald, K. H. Huggins, A. V. Williamson, H. J. Wood

1946   P. W. Bryan, H. C. Darby, W. G. East, D. L. Linton, A. A. Miller, A. Stevens

1947   J. N. L. Baker, W. G. East, D. L. Linton, R. W. Steel, A. Stevens, S. W. Wooldridge

1948   J. N. L. Baker, B. H. Farmer, W. Fitzgerald, S. J. Jones, R. W. Steel

1949   B. H. Farmer, W. Fitzgerald, S. J. Jones, L. Slater, W. Smith, Catherine P. Snodgrass

1950   P. R. Crowe, R. F. Peel, L. Slater, A. E. Smailes, W. Smith, Catherine P. Snodgrass

1951   E. G. Bowen, R. O. Buchanan, P. R. Crowe, A. C. O'Dell, R. F. Peel, Dorothy Sylvester

1952   E. G. Bowen, M. R. G. Conzen, J. N. Jennings, A. C. O'Dell, Dora K. Smee, Dorothy Sylvester

1953   S. H. Beaver, M. R. G. Conzen, J. N. Jennings, A. F. Martin, Dora K. Smee, G. T. Warwick

1954   S. H. Beaver, A. Davies, H. C. K. Henderson, A. F. Martin, N. Pye, G. T. Warwick

1955   A. Davies, H. C. K. Henderson, R. Miller, N. Pye, J. G. Thomas, H. R. Wilkinson

1956   Eila M. J. Campbell, K. C. Edwards, J. P. Haughton, R. Miller, J. G. Thomas, H. R. Wilkinson

1957   Eila M. J. Campbell, K. C. Edwards, Alice Garnett, J. P. Haughton, F. J. Monkhouse, Joy Tivy

1958   A. A. L. Caesar, Alice Garnett, E. Jones, F. J. Monkhouse, C. G. Smith, Joy Tivy

1959   J. W. Birch, A. A. L. Caesar, E. Jones, C. G. Smith, H. Thorpe, J. W. Watson

1960   J. W. Birch, F. J. Fowler, J. R. James, G. North, H. Thorpe, J. W. Watson

1961   M. D. I. Chisholm, F. J. Fowler, J. W. House, J. R. James, R. Lawton, G. North

1962   J. H. Appleton, M. D. I. Chisholm, Gillian, E. Groom, J. W. House, C. Kidson, R. Lawton, W. R. Mead, H. A. Moisley, R. H. Osborne

1963	J. H. Appleton, S. Gregory, Gillian E. Groom, C. Kidson, W. Kirk, W. R. Mead, H. A. Moisley, R. H. Osborne, Marjorie M. Sweeting
1964	K. M. Clayton, S. Gregory, G. M. Howe, C. Kidson, Kathleen M. MacIver, W. R. Mead, H. A. Moisley, Marjorie M. Sweeting, F. Walker
1965	K. M. Clayton, G. de Boer, T. H. Elkins, S. Gregory, G. M. Howe, Kathleen M. MacIver, J. Oliver, Marjorie M. Sweeting, F. Walker
1966	K. M. Clayton, J. T. Coppock, G. de Boer, T. H. Elkins, Kathleen M. MacIver, J. Oliver, R. M. Prothero, J. A. Taylor, F. Walker
1967	G. de Boer, T. H. Elkins, D. B. Grigg, J. Oliver, R. M. Prothero, V. B. Proudfoot, W. Ravenhill, J. A. Taylor, E. M. Yates
1968	J. F. Davis, D. B. Grigg, G. R. J. Jones, G. Manners, R. M. Prothero, W. Ravenhill, J. B. Sissons, J. A. Taylor, E. M. Yates
1969	J. F. Davis, C. E. Everard, D. B. Grigg, G. Humphrys, G. R. J. Jones, G. Manners, J. B. Sissons, C. T. Smith, E. M. Yates
1970	J. H. Bird, C. E. Everard, G. Humphrys, G. R. J. Jones, G. Manners, R. J. Price, J. B. Sissons, C. T. Smith, Helen M. Wallis
1971	J. H. Bird, J. C. Goodridge, G. Humphrys, G. R. J. Jones, J. A. Patmore, R. J. Price, C. T. Smith, Helen M. Wallis, E. C. Willatts
1972	J. H. Bird, J. C. Goodridge, J. B. Harley, J. A. Patmore, R. J. Price, N. Stephens, D. Thomas, Helen M. Wallis, E. C. Willatts
1973	R. U. Cooke, J. C. Goodridge, J. B. Harley, J. A. Patmore, J. L. Smith, N. Stephens, D. Thomas, E. C. Willatts, A. Young
1974	R. A. Butlin, J. I. Clarke, R. U. Cooke, J. B. Harley, T. C. Kennea, J. L. Smith, N. Stephens, D. Thomas, A. Young
1975	R. A. Butlin, J. B. Caird, J. I. Clarke, R. U. Cooke, T. C. Kennea, H. B. Rodgers, J. L. Smith, I. B. Thompson, A. Young
1976	R. A. Butlin, J. B. Caird, J. I. Clarke, D. J. Dwyer, K. J. Gregory, T. C. Kennea, Joan M. Kenworthy, H. B. Rodgers, I. B. Thompson
1977	J. B. Caird, D. J. Dwyer, K. J. Gregory, R. J. Johnston, Joan M. Kenworthy, H. B. Rodgers, D. M. Smith, I. B. Thompson, R. C. Ward
1978	J. G. Cruickshank, D. J. Dwyer, K. J. Gregory, R. J. Johnston, Joan M. Kenworthy, P. R. Odell, V. B. Proudfoot, D. M. Smith, R. C. Ward
1979	D. Brunsden, J. G. Cruickshank, D. T. Herbert, R. J. Johnston, E. W. Lewis, P. R. Odell, V. B. Proudfoot, D. M. Smith, R. C. Ward
1980	D. Brunsden, J. G. Cruickshank, A. S. Goudie, D. T. Herbert, J. H. Johnson, E. W. Lewis, P. R. Odell, V. B. Proudfoot, Judith A. Rees
1981	D. Brunsden, A. S. Goudie, D. T. Herbert, J. H. Johnson, E. W. Lewis, Judith A. Rees, P. J. Taylor, D. Watts, A. F. Williams
1982	J. A. Dawson, P. Dicken, A. S. Goudie, J. H. Johnson, Judith A. Rees, R. J. Rice, P. J. Taylor, D. Watts, A. F. Williams
1983	J. A. Dawson, P. Dicken, I. Douglas, Janet D. Momsen, R. J. Rice, K. Smith, P. J. Taylor, D. Watts, A. F. Williams

Appendix F

The Presidents of the IBG and their Presidential addresses

Year	President and University	Title	Volume of Transactions
1935–36	Charles Bungay Fawcett (University College London)	The relations between the advance of science (in geography) and the life of the community	Not published
1937	Robert Neal Rudmose Brown (Sheffield)	No address given	
1946	John Norman Leonard Baker (Oxford)	Geography and politics: the geographical doctrine of balance	13, 1947, 1–15
1947–48	Arthur Austin Miller (Reading)	The dissection and analysis of maps	14, 1948, 1–13
1949–50	Sidney William Wooldridge (King's College, London)	Reflections on regional geography in teaching and research	16, 1950, 1–11
1951–52	Alan Grant Ogilvie (Edinburgh)	The time element in geography	18, 1952, 1–15
1953	Robert Ogilvie Buchanan (London School of Economics)	The IBG: retrospect and prospect	20, 1954, 1–14
1954	Wilfred Smith (Liverpool)	The location of industry	21, 1955, 1–18
1955	James Alfred Steers (Cambridge)	The coast as a field for physiographical research	22, 1956, 1–13
1956	Laurence Dudley Stamp (London School of Economics)	Geographical agenda: a review of some tasks awaiting geographical attention	23, 1957, 1–17
1957	Robert Henry Kinvig (Birmingham)	The Isle of Man and Atlantic Britain: a study in historical geography	25, 1958, 1–27
1958	Emrys George Bowen (Aberystwyth)	Le Pays de Galles	26, 1959, 1–23
1959	William Gordon East (Birkbeck, London)	The geography of land-locked states	28, 1960, 1–22
1960	Kenneth Charles Edwards (Nottingham)	Historical geography of the Luxembourg iron and steel industry	29, 1961, 1–16

Year	President and University	Title	Volume of Transactions
1961	Henry Clifford Darby (University College London)	The problem of geographical description	30, 1962, 1–14
1962	David Leslie Linton (Birmingham)	The forms of glacial erosion	33, 1963, 1–28
1963	Stanley Henry Beaver (Keele)	The Potteries: a study in the evolution of a cultural landscape	34, 1964, 1–31
1964	Percy Robert Crowe (Manchester)	The geographer and the atmosphere	36, 1965, 1–19
1965	Ronald Francis Peel (Bristol)	The landscape in aridity	38, 1966, 1–23
1966	Alice Garnett (Sheffield)	Some climatological problems in urban geography with special reference to air pollution	42, 1967, 21–43
1967	Harry Cyril Knapp Henderson (Birkbeck, London)	Geography's balance sheet	45, 1968, 1–9
1968	Robert Walter Steel (Liverpool)	Problems of population pressure in tropical Africa	49, 1970, 1–14
1969	Emyr Estyn Evans (Queen's, Belfast)	The personality of Ulster	51, 1970, 1–20
1970	Arthur Eltringham Smailes (Queen Mary College, London)	Urban systems	53, 1971, 1–14
1971	William Richard Mead (University College London)	Luminaries of the North: a reappraisal of the achievements and influence of six Scandinavian geographers	57, 1972, 1–13
1972	Bertram Hughes Farmer (Cambridge)	Geography, area studies and the study of area	60, 1973, 1–15
1973	John Terence Coppock (Edinburgh)	Geography and public policy: challenges, opportunities and implications	63, 1974, 1–16
1974	Michael John Wise (London School of Economics)	A university teacher of geography	66, 1975, 1–16
1975	Stanley Gregory (Sheffield)	On geographical myths and statistical fables	NS 1, 1976, 385–400
1976	Jack William Birch (Bristol Polytechnic)	On excellence and problem solving in geography	NS 2, 1977, 417–29

Year	President and University	Title	Volume of Transactions
1977	William Kirk (Queen's, Belfast)	The road from Mandalay: towards a geographical philosophy	NS 3, 1978, 381–94
1978	Eric Herbert Brown (University College London)	The shape of Britain	NS 4, 1979, 449–62
1979	Michael Donald Inglis Chisholm (Cambridge)	The wealth of nations	NS 5, 1980, 255–76
1980	James Harold Bird (Southampton)	The target of space and the arrow of time	NS 6, 1981, 129–51
1981	Ronald Sidney Waters (Sheffield)	No address	
1982	James Wreford Watson (Edinburgh)	The soul of geography	NS 8, 1983, 385–99

Notes. The first President, C. B. Fawcett (1935–36), read a paper to the Institute in January 1935 but it was not in any sense a presidential address and there is no record of it being published anywhere. The second President, R. N. Rudmose Brown (1937–39), did not give a lecture to the Institute while he held office. J. N. L. Baker (President, 1939–46) read a paper to the Institute but, according to his successor, ' declined to call it a Presidential Address ' (Miller, A. A., 1948), *Transactions* 1948, 1). W. G. East (President, 1959) could not read his Presidential Address at the conference held in Southampton in January 1960 because of his absence at the time in the USA. R. S. Waters (President, 1981) was prevented by ill health from preparing his address and from taking the chair in January 1982 at the conference, which also took place in the University of Southampton.

Appendix G

Study Groups, 1983

Biogeography
British Geomorphological Research
Developing Areas Research
Geography and Planning
Higher Education Learning
Historical Geography Research
Industrial Activity and Area Development
Medical Geography

Political Geography
Population Geography
Quantitative Methods
Rural Geography
Social Geography
Transport Geography
Urban Geography
Women and Geography

Appendix H

International seminars, 1959–83

Year	Title	Place(s)	Theme	UK Leader	Numbers
1959	1st Anglo/Polish	Nieborow, Poland	Applied geography	K. C. Edwards	12 UK
1962	2nd Anglo/Polish	Keele, UK	Industrial development and urbanisation	S. H. Beaver	17 UK
1967	3rd Anglo/Polish	Baranow Sandomierski, Poland	Techniques in geography	R. H. Osborne	13 UK
1970	4th Anglo/Polish	Nottingham, UK	Geographical aspects of urban–rural interaction	R. H. Osborne	20 UK
1972	Indo/British	Delhi, India	Urban–rural interaction	B. H. Farmer	10 UK
1972	Anglo/Romanian	London, UK	Modern methods and techniques in geographical research	W. R. Mead	7 UK
1973	1st Anglo/German	Giessen, Würzburg and Munich, Germany	Applied geography	E. M. Yates	total of 40
1974	5th British/Polish	Torun, Poland	Applied physical geography	E. H. Brown	10 UK
1974	1st British/Hungarian	Nottingham and London, UK	Regional development, methods and analysis	P. A. Compton R. H. Osborne F. E. I. Hamilton	10 UK
1975	2nd British/German	Aberdeen and Newcastle, UK	Regional development	E. M. Yates R. E. H. Mellor J. A. Hellen	total of 24

Year	Seminar	Location	Topic	Organizer	No.
1975	2nd Indo/British	Cambridge, Leicester, Swansea, UK	Urban-rural interaction in geography and planning	B. H. Farmer	—
1977	2nd British/Hungarian	Szeged, Poland	Evolution of the settlement network and its impact on the environment	P. A. Compton	9 UK
1977	6th British/Polish	Sheffield, UK	Relevance of studies of contemporary environments to those of Quaternary times	R. S. Waters	—
1978	3rd British/German	Bonn, Bochum, Germany	Planning and the quality of life	T. H. Elkins	—
1978	1st British/Soviet	London, UK	Contemporary tendencies in methods and methodology	F. E. I. Hamilton	16 UK
1979	1st British/Bulgarian	Various centres, UK	Geography and environmental policy	K. M. Clayton	13 UK
1979	3rd Indo/British	Madras, Tirupath, Mysore, India	Spatial inequalities. Spatial strategies	B. H. Farmer	—
1982	2nd British/Soviety	Moscow and other centres, USSR		E. Jones	—
1982	3rd British/Hungarian	Durham and other centres, UK	Environmental management	P. A. Compton	—
1983	2nd British/Bulgarian	Lancaster, Edinburgh, UK	Geography applied to practical problems	M. J. Moseley, J. H. Johnson	—
1983	4th Indo/British	Birmingham, Lampeter, UK	Rapid social and economic change within a regional framework	D. Thomas	—

Appendix I

Field meetings

Year	Venue	Association	Outcome
1936	Lake District	The Blackpool meeting of the British Association	D. L. Linton led walks in Windermere area for three days.
1937	Derbyshire	The Sheffield meeting of the British Association	H. C. K. Henderson and Alice Garnett led excursions for three days. Council met during the Field Meeting at Ashover, Derbyshire.
1938	Cambridge	The Cambridge meeting of the British Association	J. A. Steers was unable to arrange this after the British Association. There was insufficient support for a separate meeting in September.
1946	Oxfordshire		S. W. Wooldridge prepared to lead, but abandoned because of difficulty of securing accommodation.
1947	Glasgow	The Dundee meeting of the British Association	Accommodation difficulties reported in March. A. Stevens led a week's excursions in the Glasgow area in September.
1948	The Weald	The Brighton meeting of the British Association	S. W. Wooldridge led excursions from Juniper Hall, Leatherhead for four days.
1949	Sheffield	The Newcastle meeting of the British Association	D. L. Linton led excursions for five days.
1950	Nottingham	The Birmingham meeting of the British Association	K. C. Edwards prepared to lead but cancelled for lack of support and because of cost involved and time taken for British Association and field meeting.

1951	Aberdeen	The Edinburgh meeting of the British Association	Abandoned because of lack of support. Council discussed separation of field meetings from British Association.
1952	Ireland, Galway	The Belfast meeting of the British Association	A. Farrington and Dora K. Smee led excursions based in Galway for five days.
1953	Ireland, Dublin	The Liverpool meeting of the British Association	A. Farrington and J. P. Haughton led party for five days.
1954	Forest of Dean	The Oxford meeting of the British Association	H. C. K. Henderson reported only three bookings, so presumed abandoned.
1955	No record of any field meeting		
1956	No record of any field meeting		
1957	Ireland, Cork	The Dublin meeting of the British Association	A. Farrington and J. P. Haughton to collaborate with Section E Recorder, M. J. Wise, to revive field meeting jointly with British Association. 36 attended, of which half were IBG members.

1958 onwards: No record of any field meetings, or of discussion in Council about their desirability, until 1962.

1962	Devon		Meeting on denudation chronology led by C. Kidson.

After the meeting in 1962 Council suggested that additional field meetings be held ' as a means of widening the scope of Institute activities now that membership was increasing so much '. These were in future organised by the British Geomorphological Research Group and by other Study Groups.

Note: This appendix is based on information taken from the Council Minute Books and from the records printed in the *Transactions*. It is as full and accurate as those records permit.

Appendix J

Special Publications of the IBG

No. 1   *Land use and resources: studies in applied geography.* A memorial to Sir Dudley Stamp. 1968, 272 pp.

No. 2   *A geomorphological study of post-glacial uplift with particular reference to Arctic Canada.* J. T. Andrews. 1970, 156 pp.

No. 3   *Slopes: form and process.* D. Brunsden (comp.). 1971, 178 pp.

No. 4   *Polar geomorphology.* R. J. Price and D. E. Sugden (comps.). 1972, 216 pp.

No. 5   *Social patterns in cities.* B. D. Clark and M. B. Gleave (comps.). 1973, 192 pp.

No. 6   *Fluvial processes in instrumented watersheds: studies of small watersheds in the British Isles.* K. J. Gregory and D. E. Walling (eds.). 1974, 196 pp.

No. 7   *Progress in geomorphology: papers in honour of David L. Linton.* E. H. Brown and R. S. Waters (eds.). 1974, 256 pp.

No. 8   *Inter-regional migration in tropical Africa.* I. Masser and W. T. S. Gould with the assistance of A. D. Goddard. 1975, 108 pp.

No. 9   *Agrarian landscape terms: a glossary for historical geography.* I. H. Adams. 1976, 328 pp.

No. 10   *Change in the countryside: essays on rural England 1500–1900.* H. S. A. Fox and R. A. Butlin (eds.). 1979, 190 pp.

No. 11   *The shaping of southern England.* D. K. C. Jones (ed.). 1980, 284 pp.

No. 12   *Social interaction and ethnic segregation.* P. Jackson and S. J. Smith (eds.). 1981, 244 pp.

No. 13   *The urban landscape: Historical development and management. Papers by M. R. G. Conzen.* J. W. R. Whitehand (ed.). 1981, 176 pp.

No. 14   *The future for the city centre.* R. L. Davies and A. G. Champion (eds.). 1983, 310 pp.

No. 15   *Redundant spaces in cities and regions? Studies in industrial decline and social change.* J. Anderson, S. Duncan and R. Hudson (eds.). 1983, 364 pp.

No. 16   *Shorelines and isostasy.* D. E. Smith and A. G. Dawson (eds.) 1983, 400 pp.

Note

Marketing of Special Publications was taken over by Academic Press on 1 January 1980 with the hope that sales outside the UK would increase significantly as a result.

Appendix K

The archival material of the IBG

Reference has been made in the text to the paucity of the IBG's archival material apart from the obvious sources such as the minute books of the Council (even these lack some entries) and of Annual General Meetings and the Institute's publications, notably *Transactions* and *Area*. Many of the supporting papers to which the minutes refer are, if not missing, not readily available though they may be among the mass of unsorted and uncatalogued papers that have accumulated over many years and are housed in a room above the IBG office in the RGS's house in Kensington Gore. Time and circumstances have not made it possible for me to inspect all this material even though it would undoubtedly have produced valuable information for the history. Council should, in my view, take a decision about what should be done with these papers, and how their cataloguing or disposal should be organised. Clearly many of the papers could, and should, be destroyed—old receipts, delivery vouchers and the like that have survived and have no value or relevance today. But other papers need to be inspected and the significant ones listed and retained for future use.

The work, if it is to be done at all, would be a ' labour of love ' and would need to be undertaken by someone with a knowledge of the IBG and an appreciation of the value of the work that it has done over the past fifty years. Ideally a now-retired member of the Institute living in or near London would be asked to take on this task, which could be done at his or her convenience, and over a period of some months (or even years). I do not volunteer to offer myself as a person to do this work not through lack of concern (for it could be something that would be of intense interest and satisfaction to anyone who knew anything about the early struggles of the IBG and its subsequent growth in strength and influence) but because of the difficulties and expense involved through residence in S Wales, more than 200 miles away from the IBG's office.

It is unnecessary to dwell on the reasons for this state of affairs which must be common in many learned (and not very affluent) societies, especially in their early years. It is enough to record the present position and to refer to the problems that inevitably arise where officers are located in a variety of places throughout the country and where, when officers retire and new officers take over, it is often easier to destroy or to stack away accumulated papers than to sort and pass them to one's successor. I speak with experience here, having in my time as editor of *Transactions* moved my office from Oxford to Liverpool in 1957 and then handed over my editorial responsibilities to my successor in 1960. He had, of course, all the files relating to papers then under consideration, but it seemed unnecessary to pass over to him the files relating to papers already published and, *a fortiori,* those files with correspondence about rejected manuscripts that were not being submitted again with a view to their reconsideration. Was archival material thereby lost and subsequently destroyed? One has to balance the problems of storage and relevance, and there are limits to what a body such as the Institute can keep even now that it has a headquarters office and an administrative assistant (but with far too much work to do to make it possible for her to take care of the Institute's archives in addition to all her other duties).

Officers have, therefore, faced considerable problems over the keeping of material and many of these difficulties remain; indeed in many respects they are increased very considerably by the great expansion of activity in the Council and its numerous committees, and in the study groups, all of which engender large quantities of paper.

Over the years officers have not been unmindful of the existence of the problem. From the beginning the Institute published records of its business as well as the research papers of its members—hence the use of *Transactions* as the key word of its publications throughout the whole of its fifty years of existence as a learned society. But the record as printed was inevitably brief and R. O. Buchanan in his presidential address of 1954 stated that he might ' on occasion be compelled by incompleteness of the records to rely on memory rather than on the primary document ' (*Transactions,* 20, 1954, 1). Shortly before his presidency, Council had decided to publish factual notices of members who had died (*Transactions,* 1952, vi), but the following years showed how difficult it was to obtain such notices reasonably speedily. In the late 1950s, therefore, departments were invited to arrange for the collection of the basic information necessary for a *curriculum vitae* of individual members with a special emphasis on lists of publications. So far as I am aware very few departments of geography did much, if anything, about this. Commenting on this IBG initiative T. W. Freeman, who has done so much biobibliographical work on behalf of the Working Group on the History of Geographical Thought of the International Geographical Union, wrote in an appendix to his *A hundred years of geography* (1961, 303): ' Indeed the Institute of British Geographers asks its members to provide this information before demise.

> ' Ere you mount the heavenly stair
> Detailed references prepare. '

But in practice very few of such ' detailed references ' were prepared, and the IBG must, therefore, continue to depend on the willingness of its individual members to deal as effectively and rapidly as possible with enquiries when circumstances make them necessary.

A few years later, while R. Lawton was Secretary, and arising, in part at least, from a letter from G. Humphrys about the need ' to collect and organise archival material relating to the IBG ' that does not appear to have survived in the IBG's files, a special effort was made to ensure the keeping of such material. In a letter that referred to the fact that ' the Institute is past its 40th birthday ', the Secretary suggested that ' it seems appropriate to try and bring together a lot of this material as well as to lay the foundations of a more secure and lasting record of our activities '. Certainly my task in preparing this history would have been immensely helped had the recipients of the letter reacted to it as Lawton had hoped. It is worth quoting *in extenso* from the letter which summarises so well what the position was up to 1973 and what in fact it has continued to be since then, for there appears to have been almost no response to the request sent, I believe, to all former officers of the Institute (certainly all Presidents) and to heads of departments of geography in all British universities, Lawton wrote:

' Much of this material is of an administrative nature, concerning the day-to-day running of the Institute, its conference proceedings and other meetings, and its interventions on matters of concern to the geographical profession and over issues of public interest. However, it seems to me that many important aspects of the work of the Institute, certainly up to the early 1960s, are not to be found on record, in files or formal papers, but are the result of personal and often unrecorded activities of the President, officers and members of the Council of the day.

One very great gap in our records is that we have no " Presidential Papers " and I would like to remedy this in the course of the next year or so. What I have in mind is to ask incoming Presidents in future to deposit an outline of their career and publications, together with a photograph, when they come into office and, perhaps, a short paper on leaving office on the important developments of their period of office as they see them. I am also anxious to collect similiar information retrospectively, from past Presidents and Officers of the Institute. I realise that this may be difficult for you, but I would be very grateful if you would agree to let me have such information, together with any personal knowledge of the Institute as you have known it during your period of membership which you think may not be otherwise available. '

So far as I can judge the situation, nothing very much seems to have resulted from the then Secretary's plea—certainly I do not recall doing anything about my own year as President of the Institute (1968), and this at a time when Lawton's office and mine were immediately adjacent on the seventh floor of the Roxby Building in the University of Liverpool! I have approached a number of officers during the preparation of this history, and some have been particularly helpful in their replies, though these have generally been former Secretaries, Treasurers and Editors of the *Transactions* and of *Area* rather than Presidents, whose terms of office are so much shorter (even allowing for the fact that most of them have previously served for two years as Junior Vice-President and then Senior Vice-President). Their written comments will be deposited in the IBG office so that they will be available for any research workers who wish to consult them in future; and my hope would be that future officers—and indeed members of Council, too—would be encouraged to record their overall assessment of their years of office. Annual reports, such as are regularly written and retained (and often circulated to all members), provide, it is true, part of the story but of even greater value are the accounts of the trends as they reveal themselves over a period of years coming, as they do, from those who have been particularly closely associated with the affairs of the Institute.

Many instances could be cited of the incompleteness of the history of the Institute because of the lack of written records in the IBG's archives. There is, for example, no more than the memories of some of the officers of the occasion when the Council members considered the sending of a delegation to a Vice-Chancellor of a university that had, in their view, made an inappropriate appointment to its chair of geography! But as an example of the positive value of documentary evidence about a matter of which most members must be quite ignorant there follows an account of what happened nearly twenty years ago when the IBG officers received what was described as ' A Letter from Afar ' and which happily has survived among the archives so that it has been seen and appreciated by me as well as by those who were Officers and members of the Council at the time.

' A Letter from Afar' is undated but it was written during 1964 and was signed by A. T. A. Learmouth and O. H. K. Spate on behalf of twenty-five IBG members resident in Australia. The letter was stimulated by the Secretary's invitation, in a covering note to Newsletter No. 1, to put forward views from overseas; and the signatories pointed out that nearly one-fifth of the then membership of the IBG (about 700) had addresses outside the British Isles. Such members, they observed, could not normally attend Annual Conferences and so the *Transactions* (at that time the only IBG publication apart from the newly-instituted Newsletter) was in effect their only real contact with the Institute. ' Letter from Afar ' concentrated, therefore, on a critique of the contents of the *Transactions* and the point was made that ' it does not offer overseas members what it should '. Most of the papers published dealt with British topics with what the writers regarded as a ' deplorable over-emphasis on purely empirical studies '. What they sought in a journal that purported to represent professional *academic* geography was ' more ideas. . . . much more in the way of new leads ' and more ' discussion of the real problems of method and organisation facing our discipline and for British response to the new trends so evident in America and Europe '.

Nearly twenty years later it is unnecessary to study the writers' analysis of papers published or to assess what the *Transactions* in the early 1960s were producing in comparison with ' the great theoretical activity and debate ' that were, these Australian members claimed, filling the papers of the academic geographical publications of the United States, Scandinavia, Germany and the Soviet Union. But it is worth noting that ' the plea from Antipodes ', as the writers described it, to the Council of the IBG, ' the professional body for university geographers ', was taken seriously by the Council as a whole as well as by the then Editor (B. H. Farmer) and was discussed in detail at the two Council meetings held during the Bristol Conference in January 1965. The Newsletter certainly reflected the importance of the suggestion that there should be more reporting of topics discussed at annual conferences that seemed to be of really general interest, and subsequent issues of the *Transactions* did give greater attention to general methodological discussion that perhaps helped the Institute, through its publications, to give the ' intellectual leadership ' requested by the Australian members of the IBG. Nevertheless some good and justifiable debating points were made by the Editor—in a paper dated 14 December 1964—in which he pointed out that both he and his predecessor as editor (R. W. Steel) had sought to carry out a policy arising from the fact that the IBG was ' in effect a co-operative publishing society, all members of which have, if they are in good standing, the right to submit papers for publication '. The editors, he suggested, ' take what comes, without influencing authors to submit papers to the *Transactions* rather than to other journals '; and in practice his experience during the early 1960s was that ' on most occasions when he sat down to make up an issue, the number of papers available rarely exceeded by more than one or two the number of papers he could print '. Out of this debate—in Council and at the AGM—there emerged some valuable pointers which, at least gradually and after a while, led to a different type of Institute publications. This was partly in the *Transactions* but perhaps rather more so in the Newsletters of the 1960s that later became *Area,* and in which numerous accounts of discussions and study groups, along with a certain amount of correspondence, appeared. The debate initiated from Australia also encouraged the publication of what came to be known as *Special Publications* in which whole numbers were devoted to a specific topic, often edited by a member of the Institute especially invited to do so.

Only three further comments are necessary. The first is that the above account has interest and significance, and can be recorded in this history, because the documentation is complete. It begins with a letter written in Australia in 1964 and ends with, among other things, the regular flow of ' special publication ' type volumes that continue to appear nearly two decades later. The second is that many years before it became fashionable to say that ' Council must be responsive to the membership ', Council was clearly taking very seriously the comments of some of its most remote members. Thirdly, it is of interest to note that the use of the description of the Institute as ' a co-operative publishing society ' appears to have been used first by Farmer in 1964 long before the officer of the 1970s, to whom the words are usually credited, uttered them!

Index

The index has been prepared by Eileen M. Steel